Lessons and Inferences from the Characteristics of Recent Wars

Lessons and Inferences from the Characteristics of Recent Wars

Edited by
GAUTAM BANERJEE

KW Publishers Pvt Ltd
New Delhi

Vivekananda International Foundation

ISBN 978-81-986658-8-1 Hardback

Published in India by Kalpana Shukla

KW Publishers Pvt Ltd
4676/21, First Floor, Ansari Road
Daryaganj, New Delhi 110 002
Phone : +91 11 43528107
Production : kw@kwpub.in
Marketing : sanjeev@kwpub.in
Website : www.kwpub.in

Printed and bound in India

Contents

Foreword

At a time when the global geopolitical environment has become uncertain, the world is experiencing a good deal of instability due to simultaneous wars and conflicts in Europe, West Asia and Africa. Since the annexation of Crimea in 2014, tensions between Russia and Ukraine have been building steadily. The Israel-Hamas war in Gaza, the Israel-Lebanon war, the military exchanges between Israel and Iran, have all taken place in the last three years. In May 2025, India launched an 'OP Sindoor', a counter-terrorism measure against cross-border terrorism in which drones and missiles were used in large numbers. It marked a decisive shift in India's approach of zero tolerance policy and redefined India-Pakistan rules of engagement. There is a need to study these conflicts and understand the lessons they have to offer.

Russia began its 'special military operations' against Ukraine on February 24, 2022. Thus began the first hot war in the heart of Europe since the end of the Second World War. Since then, the two sides, put together, have suffered over a million casualties and we are still counting: A wide range of new weapons have been used. Apart from hypersonic missiles, tanks and bombs, the war has seen extensive use of drones by both sides. Ukraine got hundreds of billions of dollars in military and economic support from US, NATO and European countries. Russia mobilized North Korean troops in its military operations against Ukraine. Private sector companies like Starlink and Microsoft extended technical support to Ukraine. The war became a prolonged affair going beyond 3 years. President Trump ended the US support to Ukraine and urged both sides to negotiate an end.

The Russia-Ukraine war is being studied intensely in the world capitals and by scholars for its military, political, economic, technological and diplomatic dimensions. The war is a live demonstration of how warfare is evolving rapidly in the backdrop of major geopolitical shifts, technological advancements and weaponisation of trade, finance, food, water and energy. While it is still early to draw firm lessons from the ongoing wars, it is possible to identify broad trends and draw some inferences.

The VIF requested some leading Indian military experts with practical experience and knowledge of military affairs to study the Russia-Ukraine war and identify the broad trends in modern warfare. They responded readily. We are happy to publish this collection of their articles. I hope the book will start a debate on how warfare is changing and what lessons it holds for India.

I would like to thank Lt Gen Gautam Banerjee for editing this volume. I hope that students of warfare will find it useful.

New Delhi
May 2025

Arvind Gupta
Director
Vivekananda International Foundation

Editor's Note

The present era is characterised by the global powerplay of no-holds-barred inter-state and inter-group competition. Warfare in various forms has consequently turned into a widespread pursuit among the powerful as well as the aspirational players to secure their political and economic ends. With the globalised fallouts of that pursuit spreading out on the fast track, a developing nation's defence hierarchy is obligated to take cognisance of the clearly visible 'trends' that they are destined to have to contend with in the coming days.

Lessons of war take time to crystallise, mature, and be tested and incorporated into the prevalent military concepts and battle procedures. Notwithstanding this, aggressive machinations of India's inimical powers in the neighbourhood and beyond leaves no scope for its military institution to save itself from being frozen in tactical and technological obsolescence. Appropriate responses and reactions to the observable trends in prosecution of contemporary warfare have, therefore, to be deliberated accordingly under professional scrutiny and acted upon in simultaneity.

This book, titled '*Lessons and Inferences from the Characteristics of Recent Wars*', delves into the professionally evaluated trends in prosecution of warfare in the recent era. The purpose is to draw informed inferences for the military establishment to adapt and for the nation's defence hierarchy to uphold. The book deals with the subject matter in two parts, as follows:

Part I: Strategic and Tactical Inferences from the Recent Wars (12 chapters); and

Part II: Emerging Military Technologies in Recent Conflicts and Implications for India (7 chapters).

Each of the 19 chapters in Parts I and II deliberates over the various nuances of warfighting in the modern battlefield and their appropriate assimilation into India's defence preparedness. The stage for this strategic discourse is set by the recent and on-going conflicts in Palestine, Sudan, the Caucasia, and Ukraine. These conflicts indicate that:

a. With a plethora of aims, methods, means, intensities, and mass participation in various active and passive forms, the non-state forces are becoming better equipped to engage in devastatingly violent localised conflicts.
b. In lower-key armed conflicts against the entrenched order, militias of the proletariat have easier recourses to take to arms. This phenomenon may be described as the 'proletariat-isation' of organised violence.
c. The trend is in favour of engaging in aerial/remote/stand-off attacks before committing troops to ground operations.
d. Hierarchical harness of the latest military force-multiplication effects of information, electronic, communication, cyber and space warfare is mandatory.
e. There are clear indications to show that during armed conflicts, collateral destruction of social infrastructure has come to be somewhat acquiesced if not legitimised.
f. Well- trained and motivated military rank and file is proving its centrality in the prosecution of new-era warfare.
g. Very high rates of equipment casualties in modern-era battles require corresponding back-up of competent defence industry – design, innovation and manufacture –to sustain the war effort. Further, a well-oiled indigenous defence industry is also needed to survive against adversarial 'sanctions' as well as the repudiable conditionalities of the allies' support.
h. Politics and warfare are closer to fusion than ever before, even at the functional levels – 'democratisation' of warfare, so to say. As a result, specifying the desired objectives and setting the conditions for conflict termination have to be more flexible.

Arguably, the most salient observations from the recent wars indicate that the lesser of the adversary stands feeble no more. With astute preparations, he is capable of inflicting serious injuries on his stronger enemy, enough for the latter to recoil and reconcile. Faced with covert and overt hostility from powerful adversaries on the path to progress, that could be a reckonable lesson for the military professionals.

New Delhi
March 2025

Gautam Banerjee
Editor

About the Contributors

Vice Admiral **A.K. Chawla**, PVSM, AVSM, NM, VSM, PhD (Retd.) is a former Flag Officer Commanding-in-Chief of the Navy's Southern Command and a former Captain of the aircraft carrier, INS Viraat. Highly experienced in maritime operations, defence acquisition, military diplomacy, human resource management, and training, he is an accomplished strategic thinker and author.

Brigadier **Rahul K. Bhonsle**, MSc, MPhil, MBA (Retd.) is a military veteran with 30 years of active field experience in counter-militancy and terrorism operations. Post- retirement, he has combined his military expertise with extensive study of future trends in armed conflicts to build a personal repertoire of workshops, seminars, books, magazines, and newspaper articles. His publications are internationally acknowledged, many of which have been incorporated in government policy on counter-terrorism in India. Presently, he is the Director of Sasia Security-Risks.com, a South Asian security risk and knowledge management consultancy, which specialises in future scenarios, military capacity building, and conflict trends in South Asia.

Lt Gen **Gautam Banerjee**, PVSM, AVSM, YSM (Retd.) is a former Chief of Staff, the Central Army Command and Commandant Officers' Training Academy, Chennai. Author of over a dozen books and nearly a hundred papers on military matters, the General is a senior fellow-editor at the Vivekenanda International Foundation, New Delhi.

Lt Gen **PC Katoch**, PVSM, UYSM, AVSM (Retd.), a Shaurya Chakra awardee, is a Special Forces officer and a former Director General, Information Systems of the Indian Army. From the 1971 India-Pakistan War to a Special Forces Battalion in Sri Lanka, a Brigade on the Siachen Glacier, a Division in Ladakh and a Strike Corps in the South-Western Theatre, he has been through it all. A leading defence expert, he contributes regularly to Indian and foreign publications and is an active participant in seminars at both the national and international levels.

Air Marshal **Rajesh Kumar**, PVSM, AVSM, VM, ADC is a former Commander-in-Chief, Strategic Forces Command of India. A member of the VIF think tank, the Air Marshal is a leading thinker-speaker on national strategy and force modernisation.

Air Marshal **Diptendu Choudhury**, PVSM, AVSM, VM, VSM, is a former Commandant of the National Defence College, New Delhi. An experienced fighter pilot and a member of the Royal College of Defence Studies, he is devoted to India's development of the sinews of modern air power and execution of air operations at the Command, Service and Joint Operations levels. An avid air power scholar and author, the Air Marshal is also involved in policy and doctrine formulation, air strategy development, and international defence cooperation.

Lt Gen (Dr) **V. K. Saxena**, PVSM, AVSM, VSM(Retd) is a former Director General Air Defence, Indian Army, and a noted defence analyst. A foremost authority on organisation of modern air defence, the General is a prominent speaker and an author on complex topics of modern air defence systems like the various latest means of surveillance, detection, reporting, and targeting.

Maj Gen **A.K. Chaturvedi**, AVSM, VSM (Retd.) is a noted defence analyst, speaker and author on matters of national as well as military security. He is also a leading authority on the subjects of energy, water and environmental security and has published many well- received books on these subjects. The General is one of the founding members of the Lucknow- based think tank, 'The STRIVE'.

Maj Gen **P.K. Mullick**, VSM, a former Directing Staff at the National Defence College, is one of the leading authorities and analysts of modern-era military technology. His expert lectures and volumes of professional writings on military matters are highly rated among the strategic fraternity.

Maj Gen (Dr) **P.K. Chakravorty**, VSM (Retd) is a former Additional Director General Artillery responsible for procurement of artillery equipment including those used in the current operations. He has also served as the Defence Attaché to Vietnam where he cultivated deep interest on China. A prolific writer on strategic subjects, Gen Chakravorty is a Defence Analyst and a Senior Fellow with Centre for Land warfare Studies, New Delhi. His latest edited book, 'Securing the Future, Youth Perspective on National Security Challenges' was released by the Chief of Army Staff on 22 July 2024.

PART-I

Strategic and Tactical Inferences from Recent Wars

1. Inferences from the Russia-Ukraine War

A.K. Chawla

Background

While conflict between Ukraine and Russia has a long history, the current war has its genesis in the February 2014 Euromaidan protests, instigated after Russia sabotaged Ukrainian moves for closer integration with the European Union (EU). This led to the 'Revolution of Dignity', in which Ukraine's pro-Russia President, Victor Yanukovych, was ousted. The subsequent election of anti-Russia governments in Ukraine led to Russia annexing Crimea in March 2014 by a masterful display of grey zone warfare. Russia also commenced active support to pro-Russian unrest in the Donbas, where separatists declared the independent Donetsk People's Republic (DPR) and Luhansk People's Republic (LPR) in April 2014. In subsequent years, Ukrainian efforts to subjugate the separatists failed, in part because of the considerable support in men and material received by the latter from Russia. In February 2015, Ukraine and Russia signed the Minsk II Agreements to end the conflict, which were never fully implemented. War in the Donbas, therefore, continued with periodic ceasefires, but no lasting peace, and very few changes in territorial control.

The election of the firmly pro-West President Zelensky in April 2019 marked a new low in Russia-Ukraine relations. Zelensky stood for election on a platform favouring Ukrainian memberships of the European Union (EU) and the North Atlantic Treaty Organisation (NATO), which was seen by Russia as crossing its 'red line' of Western expansion into its own 'sphere of influence'. One consequence of that was the decision by President Putin to recognise the DPR and the LPR as independent states, a move supported only by a few close Russian allies. Russia also demanded that Ukraine renounce its efforts to join NATO, but Ukraine did not back down. Based on firm intelligence of a massive Russian build-up on Ukraine's northern borders and in Belarus, the US sounded the alarm on a likely Russian invasion of Ukraine in late 2021, though much of the world community (including Ukraine) were blasé about such a possibility. On February 24, 2022, Putin announced a 'special military operation' to 'demilitarise and de-Nazify' Ukraine and launched a massive attack on Ukraine.

Not only very few countries had anticipated a war, fewer expected it to go on for so long. Now into its third year, the Ukraine War is longer and bloodier than 90 per cent of all inter-state wars since the Napoleonic Wars of the 17th century. Ominously, the situation now resembles that of the Western Front in France in World War I (WWI). Statistics indicate that once wars cross a two-year mark, they linger on for an average of three years or more. The prolonged Ukraine War goes completely against the conventional wisdom propagated after the Gulf War, which stated that future wars would be 'limited' both in time and scope, not only due to extensive use of technology but also because the 'international community' would step in quickly to quell the flames. The fact that this has not happened in Ukraine has brought out several important notables that India and the Indian Armed Forces need to take on board, as we have a somewhat similar situation confronting us on our northern borders. There being far too many lessons to be listed, only a few important ones, at the grand strategic and military-strategic levels, are discussed in the subsequent paragraphs.

Adverse Fallouts of Strategic Miscalculations

In hindsight, it is evident that everyone miscalculated the actions of each other. Ukraine assumed that Russia would not oppose its pursuit of membership of the NATO and the EU by military force. The West underestimated Russia's ability to stay the course in the face of considerable military casualties, diplomatic isolation, and sanctions by the West. Russia grossly underestimated the depth of resistance that Ukraine was willing to offer, as it assumed that its military would easily be able to capture Kiev and instal a puppet government. Russia also miscalculated the resolve and resilience of Western support as its previous encroachments in Crimea and Ukraine had only resulted in diplomatic censures. China, too, misjudged as it had banked on a successful invasion to illustrate to the US, the futility of opposing China's similar action against Taiwan.

While strategic miscalculations due to countries being politically blindsided are not uncommon, what is common to such miscalculations is that these have always proved to be extremely costly and have heralded significant geopolitical changes. A few recent examples of major strategic mistakes include Hitler's attack on Russia against the advice of his generals in 1941, which was the major cause of his ultimate defeat; Emperor Hirohito and Admiral Yamamoto's decision to declare war against the US with the attack on Pearl Harbour in 1941 despite contrary advice by the Japanese Naval General Staff, thereby dragging a 'sleeping giant' into the war much to its ultimate detriment; and the US policy to build up China economically after their rapprochement in 1972, not only to break the Sino-Soviet alliance, in which it was successful, but also in the hope that capitalism would help in replacing communism with democracy, in which it failed spectacularly.

Russia's aim to preserve its sphere of influence in Eastern Europe has also thus far failed spectacularly. Ukraine has quickly obtained a candidate status in December 2023 for admittance into the EU, just a year and a half after applying for it. NATO had agreed in principle to make Ukraine a member in 2008, but further progress had been stalled for various reasons. After the war started, Ukraine became a *de facto* member of NATO for all purposes other than Article 5 (Collective Defence) of its charter. NATO members are thus providing Ukraine with unstinted military, intelligence, and moral assistance against Russia and gradually expanding the range of weapons supplied to it, including the most modern and destructive conventional weapon systems in their possession. The war has also led two erstwhile neutral European countries, Sweden and Finland, to join the NATO, thus doubling Russia's land borders with NATO member states. Overall, the NATO, which had been fighting to find relevance after the end of the Cold War, has now been galvanised, while the European countries are rearming with an urgency not seen since the Second World

War. Meanwhile, Russia's influence in the post-Soviet space in Central Asian countries has reduced, as these states are apprehensive that similar aggression could befall them in the future. Thus, none of the states in the Collective Security Treaty Organisation (CSTO) have supported Russia's actions in the DPR and the LPR or recognised the latter two as independent republics. The cost of war has been enormous, with Russia estimated to have spent US$ 211 billion between February 2022 and February 2024.

Not just Russia, the West, too, has had to face setbacks. The cost of supporting the war in Ukraine has been huge and is growing. The US has already allocated US$175 billion in aid to Ukraine, mainly military supplies, while EU nations have given US$ 32.5 billion. Europe's energy and trade de-coupling from Russia has also caused unprecedented economic damage to its economy. The resulting hardship has led to public disaffection in the West, as illustrated by several changes in governments over the past two years. The Russia-China-Iran-North Korea axis has strengthened considerably, much to the detriment of Western interests. Russia's moribund military, after having faced serious setbacks in Ukraine, is rearming quickly and will be a formidable and battle-hardened fighting force after the war ends. US' re-preoccupation with Eastern Europe, 35 years after the Cold War ended, has also allowed China greater strategic freedom in the Indo-Pacific, especially in the South China Sea and Southeast Asia, posing a serious challenge to US' leadership in the region.

Ukraine, which the West sought to protect, has been substantially devastated, with the World Bank assessing the cost of direct war damages to Ukraine during February 2022–February 2024 at US$152 billion and the cost of national reconstruction at around US$ 500 billion. The war has created over five million Ukrainian refugees, of which 3.7 million are internally displaced, the rest having taken shelter abroad in various friendly countries. Its military and civilian casualties are estimated to be at least two million and14.6 million respectively. Ukrainians need humanitarian assistance. A part of Ukraine—the size of Romania—is now riddled with landmines, which, using conventional methods, may require more than 750 years to demine! Indeed, the effects of the war have been global, as disruption of supplies of wheat grain, oil, and LNG from Russia and Ukraine have caused inflation and food and fuel shortages in many countries. Coming on the heels of the Covid-19 pandemic, the Ukraine War has left the global economy in a fragile state.

An examination of the events leading up to the Ukraine War reveals that there were enough warning markers available to all sides, yet they blundered into war. Historically, the reasons for such blunders are many, but the most common one is a lack of debate and ground-level inputs, which can happen if decision-making is centralised under autocratic leadership. Another major problem today is the information overload, which can often obfuscate the real issues, leading to erroneous decisions. The lesson to be noted is that countries need to be alive to the strategic environment and that all arms of the government – diplomatic, intelligence, military, and civilian bureaucracy – as also intelligentsia and civil society, be harnessed to advise the national leadership regarding the implications of key decisions, especially when it relates to a major adversary. In the case of India and China, the border dispute requires to be handled with great care, as another strategic miscalculation, like the one that happened in 1962, can have serious and long-lasting implications.

Drones as a Major Instrument of Warfare

The emergence of drones as a major weapon of war exemplifies the close connection between technology and war. While drones have existed for several decades and have been used in combat since the Second World War, development and use of these have accelerated in the 21st century. The Ukraine War has seen a revolution in their use, which has had a substantial impact on the battlefield, somewhat similar to that of tanks in WWI. Beginning with volunteer drone operators in the earlier stages of the war, two years down the line, First-Person-View (FPV) drones now account for over 90 per cent of battle casualties. In fact, as per General Zaluzhny, former Commander of the Ukraine Army, "...war has changed and created a new form of combined arms that integrates radio-electronic environment control .... (to facilitate) combined operations using attack drones and cyber assets". Consequently, specialised artillery spotting and bomb dropping drone units now form integral parts of assault battalions within a brigade formation, both in the Russian and Ukrainian armies. Drones have thus replaced the manual and air observation posts of the artillery, which have become obsolete due to their vulnerability. Drones are effectively directed on to their targets, using intelligent mapping and artillery targeting software systems, such as Ukraine's Kropyva, which plots the target coordinates and directs drones on to them.

Drones owe their success to their versatility, low cost, and expendability. They come in several sizes and capabilities, ranging from small, short-range surveillance drones to very long-range drones, and are used by the soldiers in trenches to survey the battlefield ahead. Very long-range drones, such as Ukraine's Ukrjet UJ-22 and UJ-26, operated from airfields, are used to attack targets over 800 km inside Russia, while the Magura V5 sea drones are being used to attack Russian ships 800 kms from Ukrainian ports. Drones also have different capabilities and roles, which include visual/infra-red/radar reconnaissance; attack with a variety of warheads, such as armour piercing, cluster, thermobaric, etc.; conduct of electronic warfare (EW); establishment of communication links; mining/demining operations; facilitation of logistics support; provision of medical assistance; conduct of psychological warfare, etc.

Most importantly, drones are much cheaper than their targets – the Chinese-made DJI Mavic quadcopter, used extensively by both Ukrainian and Russian forces, costs between US$1500-3000 each, while each FPV drone used by Ukraine to attack Russian tanks costs US$ 400 as against US$ 800-9000 for an artillery shell, US$100,000 for a GPS-guided shell, and around US$ 200,000 for a Javelin anti-tank missile. On the other hand, tanks, armoured fighting vehicles (AFVs), infantry fighting vehicles (IFVs), mobile artillery guns/launchers, EW systems, mobile radars, etc. cost millions of dollars. The cost-effect ratio is evident from the fact that in one week, Ukrainian FPV drones are estimated to have destroyed 428 pieces of Russian equipment, including 75 tanks and 101 artillery pieces. Drones also benefit from the fact that a vast majority of these are commercially manufactured and can be easily assembled on the front line. Ukraine manufactured 1 million drones in 2024, twice the number of artillery shells supplied by the EU in 2023, and aims to enhance this number to over 1.5 million in 2025. Finally, unlike manned machines, drones are, of course, unmanned and hence, tireless and expendable. Most importantly, these help in saving precious lives.

One of the results of using drones on the battlefield has been that tanks and armoured vehicles are now deployed much further behind the front lines than used to be the case earlier. Infantry movements are also restricted and the dugouts have to be strengthened against drone attacks. However, the most significant way in which drones have impacted the Ukraine War is in their use to mount pervasive surveillance of the tactical battlefield. This kind of surveillance has deleted the element of surprise that is necessary for any attacking force to achieve success. Pinpointing of a larger assembly of men and equipment has also enabled instant attacks from both the artillery and FPV drones. A major impact of such capability on battlefield tactics of both the sides has been the avoidance of large-scale attacks by armoured forces, thus forcing both the sides to resort to attacks using small combat groups comprising a few armoured vehicles with mounted infantry. Though such attacking forces are less vulnerable to detection, they are easier to counteract and destroy from strongly entrenched defences. Consequently, the battle lines in Ukraine have almost been frozen and are likely to remain so unless a way can be found to blunt the ever-pervasive drone surveillance.

Counter-Drone Measures

Conversely, drones by themselves are not enough to hold the front lines. While much more accurate than artillery shells, especially against moving targets, these have limited explosive power, and their deployment has to be complemented with traditional infantry, armour and artillery. Anti-drone drones have also been developed to attack drones in flight. Drone aerial battles are already happening over Ukraine.

Electronic Warfare (EW)

EW has emerged as the most potent weapon against drones. Jammers are employed to disrupt the link between the pilot and the drone, thus negating its effectiveness. The drawback of this countermeasure is that costly EW systems must be deployed in large numbers, and that these have a limited number of frequencies that they can jam. Drones have responded by using less-used frequencies and frequency-hopping systems or by using pre-programmed flight paths for attacks against fixed targets, such as infrastructure. Electronic reconnaissance systems are now also being used to help plot a drone's signals back to its pilots to launch strikes against the launching stations. This again has been countered by using mobile control stations, or by using signal repeaters at intermediate stations, or relaying signals from other UAVs to mask the position of operators.

As evident from the foregoing, this cat and mouse game between the attackers and defenders is evolving daily on the Ukrainian battlefield. The inference is that battles will be won not just by the side which has better technology and higher numbers but equally by the side that is nimbler in evolving technological modifications and innovations.

The Game-changing Application of Artificial Intelligence (AI) in Warfare

The surge in common-use AI tools over the past decade is now adding to the effectiveness of modern-day weapon systems, with Ukraine being its most recent and best testing ground. As brought out, one of the most successful counters to Ukrainian drones has been the rapid development and widespread deployment of EW systems by the Russians to jam and neutralise drones. AI- embedded chips on modern drones have now started to cut the umbilical cord with the operator, thereby immunising them from the effects of jamming. This immunity would be difficult for any adversary to counter. It could also conceivably make bulky EW systems obsolete.

The most dramatic impact of AI is, however, on command-and-control systems. Herein, AI has already demonstrated very high degree of fidelity in identifying targets and allocating resources for attack, all within a fraction of the time taken by a human being to do the same task. Currently being used with a 'man in the loop' configuration, AI technology is advancing quickly to a 'man out of the loop' or a totally autonomous configuration, with human beings mainly being observers and only intervening when essentially required. This could ultimately imply many autonomous drones controlled by AI systems, searching and attacking enemy targets in relentless waves.

However, this is easier said than done, as the development of AI systems requires substantial investment in human expertise, hardware and software. For example, the networking of a variety of sensors across a battlefield requires not just the compatibility of software in the sensors but also digital systems to process the information and communications technology (both terrestrial and satellite) to disseminate it in real time. The cost of investing in AI systems, whose software mutates at an amazing pace, implies that only countries with advanced technologies and requisite resources can play this game. With China already a world leader in AI, it is imperative for India to invest heavily in this field and catch up with its main adversary.

Quantity has a Quality of its Own—The Necessity of Mass against a Major Adversary

After the First Gulf War in 1990, it became common belief that future wars would be swift and short. What was overlooked was the fact that this only holds true in wars where there is huge asymmetry between both sides—as was the case between Iraq on one side and the US and its allies on the other. The fact that conflicts between adversaries of comparable strength will not necessarily be short in duration has been proved by the ongoing Ukraine War, which is well past the two-year mark. This brings to the fore the issue of sustenance in prolonged wars, which requires a strong domestic armaments industry, as also substantial economic and human resources. As Stalin had rightly observed, 'Quantity has a quality of its own'. Indeed, mass affects endurance, as key parameters of armament and ammunition usage in the Ukraine War reveal.

With regard to artillery shells, estimates from various sources indicate that Russia has been firing between 10,000 to 20,000 artillery rounds per day over the past two years. It is also estimated that Russia started the war with a stockpile of 16 million artillery shells, of which about 8 million were consumed in the first year itself. While Russia has the largest ammunition manufacturing industry in the world and is reportedly producing three million munitions per year, it still has had to procure almost 5 million rounds of ammunition from North Korea to sustain its war effort. On the other hand, Ukraine has fired roughly 2,000 to

7,000 rounds per day. Ukraine had a very limited indigenous ammunition production capacity before the war started but has opened new factories since then and is reportedly commencing production of 155 mm shells this year. It, therefore, depends heavily on the US and the EU, which, combined, have only one-third the production capacity of Russia. The realisation that their ammunition production capacity is insufficient for a prolonged war has caused the US and European partners in NATO to open new ammunition factories and ramp up production capacity in existing ones.

The cost of artillery ammunition expenditure is not available separately. But since the costs of artillery shells from Western sources vary from about US$ 3,000 for an unguided shell to over US$100,000 for a round of guided ammunition, a rough estimate (averaging the costs of different shells) would bring the annual cost of ammunition expended to around US$ 55 billion. It is estimated that Russian shells cost between 25-30 per cent of Western ammunition, so for Russia, that would reduce this amount to about US$ 14-18 billion. Russian factories are also producing over 100 long-range precision ballistic and cruise missiles per month, but their heavy usage has meant that Russia now relies substantially on Iranian-manufactured Shahed drones. It is evident that artillery ammunition alone constitutes at least 25-30 per cent of the cost of war for Russia and over 50-60 per cent for Ukraine. Notably, this figure does not include small arms ammunition expenditure, which is more difficult to track, while other ammunition, such as mortar shells, anti-tank missiles, mines, drones, and other ammunition expended from aircraft and ships, would constitute a notably additional figure.

Another parameter that is easier to examine is the requirement of tanks and armoured vehicles. Russia is estimated to have started the war with over 12,000 tanks, either in active service or in storage. It is assessed that over 3,000 of these tanks (3,180 as per the Oryx OSINT website), mostly of the modern variety (1100 of T-72 and 100 of T-90 variants), have been destroyed so far. It is also assessed that over 6,000 AFVs/IFVs, 1,500 artillery systems, 135 helicopters, 106 aircraft, 20 ships, and one submarine have also been destroyed. This list is not exhaustive and does not include expensive equipment, such as radars, air defence systems, and

EW systems, or logistics expenditure for fuel, maintenance and repair of damaged equipment, etc. While Russia has a production capacity of 200-500 tanks and 1000 AFV/IFVs per year, the shortage being experienced by it is evident from the use of refurbished Second World War- era AFVs/IFVs (T-55s, T-62s, T-72s), as also the increasing use of non-armoured vehicles, such as the Chinese Desert Cross 100-3 All-terrain Vehicles (ATVs), and even motorcycles, which have substantially increased Russian casualties. A rough estimate of the cost of the losses in tanks can be gauged from the fact that the cost of each tank in Russia varies from US$ 1.1 million for the older versions to US$ 4.5 million for the latest ones, thus taking the total cost of only these losses to over US$ 1 billion.

Human Resources—Mass Matters

Examining warfare's most critical parameter, human resources, it is again evident that mass matters, especially in offensive action, where a 3:1 advantage is necessary for the attacker to prevail. The Russian Armed Forces had commenced the war with about 1,100,000 personnel that have expanded over the past two years to 1,320,000. This increase was helped by two mass conscriptions in August 2022 (137,000 personnel) and December 2023 (170,000 personnel), drafting of convicts from prisons (estimated to be around 100,000), and employment of mercenary forces, such as Wagner, estimated to number between 20,000 to 50,000. As per reliable estimates, Russian casualties in Ukraine have exceeded 50,000, with about 315,000 more incapacitated or wounded, the combined number exceeding the total number of personnel (360,000) involved in the initial assault on Ukraine. The Russian Armed Forces involved in the fighting in Ukraine are now estimated to comprise 415,000 troops, which implies that over 75 per cent of the initial strength of Russian Armed Forces personnel has been directly committed to the war since February 2022.

Starting the war with about 700,000 soldiers, the Ukraine Army today comprises almost 1,250,000 troops. Like Russia, this expansion has been achieved largely through conscription and the influx of foreign fighters and mercenaries, estimated to number around 20,000. Ukrainian casualties are reported to be lesser than those in the Russian Army, having been mainly involved in defence, as against the offensive battles fought by the Russian Army. However, despite this, official Ukrainian estimates of their casualties stand at over 31,000, with another 200,000 wounded or incapacitated (Western estimates put the figure at least 25 per cent higher than Ukrainian claims). The confirmed fact that there are 60,000 amputees in the Ukraine Armed Forces till now (almost the size of the British Army today) is an indication of the scale of military casualties thus far. The need for mass in recruitable manpower is clearly revealed by the fact that the average age of Ukrainian soldiers is 43—well above the desirable figure of 18-26 for a combat arms soldier. If both Ukraine and Russian casualties are combined, they are inching close to the one million mark.

Notable Inferences for India

India faces a unique strategic challenge, having long pending major boundary disputes with two nuclear weapons- capable neighbours, relations with whom remain fragile. There is, therefore, no disputing the fact that India requires a strong, well-equipped and well-trained military to deter conflict or prevail if war is thrust upon it. While this paper has examined a few observations emerging from the Ukraine War as applicable to India, many others bear more detailed study. Some of the more important ones include: the use of information warfare; the importance (and limits) of cyber warfare; necessity for high quality human resources; the need for greater jointness and integration in the Armed Forces, especially the creation of integrated theatre commands, etc.

The amount of ammunition expended, equipment lost or damaged, and casualties caused over the two years of war is proof that despite modern technology being touted as a game-changer in modern warfare, quantity has a quality of its own, especially against a major adversary, such as the one faced by India. The lesson that emerges is clear—a strong indigenous domestic arms and ammunition industry and professional human resources in adequate numbers are essential to sustain hostilities in a long-duration war.

However, the starting point of national defence has to be the enunciation of a National Security Strategy (NSS) to focus and guide the national effort in building defence capabilities, structures, and strategies. A strong indigenous military-industrial complex, supported by well-resourced research and development capabilities in both the science and art of war, is critical, both for maintenance of stamina in a long war and for finding constant technological innovations, especially on the battlefield, as has been done by both Ukraine and Russia during the Ukraine War. The current emphasis on self-reliance in defence, therefore, needs to be given further impetus, with particular focus on building capacities for production of ammunition and common use military equipment. Finally, it is important to allow all agencies involved in national security to share their free and frank opinion on important strategic issues, so that the apex-level decision-makers have the benefit of untrammelled advice from subject matter experts.

2. Unlearning and Learning: Observations from Recent Wars

Rahul K. Bhonsle

Introduction

War is a constant in human existence. Perhaps periods of peace, as enjoyed by Europe in three quarters of the century from the end of the Second World War in 1945 to the War in Ukraine in 2022, may now appear to be an oddity. While in the interim, Europe saw wars in the Balkans, Georgia, and the Caucasus, these were limited in nature and led to a belief that the continent has finally burnt the ghosts of conflicts that had racked nations over the centuries despite the Peace in Westphalia. While the rest of the world had seen frozen conflicts and real and imagined grievances flare up, Europe was in a unique peace bubble that was shattered on February 24, 2022, when legacy power Russia declared war on Ukraine, naming the same as a 'Special Military Operation'.

Further afield in West Asia, commonly known as the Middle East, wars have been a persistent phenomenon since the 1948 First Arab-Israeli War. With much interim iteration, violence has since been erupting in almost every decade, with uneasy peace in- between. On October 07, 2023, another war began with a non-state organisation in Gaza, the Hamas, launching a multi-pronged terror 'invasion' of Israel, brutally killing and maiming hundreds of innocents and taking hundreds of hostages. Israel, the military behemoth in the region, responded by unleashing the might of its air, artillery, and armour to gain control over Gaza, which continues with disproportionate losses of civilian lives on both sides.

Operational Analyses

The two wars—in Ukraine and Gaza—are conflicts of high intensity with massed use of fire power and resolute resistance. While there are many on-going smaller wars, observations from the Indian state's perspective while facing a two-front China-Pakistan challenge could best be drawn from a study of the key facets of these two military conflicts. The inferences can only be in terms of 'observations', not lessons—not yet—at this stage. That is because in military studies, drawing conclusions from an ongoing war could be too premature. Yet, for a nation having to deal with its contemporary conflict situations, it is important for India to apply these in a contextual manner.

Importantly, while the nature of war is constant—to wit, violence applied for a political purpose—its character is changing fast. Clausewitz, the doyen of the Western way of wars, highlights these truisms in the form of four continuities of war, "a political dimension, a human dimension, the existence of uncertainty and that it is a contest of wills." On the other hand, the character or the way wars are fought keep changing with geography or terrain and available instruments for violence, including the latest of military technologies, tactics, and organisations.

In the Indian context, there is a reason to first 'unlearn' some of the customarily underscored derivatives of the legacy experiences of warfare and to learn certain recently revealed ones from the wars in Ukraine and Gaza. It is in this context that this paper has been framed. The observations are preliminary notations and thus may seem concise to need further elaborations as more evidences are available to endorse or reframe the conclusions.

Rethinking Customary Experiences from Past Wars

1. Grand and Military Strategy. The aim of war is peace, not more war. The aim of waging a war or its political objective has to be 'peace' and not in creating conditions for more wars. In case war cannot achieve peace, other options, such as diplomacy, dialogue, economic coercion, and so on, could be employed rather than opening a war front. With this in view, a war aim has to be realistic. For instance, Israel's objective of 'complete' decimation of the Hamas is likely to generate even more resistance. The group is not merely an organisation but an armed movement of the Palestinian people, and that is not likely to be wiped out merely with elimination of the group—if that is possible at all. Similarly, in Ukraine, forcible occupation of vast territories as an objective is unlikely to result in peace. For wars to result in peace, impacting the will of the adversary to compromise and abandon larger goals is essential.

2. Great Power Legacy. Just as the wars, the nature, and the quantum of power change over the millennia, nations assume mantles of greatness based on several factors. These factors vary from mass and population, geography, economy, social and cultural history, ethnic evolution, technology, and due assimilation of all these. To assume that a nation-state is destined to greatness just by exercising power over a self-defined geographic zone may not be realistic here. The emergence of Ukraine as an independent nation- state is a reality which Russia had to accept and adjust to. Attempting to unite elements in Ukraine by force has only resulted in colossal harm to the people of the two nations, ruined their economies and has imposed economic hardships across the world, particularly among the developing South. Rather than blind yearnings for past 'glory', assimilating changes and renewing the elements of contemporary power equations may assume greater salience.

3. Major Economies can Sustain Long Wars. Indeed, Russia has been able to sustain the war effort for the past two years, and so has Ukraine, with the assistance of the United States and Europe. Yet, the long-term impact of bloated allocations for arming is likely to be devastating on economies, the effects of which may be expected to come about in the decades ahead.

4. Civilian Casualties can be Disproportionate. Civilians are inevitable victims of war. Though war cannot be a humanitarian enterprise, there is still a degree of proportionality; civilians being subjected to disproportionate casualties, including those of women and children, is highly questionable. Besides, targeting, for effect, needs to be more or less confined to the military domain. Israel, and to some extent, Russia, have failed to ensure the right kinds of proportionality and operational relativities. The impact is on stretching the peoples' antipathy rather than suppression of their morale, as could possibly be the aim.

5. Air Superiority versus Air Denial. The strategic equation between combat aircraft and ground-based air defence systems saw a new turn in the war in Ukraine as Ukrainian armed forces could stalemate a larger and wider war effort. In the war in Gaza, Israel and its allies, including the United States and Jordan amongst others, completely neutralised, with negligible casualties, barrages of over three hundred drones and missiles launched by Iran under 'Operation True Promise' in April this year. The ground-based air defence systems were high-technology systems like the Israeli 'Iron Dome' and U.S. 'Patriot'. Besides, in that condition, the potential targets are spread over much wider areas. This situation, however, may not apply to Indian conditions that lack that level of military capability.

6. Wars can be Sustained without National Mobilisation. Russia has sustained the war without national- level mobilisation. Ukraine has ordered a general mobilisation almost two years after the war broke out. Yet, an ongoing stalemate of sorts suggests that early general mobilisation may have produced better outcomes. Israel chose to mobilise post-October 07, 2023, which appears to be a better model.

7. Conscription. There is the belief that conscription is the answer to maintaining large standing armies. This has proved to be a myth and could well be a lesson for the proponents of the Agnipath Scheme in India. A related factor is the recruitment of foreign mercenaries. While the French Foreign Legion is an example, those recruited in it are but volunteers. Russia, and in smaller measure, Ukraine, have recruited foreign mercenaries, alluring them by the undertaking of not sending them to fight on the front line. That has resulted in loss of trust amongst the strategic partners.

8. Role of Private Military Corporations [PMC]. Private militias have been hailed as alternatives to mobilised conventional forces. Indeed, these have played various roles in some of the civil wars, for instance, in Africa. But Russia's employment of the PMC Wagner Group, controlled until 2023 by Yevgeny Prigozhin, proved to be a double-edged sword—fighting on the front line in 2022 and rebelling against Moscow later. PMCs are hardly a substitute for professional militaries, and experimentation with this distraction is unwarranted.

Operational and Tactical Facets

1. Attrition and Mass versus Manoeuvre. The war in Ukraine has led to the conclusion that mass, including massed fire, has spelt the end of manoeuvre, thus leading to apparent irrelevance of the modern tank. Indeed, the Ukraine war has seen massed fire dominate the battlespace, leading to heavy demand on artillery munitions and missiles. But this was more of a function of the warfighting tactics of the two sides in replicating the Soviet era concepts in a limited manner, short of the gamut of outright war – 'special operations' so to say. In the Indian scenario, as in most of regular warfare, armour and mechanised operations will remain relevant as key instruments of land warfare. Armour would remain a determinant factor in terrain and situations obtained in sections of the Western front with Pakistan as well as on the Northern borders with China. Employment customisations would, however, be obviously needed.

2. Numbers versus Technology. Russia employed large numbers of Iranian Shahid-191 and other types of drones, as well as North Korean artillery ammunition. In the same vein, the Ansarullah or Houthi in Yemen have employed relatively low technology drones and missiles to target defenceless merchant shipping. How effective these low technology weapons used in large numbers are needs careful assessment.

3. Innovations 'On the Fly'. There have been admirable innovations by the Ukrainians 'on the fly' and by the Russians in a slightly longer timeframe. These include civil production of drones and innovations of significance, such as the instruments of 'First Person View' or FPV, GPS- enabled dumb munitions, and so on. In Ukraine, several drone manufacturing 'plants' have come up in homes and basements. While this is an inevitable dimension of modern wars, such innovations can at best fill up certain tentative sundry gaps but cannot provide the war-winning edge. Thus, makeshift inventiveness alone cannot be a war- winning strategy.

4. Time for Orientation and Training. Training and orientation for newly inducted weapons is a time-consuming exercise and may take months to over a year to be effective. This is more relevant in the case of Ukraine, which operated mainly Russian equipment in the past, and so its personnel required extensive orientation and training. A realistic timeframe needs to be envisaged for that purpose; mere announcements of allotment of weapons to Ukraine by the United States and other allies should not drive higher expectations. On the other hand, the Israel Defence Forces, which have been using American weapons and equipment, require far lesser time for orientation and employment of US assistance provided during the war in Gaza.

5. Technology versus Human Factors in Wars. Recent wars have confirmed that the human factor remains the primary determinant in warfare. Technology is only an addendum to efficient war- waging tools at the hands of the military personnel. Thus, focusing on training of personnel in the use of weapons with integration of force multipliers assumes importance.

6. Urban Conurbations. Sun Tzu's wise advice to avoid cities was ignored in both wars – Ukraine and Gaza. Yet, the dilemma remains as to how to winkle out the resolute defenders entrenched in urban conurbations. How this can be done is a factor that has immense consequences for war on the Western front for India. This matter needs a larger debate.

Learning Derivatives from the Recent Wars

1. Grand and Military Strategy

a. **Frozen Conflicts and Broken Peace.** Frozen conflicts can erupt, and broken peace will collapse, while armistice can be an interim halt to violence. This aspect must be taken to a logical conclusion to remove residual political objectives, which can lead to another phase of warfare. This is an enduring lesson from the Ukraine and Gaza wars.

b. **National Leadership and 'Will'.** Ukraine's President, Volodymyr Zelensky, is a foremost demonstration of how national leadership can resolutely stand up against aggression. Zelensky has also excelled in mobilisation of resources for his armed forces from abroad. Without his unique diplomatic thrusts, Ukraine may well have had to face greater challenges or could have succumbed to the Russian invasion. At the same time, Russian President Vladimir Putin, despite a failed attempt to seize Kyiv in 2022 and in the face of heavy manpower and equipment losses, has sustained the war effort by mobilising national and international resources, thereby sustaining his war objectives. Israel's war leadership by a committee is a model that will have to be studied with greater deliberation to examine how it impacts the direction of wars.

c. **Strategic Alliance and Axis of Resistance.** Modern wars need mobilising of allies. While the United States and Europe rallied behind Ukraine and later, Israel, Russia had to weave its own network of partnerships with Iran and North Korea providing valuable military support, albeit of tendentious quality. China, India and many countries in the Global South have offered political support to Russia. At the same time, Iranian drones, like the Shahid 129 and 191, have provided favourable cost benefits to the Russians. In the Gaza war, Iran's so-called 'Axis of Resistance', to include Syria, the Hezbollah in Lebanon, Iraqi militia and Ansarullah or Houthis of Yemen, has created a major challenge not just for Israel but international maritime trade passing through the Red Sea. Thus, even large powers need allies.

d. **Strategic Information Campaign.** Information as a strategic tool was evident more so in the war in Ukraine. While Kyiv employed this tool masterfully, Russia did not lag behind with its mention as well as occasional working of the nuclear option acting as a restraint on Western support. On the other hand, Israel could not weave in a favourable narrative in the operations, resulting in loss of crucial support.

e. **Strategic Surprise and Deception.** Sun Tzu's maxim that all warfare is based on deception remains relevant. Obliviousness of this principle has inflicted a heavy price on Israel that was completely surprised by the Hamas terrorist offensive on October 07, 2023, in Gaza. The famous Israeli intelligence capability failed dismally, and that was a factor in Israel's response of overwhelming revenge. Ukraine, on the other hand, was benefitted by intelligence from the United States to anticipate the launch of Russian operations on February 24 and thus perhaps could face off the first wave of Russian offensive to capture Kyiv.

f. **National Defence Industrial Base.** A national defence industrial base is essential for large powers and an inevitability for India. While the base need not be completely indigenous, as it is aspired by the Indian national leadership, it should be solidified over durable partnerships with friendly nations. India's dependence on Russia would have been viable in case of subcontinental warfare, but when Moscow is itself involved in Ukraine, broader collaborations have proved unviable. Today, in expansion of military industrial capacity, India's dilemma is with engagements with the United States and Europe. For India, sustainable defence industry partnerships must be sufficiently broad-based. As to what such a network will shape-up to be requires separate deliberations and debate.

g. **Ammunition.** Munitions, particularly artillery ammunition, have emerged as a strategic factor in sustaining recent wars. This is a function of attritional warfare, but may cover larger inventories where manoeuvre is involved.

h. **Missile and Drone Defence.** As an addendum to the above- listed strategic lessons, missile and drone defence has emerged as a vital strategic asset on its own, besides its tactical import.

2. Operational and Tactical Issues

a. **Defence is the Stronger Form of Warfare.** Clausewitz's contention that defence is the stronger form of war has once again been proved in the war in Ukraine. Both sides learnt their lessons to beat-back offensives by their adversaries. Lack of appreciation of that sense was evident when Ukraine launched its offensive in 2023 and was thoroughly defeated by Russia by the latter's adoption of layered defensive networks with mines and obstacles. The significance of secured firm bases for launching attacks was also evident in these operations.

b. **Emergence of 'Uncrewed Systems'.** Every war throws up secondary platforms which assume significance. While use of 'uncrewed platforms', such as Unmanned Aerial Vehicles or drones, has become widespread, these have emerged as a mainstay of the Ukrainian stalemate. Multiple forms of usage of drones have emerged, from reconnaissance and surveillance to one-way or 'suicide' missions that would now be an essential armoury for nations engaging in future wars.

c. **Integrated Battles**. Integrated combined arms teams, the lack of which prevented both sides from breaking through in the war in Ukraine, has been underlined. The Indian Army is working towards 'Integrated Battle Groups' or IBGs, but so far, that applies only to the land forces. Astute integration of air and helicopter for fire support and manoeuvre needs serious consideration. For prosecution of rapid precision operations with minimal losses of men and material, integration to multi-domain war- waging capability is a leap that the Indian Armed Forces would have to take.
d. **Tactical Integration of Drones.** Integration of drones at the tactical level is set to change the military tactics. Particularly, the FPV tool can provide tactical units and sub-units with a high level of battlefield transparency, and that may revolutionise the tactics of fire and movement. This aspect needs consideration.

Conclusion

War is a human event and thus, a dynamic sphere of activity, which is ever evolving. Modern wars entail the use of multiple elements or 'domains' as these are usually known as. Orchestrating these elements would require an acme of broader professional skills among the military commanders. Suffice to say, modern era conflicts have exacerbated to such higher complexities that these require to be specifically and astutely surmounted by the masters of contemporary warfare.

3. Characteristics of Recent Wars: Trends and Inferences

Gautam Banerjee

"When the pace of change accelerates, the militaries that change and adapt are likely to gain massive advantage over potential enemies who are less agile."

– Lt. Col. Scott Stephenson

Preamble

This brief is an assessment of nations' strategic obligations in the emerging world order and how such obligations are transmuted into military imperatives. Recognition of these transmutations is mandatory to ensure that political application of military power, its applications at the strategic and tactical levels, and the corresponding modelling of military structures remain aligned to the national security objectives - at affordable costs.

Analysis of the military implications of the emerging era's societal, political, technological and economic determinants begins with the understanding that the sanctified *Principles of War* and the fundamental concepts of their prosecution remain eternal in their spirit and practice. Even the various sub-sets of regular warfare, namely, sub-conventional, irregular, militia, subversive, and mercenary operations, as well as the parallel targeting of civil infrastructure, industry and trade, have been, as military history reveals, by and large, ruled by such fundamental concepts. Accordingly, any assessment of the sensitive matters of national defence is best begun from the 'first principles'. This keeps the assessment from being distracted by unripe prophecies that might bring some fleeting relief to the ever-beleaguered defence decision-makers but only at the cost of serious consequences of mis-interpreting the strategic signatures of the foggy and indefinable kind.[1]

The assessment here is discussed in three parts, as follows:

a. Part I: Politics of Military Power in the Emerging World Order;
b. Part II: Strategic Implications of New Era Politics of Warfare;
c. Part III: Ruling Inferences from the characteristics of the wars waged, and being waged, during the recent years.

Part I: Politics of Military Power in the Emerging World Order

Politics of Contemporary Warfare

Incessant warfare in a globalised order is destined to forge new alliances, rehash the global financial systems, disrupt existing economic ties and re-invent supply chains. This order would also lead to gradual spread of multiple, autonomous centres of technological and industrial growth for the developing countries to draw from. The subject being vast, this assessment would have to be focused on the key markers of the recent developments in the application of military power.

Notable characteristics, as observable in the politics of the emerging world order, are listed under the following paragraphs.

1. **Territorial Hegemonism.** There are suggestions that in the contemporary era, the typical territorial expansionist ambitions among powerful contenders stand superseded by the lure of economic domination. This notion, however, is differently qualified by the panorama of global conflicts. As the US-NATO, Chinese and Russian policies of engaging in various forms of geographic-territorial usurpations reiterate, territorial hegemonism remains, as ever, as the main recourse to gaining monopoly over the cross-border political, economic and strategic resources. Instances of territorial hegemonism are thus in continuous play, as exemplified by over four dozen significantly destructive armed conflicts that engulf more or less the entire African continent as well as substantial parts of Asia and Europe.[2] In the Asia-Pacific, China makes no bones about its intent to carve out its regions of 'sovereignty' and 'influence' at the

expense of the US' global hegemony. The larger ambit of conflicts in East Europe, with Ukraine-Crimea at its centre stage, is another new-era reiteration of the persistency of territorial ambitions.

2. **New Era Conflict Mechanisms.** With spreading ideals of human rights, abhorrence of the sufferings of war is becoming increasingly universal. At the nationalist levels, however, this abhorrence has not diminished the allurement of power and domination over the vying co-habitants. The spread and scales of armed conflicts in the emerging era are to be determined by this contradictory setting. The trend is characterised by varying shades of political instigations, commercial allurements, patronage of affiliates and provision of war wherewithal to the contestants and their proxies while preaching 'peace' in crassly self-defined terms. The Chinese, Iranian, West Asian and Russian belligerents are some prominent examples of that trend. Conflict mechanisms in the emerging era—in terms of diplomacy, force-structure, transportation, technological instruments and logistics—are to be construed accordingly to manage this contradiction between war-abhorrence and war-instigation.
3. **Politicisation of Military Strategy.** Trends of blurring the distinction between the bounds of political control of war and its professional execution have been witnessed before, with undesired implications. The US Government's jaywalking into a post-invasion quagmire in Iraq-Syria, much against military advice, is one recent example. Similarly, Russia's 'Special Operations' in Eastern Ukraine has been but a superfluously (dis)organised rampage against an adversary who, contrary to wishful expectations, refused to submit. Both these campaigns were launched at political insistences, but as the resistance escalated into deliberate military contests, the aggressors were forced to observe the classical principles of war, balance their force-compositions and revert to regular fortifications, battle tactics, air operations and logistics. That underlines the hoary adage about the dangers of falling into the lure of politically expedient but professionally untested concepts of warfare.[3]
4. **Forging Alliances in Preservation of a Rule-based Order.** The rise of challengers against the sole superpower's authority, particularly

within the regions of the challengers' interests, has been witnessed in the recent years. The lead challengers are China in the Indo-Pacific region, Russia in East Europe and Iran in West Asia, all of them authoritarian military powers who protract from their bonded minions. The challenge from China's dictatorial adventurism is particularly worrisome as it is intent on replacing the globally preferred rule-based order with a partisan version of a China-dominant order. This situation gives cause for the global stakeholders to forge various counter-balancing 'strategic partnerships'. The Quadrilateral Security Dialogue (QUAD), the Freedom of Navigation Operations (FNOPs), the Australia-UK-US (AUKUS), the US'Taiwan Policy Act of 2022, the UK-Japan Defence Agreement 2023, and the most recent Indo-Pacific Security Initiative (IPSI) are some prominent expressions of this concern. These partnerships are aimed at instituting measures to contain the rising security challenges in the affected regions. China's repudiation of a stable international order, North Korea's nuclear brazenness and Iran's destabilising interventions in West Asia are some examples of such new security challenges. With the threats rising, recourse to strategic partnerships could evolve further into big power-led military and economic alliances. This aspect would need to be managed to protect national interests.

5. **Resurrection of Conventional Deterrence.** During the second half of the 20th century, nuclear deterrence prevented wars from being escalated to 'total war' situations. With nuclear brinkmanship settling into somewhat a 'rationalist' order in contemporary political shadowboxing, the hugely escalated capabilities of 'conventional deterrence' have re-claimed its past muscular status. Indeed, with pinpoint accuracy and being highly destructive and yet, less harmful to mankind in the long run, the modern-era conventional forces and their weaponry have the ability to deter and regulate the intensities of conventional and even sub-conventional warfare as these escalate beyond the limited or skirmish operations. China's presently stalled bellicosity against India and reciprocal restraints observed in the Russia-Ukraine war are two distinct examples of conventional military power- deterring escalation – in the first instance, China's

aggressive activities stand subdues, if tentatively, while in the second instance, the Ukrainian alliance is deterred from hitting deeper into Russian hinterland, even as the latter flouts the limits of the norms of international acceptability.

6. **Conflict Space below the Nuclear Threshold.** It is, by and large, universally accepted that the option of nuclear warfare stands capped at posing deterrence against existential threats against any of the belligerents. Major power conflicts have, therefore, had to assume the forms of limited, 'grey' and sponsored 'proxy' wars of varying strategies. These kinds of conflicts are particularly devastating when the combatants are aided by their respective sponsor's advanced information warfare capabilities and modern military technology. As seen in the Western alliance's military advisors' covert support of the Ukrainian war machine, limited intervention from the allied powers could also be possible as long as it does not provoke nuclear escalation from the adversary.
7. **Spread of Civil Wars.** Instigated by political, ethnic, religious and economic ambitions of parochial nature, the emerging era is witnessing a widening spread of violent internal conflicts. Herein, the contending groups find 'justifications' for their cause to be fixated and indelible. That leaves little room for mutually acceptable reconciliation and goes on to provoke armed conflicts, which continue, in varying tempo, for generations. Already there are over 110 major civil wars going on around the globe—Syria, Somalia, Myanmar, Yemen, Sudan, Congo, Armenia, and Colombia are but a few examples.[4] Any of these might flare up to call for greater degrees of intervention from the global powers and their allies. Thus, while civil wars continue to engulf significant parts of Africa, resulting in heavy casualties and torturous displacements, recurrence of unrest and organised violence, active and simmering, are turning endemic in parts of West and East Asia.[5] It is more or less certain that various hues of internal discord would continue to spread in the emerging world order, many of which could result in the outbreak of extremely violent contingencies like ethnic mayhem and mass displacements. With the United Nations neutralised in its prime authority to undertake pacification operations,

the militaries of significant powers would have to be geared up to control such situations.

Politicisation of the Rules of Warfare

'Politics of Warfare', as discussed above, leads us to the phenomenon of 'politicisation' of the rules of warfare. These rules of warfare are sanctified to control the human misery that any war inflicts upon the victors and victims alike. Conversely, the rise of the adversary's political ambitions, backed by the belligerents' possession of formidable destructive capabilities, is liable to trigger irrational breaches of the established rules of combat. In the emerging era, this trend of politicisation of the rules of war is likely to pose added challenges to the management of escalatory control over warfare. Notable trends observed herein are discussed in the succeeding paragraphs.

1. **'Normalisation' of Scorched Earth Tactics.** A rather sinister trend in the politics of warfare is that of 'normalisation' of deliberate targeting of civilian settlements and national infrastructure. Whereas such instances had been but regretful exceptions in the past, there is presently an observable trend of viewing these, in the name of 'unavoidable collateral damage', as marginally legitimate military targets.[6] In the emerging era, organised military action would need to be distinguished from gross savagery and further rationalised through deliberate command and control mechanisms. Leadership in the emerging world order has to recapitulate what even the savage warlords of the past knew: Military power is meant not for destruction of man's labour but to harvest a new range of opportunities against regretful, minimum and unavoidable levels of damages.
2. **States' Recourse to Quasi-military Forces.** In the tradition-bound military ethos, the immorality of taking recourse to proscribed methods in use of force is severely disdained and firmly repudiated. That leads many of the politically diehard regimes to execute their impious, weaponised schemes through quasi-military and grey militia forces operating outside the nation's more conservative military institutions.[7] This trend is exemplified by Iran's Islamic Revolutionary Guard Corps (IRGC), Russia's 'Green Men' and the

Wagner Group, the militarised elements of US' Central Intelligence Agency (CIA), the 'Academi' (Blackwater) and the muscular groups of defence contractors, Pakistan's multitude of Jihadi Mujahideen groups, Sudan's paramilitary 'Rapid Response Force', China's 'People's Militia', Africa's ethnic marauders and arguably, even the UK's 'G4S'. Unbound from the military's orthodox underpinnings, these forces are free to operate across the proscribed limits without being formally accountable for their acts.[8] Many times, this trend also leads to power conflicts between the regular and quasi-military forces, with serious consequences for the citizenry.[9]

3. **Mushrooming of Renegade and Private 'Armies'.** Another trend, aided by lackadaisical state control and easy access to weaponry as well as funds, is the mushrooming of renegade and private 'armies' that operate to impose their dogmatic agendas.[10] Sudan stands devastated by an internal conflict between her paramilitary and regular forces.[11] Similarly, bloodshed and civic strife in the Congo, Angola, Rwanda, Syria, Yemen and some other parts of Africa and West Asia are worrisome examples of factionally prejudiced internal conflicts that rend the afflicted nations with famines, collapse of medical services, mass displacements, breakdown of civil services, and even massacres. Many times, these renegade forces freeze their mutual animosities to forge opportunistic and even more deadly alliances, including securing neo-state sponsorships, to get out of tight corners before reverting to their usual trade. There are also instances of some such factions gaining enough clout to run renegade governance – the Boko Haram in Nigeria, the Islamic State in Syria, Hamas in Gaza, Hezbollah in Lebanon, Houthis in Yemen and the Ethnic Armed Organisations (EAOs) in Myanmar are some leading examples. In the coming days, it would be a harrowing task for the regular militaries to restrain such renegade forces from usurping the affected states' legitimate control over the nationalistic causes—that of fostering internal stability and unobstructed sovereignty.
4. **Test of Military Codes of Conduct.** In the contemporary period, the urge among the non-state, and even some state factions, to impose their bigoted ideologies—Islamist and various ethnic

bigotry particularly—over others has escalated. Organised, trained, equipped and venomously indoctrinated, such factions are casually contemptuous of the moral conventions of warfare. Use of terror as a policy, hostage tactics and fronting human shields to tie the hands of the state forces are some such observable trends. These fanatic factions have to be neutralised at some stage by lawfully mandated national militaries. In that process, militaries being turned loose to perpetrate proscribed acts of retaliatory atrocities have been evidenced in the former Yugoslavia, Syria, Nigeria, Rwanda, Myanmar, etc. In the ensuing violence and counter-violence, the hoary ethos of military conduct could come under threat of blurring its distinction from organised barbarism.[12] That indeed would be a serious matter—it would be suicidal for the world order to suffer the grave consequences of regular militaries falling off their moralist perch to turn into gangs of uncontrollable bloodletters. Indeed, that places an additional burden upon the new era military leadership.

Technological and Economic Fallouts on New-era Warfare

Galloping developments in technological innovations and stronger economic regimes have triggered avalanches of bloated trade and commercial ambitions among the people. In the modern era of individual and group empowerment, governments are obliged to respond to that kind of exponential rise in their people's demands if they have to hold on to political power; this is true even in non-democratic societies. But when the pressures of people's expectations exceed the reservoirs of any nation's indigenous resources, there arises the urge of grabbing external sources—preferably through genuine as well as deceitful commercial dealings, and failing that, through weaponised manipulations. In such instances, wars sprout when partisan ambitions are rendered unworkable either due to inherent impracticalities or strong opposition from contending parties. This phenomenon is marked by the following recent developments:

1. **Rise in Global Arms Trade.** The combined globalisation of technological handles and profitable arms trade, legal or otherwise, has led to weaponisation of a plethora of non-state factions—

rebellions for causes, noble as well as diabolical, as one might view these. A reckonable rise in bloodletting confrontations across the global trouble spots is a disconcerting fallout of that situation.

2. **Growing Influence of Defence-Industrial Conglomerates.** Commercial motivations, as witnessed during the long years of the Gulf Wars as well as the on-going Russia-Ukraine War, offer indications of growing clout of the political-military industry conglomerate over the conduct of modern-era warfare. Many among the top political thinkers opine that besides political ambitions, the influence of the US-Europe defence industry has also contributed to the same: firstly, by stoking the Russian attack on Ukraine; and secondly, in prolonging the senseless slaughter and destruction that goes on in other hotspots in the Middle East and Central Africa. The opinion is construed from the alleged lobbying activities of the major defence dealers, manufacturers and contractors, like General Dynamics, Boeing, Lockheed Martin, Black Rock, etc. and their NATO connections, which are stated to profit from huge orders against defence recoupments and reconstruction of destroyed infrastructure.[13]
3. **Flow of Defence Hardware.** The above-mentioned possibilities apart, there is also a matter of concern in defence circles that points to military commanders' operational options being limited by conditions of supply of military hardware. As war stocks deplete quickly in the intense engagements while production remains regulated by long-term principles of stocking, defence manufacturers could force-feed their in-stock weapons into the supply chain—with good profits. This would be indicative of a situation when the market of military hardware comes to rule over preferred strategy and military tactics. That indeed would be a serious situation, which could further be dangerously exacerbated by political manipulations.

Matters discussed in Part I above are destined to flow into substantial implications on contemporary military strategies. This aspect is discussed in the following Part.

Part II: Strategic Implications of New Era Politics of Warfare

Determinants of Military Architecture

As an instrument of sovereignty, the options and methods of military force application are to be revisited in tune with societal, political, technological and economic determinants of the time. These determinants dictate as to 'why' one has to engage in warfare, 'what' might be its objective(s), and 'how' might one secure that objective with the least violence and destruction. The architecture of a nation's military organisational framework, its man-weapon-machine integration, selection and training of warriors, and the motivational core of the military institution are determined accordingly. Therefore, a discussion of the emerging nuances of warfare should begin with a review of the contemporary era trends of strategic applications of military power. It will be observed that contemporary-era conflicts are resonant with continuities from the reigning principles of strategy, and that there are but limited 'surprising discoveries' as such.

Appraisal of Recent Wars

Afghan Wars. In a case of strategic failure, the Soviets, having tactically subdued the adversary, found their desired political end-state unachievable against unyielding and externally supported native opposition.[14] The America-led Western powers had a similar experience in 2021 when they had to recuse from Taliban's Afghanistan without achieving their political objectives. These cases are but new-era reiterations of the fact that indigenous masses of fanatic religious-cultural indoctrination, when sustained by inflow of information age instruments coming from common-cause alliances, can neither be freed from bigotry or 'democratised' nor be triumphed by hard military power alone, unless it is dove-tailed into a negotiable political end-state.

West Asian Wars. The US-led invasion of Iraq and its follow-up operations (2003-11) offer certain modern era tactical reiterations. Herein, after the Revolution in Military Affairs (RMA)- induced military campaign succeeded, the victors got caught up with complex mixes of local political, religious and social conflicts when the power of RMA stood marginalised. In the foreseeable future, deep-rooted regional, political, ethnic and religious alliances and animosities among nearly a dozen state and non-state belligerents are expected to keep the region in multi-dimensional discord. Frequent military flare-ups among the regional and extra-regional stakeholders of this strategically vital region would thus have to be prepared for. Accordingly, military interventions in the emerging era, in order to reign-in those factions that remain obdurate, have to be buttressed with inclusive participation of indigenous power centres. That could be a tedious haul for the world powers and their allies.

The Kargil Conflict. This limited conflict offers certain key lessons on the emerging era war. Having been thwarted in its frequent attempts to wrest Kashmir by means of conventional attacks and terror tactics, Pakistan's leadership had taken to infiltration of regular-irregular forces in order to extend its occupied areas of Kashmir. This led to a military conflict even while both the adversaries exercised certain restraints to avoid escalation to nuclear exchange. As India unleashed regular operations to evict the intrusions, Pakistan was left with no choice but to concede defeat. Finally, US' 'advice' forced Pakistan to withdraw its remaining doomed infiltrators. Notables here are: one, conventional deterrence caused the revisionist aggressor to resort to sub-conventional options; two, sub-conventional aggression could well be defeated by means of conventional operations; and three, this instance established the fact that it is possible to conduct conventional military operations without triggering nuclear exchange and suffering its global fallouts. The notion that conventional power had lost its salience was belied thus.

Russia's 'Special Military Operations'. After some intense fighting over two years, this war has reached a state of strategic stalemate where both sides are content to hold what they have while engaging in intermittent localised tactical-level operations to keep the guns hot. This has given Russia the time and opportunity to consolidate its political grip over the captured Russian-majority areas of Ukraine. With possible thinning out of Ukraine's military supply lines, this war could turn out to be an example of Russia's strategic application of moderated military power to achieve its political ends. This must be a significant pointer to those nations who stand vulnerable to their powerful adversaries' expansionist ambitions. Conversely, it is also likely that Ukraine's military resolve, if sustained by its allies' robust political and economic assistance, could wear out the aggressor; and that could derail the ambitions of the expansionist powers.

Israel-Hamas-Palestinian Confrontation. This is a case of a nation deploying conventional forces to decimate its quasi-military enemies.[15] The targeted anti-Israel forces—the Hamas, Islamic Jihad, Hezbollah, etc.—who are liable to adopt crass acts of brutality, are built with well-trained and radically instigated fighters, modern weaponry and huge funding. On the other end, Israel's retaliatory mass-destruction of Palestinian settlements has invited widespread consternation. But sublime considerations have not been able to divert either of the adversaries' resolve to extract bloody revenge against the opponent's weaponised brinkmanship. Over long periods of the recent decades, this kind of deliberately foisted and sustained terror-hostage-humanitarian situations had begun to be witnessed mostly in Africa and West Asia. Presently, such breaches against the established norms of warfare seem to be turning into a shadowy practice even in regular armed conflicts. This could be a new-era trend—that of a democratic nation adapting to the proscribed methods of using conventional military means to disable armed militant factions from forcing their objectives through acts of terrorism. Notwithstanding this disturbing trend, just as Israel's success in the killing fields is unlikely to bring lasting peace as long as the root causes of fanatical hatred among either of the belligerents are not assuaged, so would be the case elsewhere too.

Some Significant Strategic and Tactical Reiterations. The preceding appraisal offers certain significant reiterations:-

a. Fixation with the concept of 'short and intense' wars stands repudiated; and so is the relief it permits to those nations who possess but limited capacity for prolonged conflict.
b. Universal dismay has not come in the way of the belligerents to inflict collateral destruction and blow up humanitarian crises, when considered necessary.
c. Military campaigns require profound ways of preparing the society to reconcile to the inevitable setbacks, deprivations and manipulative misinformation. Towards that end, extensive authentication of the information domain from the trusted media would be mandatory.

Russia's use of Telegram channels and Ukraine's use of social and traditional media to explain setbacks and reassure their peoples are some examples. Selective censorship to safeguard sensitive interests would still be needed.

d. This appraisal reaffirms that the advantages of modern intelligence, surveillance and cyber technologies can be assimilated through tactical adaptations. And yet, these sub-sets of conflict cannot be the magic alternatives to classical conduct of regular warfare.
e. By sharing reconnaissance, communications and intelligence data, advanced powers can radically enhance the military capabilities of their middle power allies.
f. Politically determined supply of weaponry and equipment, as selectively made available from the allies' stockpiles, can prolong a war but might not conclude it in favourable terms.
g. Autonomy in indigenous defence manufacturing could diminish the effects of sanctions. Russia, China, Iran, and Türkiye are some examples.

Centrality of Classical Military Power

Many among the new era analysts are liable to advance wishful alternatives to the catastrophic burdens of classical military power. The motivation is to address the ever-rising human and material costs of maintaining, modernising and unleashing conventional military power with what are considered to be more expedient means of achieving the purpose of national defence. The idea is enticing, no doubt, particularly so to the resource- constrained nations that are destined to defend against more powerful adversaries. The proposition goes awry when such means of stand-off, information, cyber and trade war options are purported to compensate for the deficits of hard, destructive and high-cost military power. As the nature of military campaigns in the contemporary world order reiterate, such convenient options are workable but only to the extent of performing the roles of modern force multipliers in aid of hard military power. As ever, hard military power remains the sole arbitrator against injustice and affront in this dog-eat-dog world, and the only alternative to escape from the excruciating costs and catastrophes of war would be to submit to the much larger perils of yielding to transgression!

Strategy of 'Shadow Warfare'

Shadow warfare has assumed profitable salience in the emerging world order. Incremental usurpation of territorial, political and economic rights of cohabitant nations, situated in what is arbitrarily declared as the perpetrators' regions of 'dominance', is a kind of shadow warfare. The trend is exemplified by some of the main proponents of expansionist and hegemonic aspirations—China, Russia, Iran and Türkiye, for example. China's strategy is remarkable, wherein the affronts remain below the underdog's red lines of sovereign concerns, and yet, over time, they get 'normalised' by the arbitrary usurpations into the 'realities' of new territorial, economic, political and social status quo. With its neighbourhood possessing but limited military capabilities, China would be unstoppable in its multifaceted expansionism. As history tells us, its appetite would grow in the coming years—till it over-stretches itself.

Ukraine has already suffered the consequences of Russia's shadow aggression in Crimea, Donbas and Luhansk regions. Presently, Taiwan, Vietnam, the Philippines, India, Japan and many other Asian and African nations are victims of various forms and degrees of China's shadow aggression. For its low-commitment-high- return results, the trend is likely to gain salience in the years to come. Nations of moderate military capacities have to find appropriate responses to this strategy. The point to note here is that shadow warfare also offers to the modest powers, many out-of-proportion capabilities to retaliate and hurt the interests of their powerful adversaries. Such examples are galore in the West Asian and African theatres. Given China's military arm-twisting policies, shadow warfare could well get sparked by the hapless defenders in the China Seas theatre.

Defence Research, Production and Maintenance Industry

As militaries add to their arsenal of 'intelligent' hardware, there is a concurrent thrust on modernisation of the possessed stocks of standard weaponry and war equipment. Consequently, nations are undertaking accelerated efforts to recoup the irregular forces' hardware deficiencies. The global defence industry is already being run in top gear while the dormant production lines and the rusted supply chains are being resuscitated. In this context, global reinforcement of defence production lines against Russia's withdrawal from the treaty on 'Conventional Armed Forces in Europe' (CFE), as also its counter-actions from the US-NATO partnerships, are some significant developments.

Part III: Ruling Inferences from the Characteristics of the Wars Waged, and Being Waged, during the Recent Years

Imperatives at the Tactical Level

The strategic implications discussed in Part II above set the stage for identifying certain key inferences related to tactical imperatives for the military of the coming era. These are listed in subsequent paragraphs.

Prosecution of Regular Warfare

Inter-relations: Conventional and Sub-conventional Wars. As ever, substantial parts of the globe may be expected to continue to engage in inter-state as well as internally and externally instigated militancy, aimed at upstaging the existing order through various forms of conventional and sub-conventional violence. Further, a phenomenal rise in the use of modern conventional weaponry to prosecute sub-conventional conflicts and anti-militancy actions would be a natural fallout of that situation. As the belligerents access high-technology weaponry and modern tools of violence, deployment of formally trained and equipped regular military forces would have to be the afflicted states' principal recourse to safeguard their constitutional aspirations.

Firepower Options. Dispersed, strong and defiladed fortifications have led to the militaries' increased dependence on stand-off, high-destruction, precision and obviously, high-cost weaponry. The purpose herein is to saturate targeted objectives with near-total destruction before the troops are unleashed to finish the task. The roles of tactical manoeuvre, artillery firepower, air strikes, missiles and drones in destruction and interdiction operations have thus assumed added magnification in prosecution of war.

Centrality of Air Defence. As a corollary to fire power options, the purpose of air defence, too, has found a high level of centrality in modern warfare. The development of National Advanced Surface-to-Air Missile System (NASAMS), the Patriot and Iron Dome Systems, Hi-Mobility Artillery Rocket System (HIMARS), US-Norway's Short Range Air Defence System and Iran's new Zoubin System, followed by a Ukraine-Poland four billion air defence deal, are some indications of this trend.

Contemporising the Civil Defence Organisations. Alongside strengthening air defence systems, it is also necessary to organise appropriate civil defence systems for the security of civil infrastructure, backup installations for the critical systems and facilities for public mobilisation.

Salience of Cutting-edge Electronic Warfare. Russia could manage against Ukraine's network-centric and cyber warfare restrictions by elevating electronic warfare capabilities into its traditional tactical countermeasures. In future warfare, this aspect would demand greater attention by means of deliberately planned and provisioned electronic defence preparedness.

Harness of Space Power. As evidenced from recent military operations, robust orbital arrays of space assets are a crucial factor in the effectivity of military prowess. Satellites dedicated to provision of real-time surveillance, reconnaissance and targeting, aided by robust networks of communications, can significantly influence the courses of modern warfare. Space power has thus emerged as an effective means of influencing the equation of military power as well as the course of hostilities across the world. Build-up of space capabilities is, therefore, one of the primary goals of bolstering national defence.

Dependence on Boots on Ground. Contrary to wishful notions, the roles of professionally structured and experienced troops in covering the wider facets of modern warfare have actually expanded. Consequently, there has been much debate in the strategic circles over deployment of friendly forces' boots to fight their ally's war. The summary opinion is that no power would like to commit its troops to such assignments, even if it would be permissible for them to meet the partner's material needs. However, such conclusions are not always sustainable. When stakes are strong enough and rewards are significant, strategic partners would, no doubt, commit their troops, either directly or from behind a facade, in wars against their common enemies. Presently, there are over 300 nations where foreign military contingents are stationed with the purpose of performing the role of bases for training and advisories on their allies' military operations when the need arises.[16]

Rise of Limited Objective Skirmish Actions

Political, economic and social stakes in full-scale warfare having become prohibitive, there is a rising trend to opt for grey and skirmish- level military operations with regular military back-up to upstage the opponent over time. The Taliban in Afghanistan, China in the China Seas and along the Indo-Tibet border, Russia in Crimea and Ukraine, Islamic militants in Sahel-Central African countries, and quasi-military forces in Iran and Yemen are some notable practitioners of such grey-zone skirmish actions—with varying results.

Rising Opportunities for Stand-off, Deniable, Disruptive Attacks

Masked use of rudimentary technology and mass-produced versions of explosive devices, rockets, drones and missiles in perpetration of stand-off attacks against soft targets has gained favour among the trouble- making non-state, and even some state, actors. Herein, rogue fighters try to disrupt routine commerce, transportation, manufacturing, social activities, and even civic infrastructure, and so create terror situations to hold the stable order to ransom. Hamas' and Houthis' mass use of country-made rockets and drones to disrupt their enemy's socio-political stability are some examples. Examples also come from the stand-off, faceless drone attacks against military and civilian targets by the states of Ukraine, Russia, Iran and Türkiye.

In regular warfare, unless the standard tactical practices are overlooked, such attacks might not go beyond infliction of temporary setbacks of nuisance value.[17] But the situation of perpetual hostility and piracy of the kind seen against global shipping in the Red Sea, Persian Gulf, and the Arabian and the Mediterranean Seas could further spread over to other chokepoint passages like the Malacca Straits, Panama Canal, and so on. The recent formation of a Red Sea coalition of US-led 'Operation Prosperity Guardian' to deal with this kind of situation is a pointer.

Similarly, threats to socio-political stability, particularly of the kind seen in West Asia and Africa, could instigate new causes of turmoil in larger parts of the globe. Unless this kind of perpetual state of inter- and intra-state hostility is moderated in the coming days, highly destructive grey-zone activities against even routine civic functions could spread across the vulnerable regions. Nations have to put their heads together to address this malaise.

Interpretation of Military Intelligence

The modern era is witness to the rise of unlimited and unaccountable sources of information. This leads to information overload, much of which is conjecture, exaggeration and fake. Easily accessible, these inputs tend to divert the highly professional and tedious processes of assimilation, interpretation and dissemination of military intelligence, particularly at the tactical levels. In intelligence assessment, dependence on technically generated information with limited interface with professional military insight leads to the appearance of grey and black spots. Then, there is also the trend of injecting politically feel-good notions into hard but discomforting military intelligence. Such ambiguities result in misleading intelligence appreciations, and consequently, compromise the sanctity of operational planning.[18]

The situation is exacerbated by the recently necessitated overlap between strategic and tactical military intelligence, and the overlapping core competencies among the state's various intelligence gathering mechanisms. In the emerging era, rather than resorting to the easy way of lamenting 'intelligence failure', it would be mandatory to address the real, still unaddressed infirmities of the modern-era intelligence system. In this process, deliberate upgrade of the military intelligence system, as aligned to the parameters of modern-era warfare, has to be a foremost undertaking.

Looking at Future Wars

Just as the fundamental determinants of mankind's civilisational existence remain more or less eternal, so is also the case with warfare. Warring, after all, has always been an intrinsic sub-set of human existence, its significance being in its prevention, and when that effort fails, in successful termination, as early as practicable, of its violent, destructive prosecution. Achieving that end in the emerging world order requires refreshing the dated definitions of 'peaceful co-existence', 'modernisation' and 'application of military power', while saving from misinterpretation of the repackaged, if catchy, military ideologies.

Delicate equations of power in an increasingly turbulent world order call for the state and its military hicrarchy to conjointly regulate the ever-escalating triggers of warfare, refresh the military doctrines, and strategise over the rising issues of national defence. That would be a prerequisite for building up the nation's due military preparedness, moderating the adversary's military arrogance and foiling inimical military adventurism.[19] Similarly, higher levels of political insight and diplomatic astuteness would be the prerequisites to manage intimidating possibilities of direct military clash among the large as well as mid-level powers, even possibilities of nuclear exchange, as these are being perceived among the contemporary strategy analysts.[20]

Notes

1. Post-independence, India had sought to adopt a policy of 'peace and friendliness' with aggressive adversaries as an expedient alternative to the burden of military preparedness.
2 Wise Voter Review, *Countries Currently at War, 2022*, www.wisevoter.com.
3. Valdai Discussion Club, *Warfare in a New Epoch, Moscow*, October, 2023.
4. The Geneva Academy, *Military Briefings*, November 2023.
5. Some of the more significant civil wars, with no end in sight, rage in the Central African Republic, Ethiopia, Libya, Mali, Somalia, South Sudan, Palestine, Yemen, Syria and Myanmar—the list is long.
6. The Battle of Britain, Dresden bombings and atomic attacks on Hiroshima-Nagasaki are some well-known examples. Russia's destruction of civil infrastructure in Ukraine and Israel's 'levelling' of the Gaza Strip are some recent ones.
7. Nazi Germany's SS and SA, the Italian Blackshirts, the Kosovo Liberation Army, Pakistan's Razakars and the Federal Investigating Agency are some more examples.

8. Sean McFate, *Mercenaries and War: Understanding Private Armies Today,* National Defence University, Washington, D.C. December 2019.
9. Hostility among the military and paramilitary forces in broken-up Yugoslavia, that between the Iranian Armed Forces and the IRGC, between the Sudanese military and its Rapid Reaction Force and the Russian Army and the Wagner Group are some recent examples.
10. Some well-known private armies are: the Kurdish Peshmerga, Iraq's Ansar al-Islam and Al Sadr's Mahdi Army, the Tehreek-e-Taliban (Jihad) Pakistan, Lashkar-e Taiba, the Hamas, Hezbollah, Houthi, Boko Haram, Myanmar's Wa State Army—the list is long.
11. The warring parties are led by fallen out generals of the paramilitary Rapid Support Force (RSF) and the Sudanese Armed Forces (SAF).
12. Civil wars in Sri Lanka, Sudan, Kosovo-Serbia and the most recent bloodbath in Israel-Palestine are some examples of militaries contradicting their culture of sparing non-combatants.
13. In this dispensation, the donors are stated to stand profited at the cost of the recipients even if such expenses are to be met from grant of 'loans', leases' etc. Reportedly, 30 per cent of Ukraine's fertile basket of agricultural assets stands bequeathed to M/S Dupont, Cargill and Mosanto, all owned by the Black Rock management. www.kennedy24.com
14. Anthony Cordesman, *Learning the Right Lessons from the Afghan War,* September 7, 2021 (acordesman@gmail.co)
15. India has been tackling externally instigated militancy with conventional forces.
16. *Journal of Conflict Management and Peace Science*, Vol 40, Issue 6, November 2023. Even in the Ukraine War, there is selective presence of foreign troops.
17. In 2020, Armenian forces suffered heavy losses from Azerbaijan's conventional use of drone attacks only because it had overlooked the basics of balanced force-structure.
18. Some examples of premature propaganda vitiating the political-military decision-making inputs are: one, till the very last, the US forces were purported to be gaining over Afghanistan's Taliban insurgency; two, millions of Afghans were purportedly 'dying of starvation'; three, Russia was on the 'verge of defeat' in Ukraine, and so on.
19. Valdai Discussion Club Report, *Warfare in a New Epoch,* October 2023.
20. 'Military Aspects Emerging World Order', VIF Journal *National Security* Volume VII, Issue I, January-March, 2024.

4. Changing Trends in Warfare

Prakash Katoch

An Overview of Major Wars

The increasing race for world domination is leading to global realignments. America wants to lead with its own 'Rule-based Order' and subjugate Russia and China, but US actions have brought them closest ever. With the aim of becoming a top superpower, China is flexing muscles in the South China Sea (SCS) as tensions mount over Taiwan. With the US and NATO increasingly violating Russian redlines and Russian submarines operating near Florida—the US Coast, another Cuban Missile Crisis appears to be in the making although Russian President Putin says, 'America need not worry'.

The Israel-Hamas war continues. Hamas has "conditionally" agreed to negotiate the ceasefire proposed by the UN Security Council (UNSC). However, indications are that the 'conditions' would not be accepted since Hamas wants Israel to release its 8,900 plus prisoners as part of the hostage swap. Israel-Hezbollah hostilities have escalated. The US and the UK continue to attack Yemen. The US and Israel are concerned about Iran producing more weapon-grade plutonium. The volatile situation in Sudan is conducive for the IS to again establish itself there. Myanmar is in the throes of a civil war, and Pakistan is losing its grip in Khyber Pakhtunkhwa-North Waziristan to the Taliban.

The above developments and how these impact India would be of special interest to Indian policy makers and the Indian military. Some of these issues are discussed in the succeeding paragraphs. In that, an overview of major war-like situations across the globe would be an appropriate starting point.

Ukraine War

This is not a Russo-Ukraine war but a US-NATO war (Ukraine being their proxy) on Russia. With NATO's expansion posing an existential threat to Russia, Moscow was pushed into launching its Military Special Operations (MSP). Herein, the American interests include weakening Russia militarily and economically; denying Russia access to the Black Sea; protecting own investments (land-agriculture, minerals, biological R&D) in Ukraine; expanding NATO further—making new members dependent on American arms; increasing Europe's security dependence on the US; and taming China similarly.

The war is a mix of 20th and 21st century warfare, holding frontlines replete with trenches and tunnels, land, sea, air and space activated StarLink satellites facilitating Ukrainian operations. It has rejected the belief that technological advancements as well as increased lethality and precision of weapons will force modern era wars to be short and swift. It reflects the changing character of war. These changes are in terms of high intensity multi-domain operations, heightened Control, Communications, Computers, Intelligence, Inter-operability, Surveillance & Reconnaissance (C4I2SR), and employment of hitherto unseen Artificial Intelligence (AI)-driven systems, hypersonic and advanced autonomous weapons inflicting unprecedented high level of casualties. All this necessitates changes in the methodology of warfighting.

Along with the US-sponsored sabotage of Russian Nord Stream Pipelines, underwater drones have been used to attack Russia's Kerch Bridge link to Crimea. Both sides are using aerial drones extensively. Ukraine has been losing 10,000 drones on an average every month. Jamming has emerged as a very effective new counter-drone measure. Fearing Russian incursions, six NATO countries plan to erect a 'drone wall' from Norway to Poland. Because of heavy losses, helicopters flying close to the frontline are allowed only in emergencies like casualty evacuation. Significantly, Ukraine has added a branch to its armed forces dedicated to drones.

US weapons, including M-1 Abrams tanks, Switchblade drone, Patriot air defense missiles, M-777 howitzers, Excalibur guided 155 mm artillery rounds, HIMARS precision missile, GPS-guided bombs and AI-aided Skydio drones have fared poorly because of Russia employing electronic warfare (EW), cyber warfare, and artificial intelligence (AI) countermeasures. Ukrainian air defence is no match for the Russian Kh-47M2 Kinzhal hypersonic ballistic missiles. Artillery ammunition expenditure is very high—10,000-20,000 rounds being fired on a single day. Glide bombs helped Russia breach consolidated Ukrainian frontlines, inflicting 1,000 casualties every day in one instance. Russia used mines extensively to block Ukraine's counter-offensive. Periscope machine guns have emerged on the scene.

AI-enabled voice transcription and translation services are processing intercepted communications and automatically highlighting information concerning enemy forces. The danger of being located has forced dispersed dug-down deployment, even moving to alternate locations frequently.

Russian casualties were high in the first two weeks of launching the MSP because Ukraine successfully targeted Russian command posts. But thereafter, Russian casualties reduced dramatically, averaging just 10 per cent of Ukrainian casualties.

Both Russia and Ukraine are using mercenaries, and there is evidence of Western regulars operating in Ukraine as trainers, logistics managers, and incognito participants in operations.

The West is supplying long- range weaponry to hit deep inside Russia, as also F-16 fighter aircraft. On May 22, 2024, Russia released footage of the Russian multipurpose naval fighter, Su-30SM2, equipped with 2 x R-77-1 and 2 x R-37M missiles and designed to destroy high-speed aircraft at more than 300 km range, which the F-16s cannot match. Ukraine has managed to target a Russian S-400 AD missile location.

Russia's President, Putin, says he doesn't need to use nuclear weapons, but if Ukraine starts attacking targets deep inside Russia with long-range missiles, he may be forced to consider the same. The long-range weapons that the US, the UK, and France have provided Ukraine with need satellite reconnaissance data that Kyiv lacks. In effect, the supplier states have control over the client's target selection.

Israel-Hamas War

There are insinuations that Israel had advance information of the Hamas' attack on October 7, 2023, which was not taken seriously. The border units of Israel were not alerted. Hamas was thus able to successfully breach the hi-tech barrier (running above and below the ground), which separates Gaza from Israel.

Hamas has constructed a labyrinth of 500 km of underground tunnels. Fighting through such an elaborate tunnel network required new innovations by the Israel Defence Forces (IDF). Clearing all the tunnels would have invited many casualties, which is probably why Israel opted for mass bombings.

Media subterfuge is on full display here. It is said that the previous Israeli government under Prime Minister Netanyahu had funded or allowed funding of the Hamas, which helped in arming this organisation. This is similar to allegations of the US training and arming the Islamic State in Turkey. Conspiracy theories abound that the IDF have captured two Chinese military engineers from these tunnels. Fingers have been pointed at Mohammad Deif, the military head of the Hamas, who lived in China for many years and is married to two Chinese Muslim women.[1] Believable or not, war gossip has become a dangerous pastime.

Israel used AI to mark suspected Hamas and Palestinian Islamic Jihad (PIJ) operatives under the 'Lavender Program' through mass surveillance on most of Gaza's 2.3 million residents. The use of this method despite an error rate of 10 per cent has caused unwanted collateral damage. An investigation report, citing two sources, states that the IDF has decided that for every killing of a 'Lavender'—marked junior Hamas operative, killing of up to 15-20 civilians in the process could be acceptable; on several occasions of selectively targeted assassinations, the permissible numbers could be more than 100 civilians.

Permanent ceasefire appears to be a chimera since the 'two-state solution' is not acceptable to the US and Israel. Netanyahu is unlikely to achieve his aim of total destruction of Hamas. Mass killings and political disagreements in the post-war Gaza plan have resulted in six resignations in Israel's War Cabinet. Concurrently, Hezbollah has been attacking

Israel with drones and rockets, and Israel has been bombing Hezbollah locations in Lebanon.

Only Argentina, Australia, Canada, the European Union (EU), Israel, New Zealand, Paraguay, the UK, and the US designate the Hamas a terrorist group. The world is divided over 'Gaza Genocide', with over 40,000 people already killed since October 7, 2023. Related rulings by the International Criminal Court (ICC) and the International Court of Justice (ICJ) have made the US and Israel pariahs in the eyes of many. This is not surprising considering that in the Vietnam War alone, America killed around two million Vietnamese men, women, and children.

Red Sea Conflict

The Houthis had announced they would attack vessels to and fro from Israel if there was no ceasefire in Gaza. They have been attacking ships while the US and the UK have been bombing and firing missiles at Houthi locations in Yemen with a broader message to Iran.

Israel aerially attacked the Iranian consulate in Damascus, following which Iran attacked Israel with drones and missiles, damaging some Israeli airbases. Despite giving advance warning to the US and Israel, Iran's hypersonic missiles were able to penetrate western air defences to hit targets in Israel.

The Houthis have been able to down six US MQ-9 Reaper drones since September 2023, one of which appears electronically in pictures as unharmed—similar to Iran electronically capturing a US RQ-170 drone in 2011 and replicating it. Yemen also hit US aircraft carrier USS Dwight Eisenhower.

Western Pacific

China has been undertaking live firing exercises around Taiwan and periodically intruding into Taiwan's airspace and the Taiwan Straits. China is flexing muscles both in the South China Sea (SCS) and East China Sea (ECS), besides increasing tensions with Japan. The Chinesc Coast Guard has been entering the Japanese-controlled disputed islands—for a record 158 consecutive days in recent months, surpassing the record of

157 days in 2021. Chinese fighter jets recently circled a Dutch frigate and approached a Dutch helicopter during a patrol in the ECS.

China continues with its grey zone tactics in the SCS to harass foreign ships. Tensions between China and the Philippines are high with Chinese Coast Guard vessels using water cannons, injuring Filipino crew members, and seizing food packs airdropped to the Philippine outposts. At the recent Shangri-La Dialogue, the Philippines President warned China against crossing the line into "an act of war", but despite tensions, the Philippines reportedly wants robust trade with China. On June 6, 2024, Vietnam demanded that China's survey ship, Hai Yang 26, exit from its illegal survey operations in Vietnam's EEZ.

At the summit with US President Joe Biden in San Francisco last December, Chinese President Xi Jinping told Biden that Beijing will reunify Taiwan with mainland China, but the timing had not been decided. Xi repeated this resolve in his New Year address. Later, *meeting a former Taiwanese president in April 2024, Xi said that* outside interference can't stop Taiwan's reunion with China.

US lawmakers have been visiting Taiwan. The new US$ 8 billion US military aid package to Taiwan will 'boost confidence' in the region, the US media said on April 23, 2024. Vessels of the US and its allies have been sailing in the SCS. America is closely monitoring Chinese military activities and even maintains US Special Forces' presence in Taiwan's Kinmen Islands, located less than 10 km off China's mainland.

The US Indo-Pacific Command recently announced its 'Hellscape Strategy'. It is aimed at using swarm drones, submarines, surface ships, and other classified capabilities to swarm the Taiwan Strait to restrain the Chinese forces for a month, thus allowing the US and its allies to mount a full response. *The Washington Post*, however, states that the People's Liberation Army's (PLA) rapid expansion and US military budget constraints present significant challenges in implementing the Hellscape Strategy.

The US Defence Department has proposed 5 bn in military aid to Taiwan in its 2025 budget. Meanwhile, America has been holding the US-Japan–South Korea and US–Japan–Philippines trilateral summits, besides engaging in diplomatic talks with China.

Sudan

Civil war between two rival factions of the military government of Sudan—the Sudanese Armed Forces (SAF) under Abdel Fattah al-Burhan and the paramilitary Rapid Support Forces (RSF) under the Janjaweed leader, Hemedti—broke out on April 15, 2023. Sudan is undergoing the most dangerous humanitarian crisis in the world. Almost 18 million Sudanese (one- third of the population) face life- threatening levels of food insecurity. By the end of May 2024, around 11 million people were forced to flee their homes or left Sudan. Healthcare is critically affected, and there is severe shortage of medicines and vital supplies.

Sudan and China established diplomatic relations in 1959. Both are close allies, supporting each other during internal crises and international controversies, like in the Second Sudanese Civil War. The US' policy on Sudan is facing pressure from Democratic and Republican lawmakers to do more to help end the war. This issue also needs to be viewed against the backdrop of China's increased influence in Africa.

In 1993, the US designated Sudan a "State Sponsor of Terrorism" for supporting international terrorist groups, including the Abu Nidal Organization, Palestine Islamic Jihad, Hamas, and Hezbollah. But some reports indicate that the Islamic State, purportedly linked to the CIA, is looking to reestablish its main base in Sudan. This may not be surprising with both America and China using terrorists to advance their respective national interests.

Myanmar

Myanmar is witnessing increasing violence. Myanmar's government army is combating multiple Ethnic Armed Organizations (EAO) and the People's Defence Force (PDF), the armed wing of the rebel National Unity Government (NUG). The Arakan Army controls the majority area of the Rakhine State and more than one-third of the adjoining Chin State. The government has ruled that men aged 18-35 years and women aged 18-27 years must compulsorily serve a minimum two years in the military.

On May 6, 2024, the UN stated that the conflict has forced out three million plus people in Myanmar from their homes—a 50 per cent surge in the last six months. Fighting intensified in October 2023 when EAOs and the PDF launched major offensives in Shan and Rakhine states to overrun many military outposts and take control of key towns near the China border. In recent weeks, the military has also been battling ethnic Karen groups for control of Myawaddy, a major trade hub bordering Thailand.

The violence has resulted in thousands of refugees pouring into India and China. China is supporting and arming the junta as well as the EAOs in Myanmar (its involvement is also suspected in aiding the insurgents and terrorists in India, particularly in Manipur state). American support in arming the PDF in Myanmar is ambiguous, although the US and its allies have been calling for restoration of democracy in Myanmar.

The Myanmar military has killed around 5,000 people since the coup and 20,000 plus are in detention. The majority of refugees entering India get located in Mizoram because the ethnic Chins inhabit both sides of the border. Having lost control over their military posts, Myanmar military stragglers are pouring into India and Bangladesh; these are being repatriated by both countries. The situation adversely affects India's national security.

Afghanistan-Pakistan

The Tehreek-e-Taliban Pakistan (TTP) has become the bane of Pakistani security forces for frequently targeting them. Pakistan experienced a dramatic increase in TTP-led attacks since the Taliban took control of Afghanistan in August 2021. Since then, the TTP has claimed the merger of 47 Pakistani Taliban factions, sectarian groups, and Al- Qaeda affiliates.

By mid-March 2024, the TTP had killed about 2,000 Pakistanis, including police and military personnel. The Hafiz Gul Bahadur (HGB) group has joined the TTP to launch attacks in Khyber Pakhtunkhwa (KPK) and North Waziristan. The HGB group is also linked to the Haqqani Network and Al- Qaeda. On May 25, 2024, the HGB killed more than 25 Pakistani army personnel and burnt several vehicles in an attack on a post near the Durand line in North Waziristan and occupied the post.

KPK is virtually under the control of the TTP-HGB. Babar Ali, a senior TTP commander, says, “Entire country (Pakistan) is now under our control, we are present in every corner of Pakistan.” The TTP and the HGB have been trending the idea of “Ghazwa-e-Hind” on social media since mid-March 2024. Turning Afghanistan-AfPak into a crucible of terror has allegedly been an American design. The Taliban, the Haqqani Network, the TTP, the Al- Qaeda, the Islamic State (IS or ISIS), the HGB group, and the Pak-based terror groups are all interlinked.

The US-UK support to Pakistan is a counter-pressure against a rising India. The CIA and the MI-6 continue to maintain links with Pakistan's ISI as a pressure point to tame India. Pakistan will keep stoking terrorism in Jammu and Kashmir, as indicated by the terror attacks coinciding with the swearing-in of a new Indian government.

Issues of Interest to India

Sanctity of International Organisations. The UN General Assembly (UNGA) is sans due authority. The manner in which UN resolutions related to Ukraine and Gaza have been vetoed shows how toothless the UN is. The same goes for the response to the rulings by the ICC and the ICJ (a UN organ). Earlier, on July 12, 2016, China trashed the ICJ ruling on SCS in favour of the Philippines. Related to this is the many foreign nations' irrelevant support for India's 'permanent' membership of the UNSC, ignoring the fact that China will veto any such move.

Geostrategic Contestations

Ukraine. The US wants the Ukraine war to continue for a long time. The recent US-Ukraine 10-year security pact (precursor to Ukraine's NATO membership) and the G7 decision to “loan” US$ 50 billion to Ukraine using frozen Russian funds confirms this unequivocally. The loan fools none since Kiev can never pay it back even if using frozen Russian funds and could amount to economic highhandedness. Moscow calls the G7 move as criminal and states that “our response will be painful”.

Russia. Despite sanctions, Russia is the fourth- largest economy in the world in terms of Purchasing Power Parity (PPP). The US external debt is rising exponentially, but with the war continuing, American arms manufacturers and oil producers are raking in billions of dollars. Concurrently, European economies are weakening, making them more dependent on Washington for security.

Gaza. Ceasefire in Gaza is unlikely while Israel-Hezbollah hostilities are escalating. Hezbollah, too, has a network of tunnels, which made Israel suffer considerable casualties during its ground offensive in Lebanon during 2006. Therefore, Israel might resort to heavy bombardment before launching a ground offensive against Hezbollah.

Iran. Many analysts believe that the US is prepared to bomb Iran in case the latter goes nuclear. But the possibility of China testing an Iranian nuclear weapon on its soil cannot be ruled out—just as it tested a Pakistani nuclear device at Lop Nor (Xinjiang).

China. The chances of the US brushing off Putin's warnings while confronting China raises many concerns. These relate to the strength of the Russia-China partnership; their advances in space, cyber, and electronic warfare and hypersonic capabilities; and the capacity of the US war machine and production lines to cope with conflict on two fronts in parallel timelines. The reason for this could be America's belief that she can use strategic partners to fight China—like Ukraine fighting Russia—while keeping the US mainland safe.

Taiwan. China probably awaits an opportune time to capture Taiwan, possibly by a combination of force, destabilising machinations and political dislocation. Opportunities might come from severe escalation in the Ukraine war and Russia targeting countries that supply weapons to Ukraine—whether nuclear weapons come into play or not. According to some analysts, China has adequate capability to overcome American air defences to target US vessels and submarines in the SCS. In case of war, Taiwan (1/16th the size of Ukraine) could be completely crippled or even abandoned at some stage.

India. Besides relentless hostility from her immediate neighbours—China and Pakistan-India is on a hard turf in geo-strategic terms:

a. It is evident that America wants India to collaborate in its confrontations with China. India is the only Quad member having land border with China and this could be the reason that the joint statements from the Quad have never directly indicted China. The

US has, therefore, gathered the 'SQUAD' grouping minus India. India also stands denied of access to processed sonobuoy data from its US-sourced P-8 Poseidon surveillance aircraft. Meanwhile, amid the likes of George Soros' funding of India's image-tarnishing rhetoric, the 'Five Eyes' intelligence grouping of white nations leaking allegations against India and the brazen harbouring of Sikh separatists by Canada and the US, the *OpenAI* has reportedly discovered an Israeli company meddling in India's general elections.

b. America marks China for illegally claiming Arunachal Pradesh, but it has not supported the idea of 'One India'. The CIA and the MI-6 maintain strong links with Pakistan while the US has never, in real terms, clamped down on Pakistan to stop its proxy war on India. Britain was complicit in the partition of India that has left territorial disputes besides allowing a troublesome China to share a border with Pakistan it never had. Even if it may be politically incorrect to state so, there are concerns in many informed quarters that the US-UK would not mind seeing India fragmented further. These inimical forces might be looking at possible strategic and economic profits in an India-China conflict, selling arms and enabling NATO's Indo-Pacific pivot, while saving themselves from direct involvement – *a la* Ukraine.

Future Warfighting

Wars may not be short and swift despite being hi-tech with increased lethality and precision weaponry. Operations will be five dimensional: aerospace, land, sea, cyber, and electro-magnetic (EM) in various forms of C4I2 Warfare, Electronic Warfare (EW), Cyber Warfare and operationalised Cyber Space. Space combat like hypersonic missiles, cyber space combat, robotic combat, and nano-technology combat are recently added forms of combat. All these would necessitate changes in the methodology of warfighting.

High intensity multi-domain operations, heightened C4I2SR, employment of AI-driven systems, hypersonic and advanced autonomous weapons would be in play, inflicting unprecedentedly high levels of casualties. Mass use of swarm drones and missiles should be expected—

China follows this concept. Surface and underwater drones having long ranges and endurance would be extensively used in the air and sea. Use of robots on land can be expected; China has developed a machine-gun-carrying robot. According to one report, the US is working on robots to contain its 'first line' of casualties. However, the man behind the machine will remain as important. Notably, in both the Russian and Ukrainian forces, the short-term soldiers have proved to be mere cannon fodder.

Air battles would involve drones and hypersonic missiles. Slow moving helicopters would be easy prey when flying close to the frontline. Effective use of EW might disrupt communications, radar systems, and other electronic equipment. Jamming is found to be most effective against drones, communications, and GPS signals. Counter-drone systems would need to cope with swarm drones, possibly in hundreds. The combined use of EW-cyber-AI would ensure success; this capability must be constantly upgraded since technological advances in these fields would continue.

Intelligence systems and information warfare will be increasingly important. AI systems are of use in facial recognition, voice transcription, and translation services to process intercepted communications. In June 2023, Russia downed a Ukrainian aircraft using its AI-controlled S-350 Vityaz anti-aircraft missile system. The US Army's project, 'Real-Time Threat Forecasting', wants the system to predict what the enemy will do just minutes before they actually do it.

More dispersed deployment is needed with the headquarters divided into smaller functional entities, dug down and moved frequently. The same is true for command and control systems and mobile command posts to enable distributed processes of collaboration and synchronisation. Tunnelling and tactical innovations to tackle tunnels assumes importance; China and Pakistan have adopted extensive tunnelling. India must conceptualise and operationalise a tunnelling strategy and examine specialised weapons like periscope guns, stun gas, etc. to deal with this.

The use of terrorists and mercenaries as proxies will continue, including by the US and China. With growing Chinese influence in India's immediate neighbourhood along with instability in Pakistan and Myanmar, which China would use to wage a hybrid war, this matter is important to note. The army needs to revive its technical support capabilities and expand it to cover land borders with all the neighbours. Note must also be taken of the methods adopted during the recent Hamas attack on Israel.

Russia has been firing S-400 on "practice" targets—is India doing so? Ammunition expenditure, especially artillery, would be very high, necessitating adequate production, logistics, supply and stocking in the battle zone, with requisite protection. Armies should review their organisations to meet the requirements of de-centralised and dispersed command and control, be adept in functioning with minimal communications—encrypted without compromising speed—and should organise their air defence, information warfare, drone operations and the rest of the war-like functions in a modernised, efficient manner.

Conclusion

The advent of artificial intelligence, autonomous and precision weaponry, and stealth and hypersonic missiles systems point to fundamental changes in the manner of prosecuting warfare and the methods the military forces have to master to fight. Herein, the combined use of EW-Cyber-AI is a potent winning tool. The need of the hour is to draw inferences from the recent trends of warfare and adapt these to own ground realities.

Note

1. https://sundayguardianlive.com/top-five/chinas-is-the-hand-behind-hamas-attack-on-israel.

5. Contemporary Wars: Recent Trends

Rajesh Kumar

Introduction

The ongoing wars between Ukraine and Russia as well as Israel and Hamas have shown that conventional wars between two states can also be prolonged. It has also thrown light on the importance of home grown weapons and tactical solutions. Prolonged wars generally turn into wars of attrition. These then lead to rapid depletion of resources, the most critical of these being manpower and ammunition. Large amounts of damage also occur to equipment that needs to be quickly replaced. The nation's economy is required to shift to a wartime economy that will then orientate itself to securing supply chains for the manufacture of equipment and ammunition.

In this essay, certain notable trend-indicators that emerge from the recent wars, particularly the Russia-Ukraine war, are highlighted. The discussion is focused on the strategic and tactical adaptations made by the warring forces and the applicability of these under India's strategic circumstances. Certain policy imperatives to reap the benefits of the trend-indicators are also briefly touched upon.

Strategic Level Trends

Armament Production. In the case of India, as indeed elsewhere, it is obvious that certain supply chain components could be under the control of states or entities that are inimical towards own nation. Hence, alternate sources of supply have to be secured and strategic stockpiling needs to be carried out. It is also evident that home grown weapons with production facilities located within the country are necessary alongside all the technologies needed to continue indigenous production. Some facilities of licensed production like SU-30 should be kept alive under low production rates to preserve manufacturing talent and retain the ability to ramp up production in crisis situations.

Scaling and Stocking of Munitions. Broadly speaking, India should look afresh at her scales of ammunition stocking, and rather than mandating just 10 days' reserves for limited wars, increase these to higher scales. Facilities to produce the high consumption artillery and infantry weapon ammunition have to always be in good states of function and equipped with capabilities of ramping up production at short notice. In the past, such production facilities were secured by locating these in- depth, but with modern conventional ballistic and cruise missiles possessing the capability to target in-depth areas, the production plants need to be duplicated to gain redundancy wherever necessary. Such facilities would preferably be located in different theatres of war; that would also permit feeding of the diverse theatre-specific needs.

Reserves of Manpower. For manpower management, high attrition must be anticipated. Reserves must be available for quick call-up. India has not exercised any reserves call-up exercise for many decades. Considering the rapidly changing geopolitical scenario, this process needs to be activated. It is also seen that at the outbreak of war, the most experienced and talented manpower is deployed closest to the action and tends to suffer casualties. This needs to be replaced quickly by experienced people and not just the freshly trained recruits. Thus, the importance of ready reserves of manpower and equipment cannot be over-emphasised in attrition wars.

Concept of 'Tour of Duty'. The Indian armed forces are being reduced in strength and are also being brought under a 'tour of duty' concept named 'Agniveer'. This concept needs a review as wartime needs highly robust soldiers of quality and commitment, and that cannot be expected from personnel who are made to believe that their stay in the armed forces is but a temporary one. Even Russian soldiers, who are considered to be coming from one of the most patriotic populations in the world, refused to renew their contracts during the 'Special Operations' in Ukraine and had to be offered extra bonuses to prolong their engagements. The Russian economy that generates resources through the sale of energy could afford to do so. India, on the other hand, could well be importing even larger amounts of expensive energy to keep her war machine running. India, therefore, may not be able to afford that same option. This calls for a review.

Quality of Personnel. Besides the Russia-Ukraine war, in many other ongoing wars, the quality of military manpower has been called into question. In the current Gaza conflict, this applies to even the Israelis, as it has been evidenced during certain phases of the Israeli operations. It is particularly found among the reserves who had done their minimum compulsory duty. Long-term professional soldiers would always be the best bet in any war. The Indian armed forces have to be manned with the best and highly committed personnel to retain their sole advantage that they have over India's principal adversary, a vastly better equipped China—that of motivation, professional dedication, and skill.

Targeting in Urban Terrain. Another major trend that has emerged during recent wars has been the spread of combat to the urbanised terrain. With the general trend of urbanisation across the globe, urban spaces have become the new defensive strongholds that are difficult to bypass and isolate. Amongst the many other obstacles and urban fortifications that the adversary can take cover from, targeting for effect becomes very difficult. Therefore, there is a need to devise new ways and technologies to gather targeting information in urban settings. Even in open areas where satellite information can reveal enemy positions, the requisite mobility for the deployment of war-like assets requires a larger number of satellites and persistent intelligence gathering platforms to ensure that the forces remain well inside the adversary's OODA (Observe, Orient, Decide and Act) loop. Failure to do so could dramatically increase casualties in the securing of the chosen objectives.

Professionalism and Technological Tools. In addition to the wishful assumption that future wars would be limited, another fallacy that had gained ground amongst the higher decision- makers is that technology would assist in greatly reducing the manpower needed to conduct future wars. The replacement of large sections of any standing military with technology is thus seen as a short-term opportunity to save personnel costs. The October 2007 Hamas' attack on Israel has shown—if at all that proof was necessary to bring home the understanding—that technology can be blunted by ingenuity, and that technology cannot replace the inductive reasoning ability of professionals in the foreseeable future. Even when unmanned technologies and artificial intelligence are boosting human efforts, the following analysis by Russian experts who are observing the war effort is insightful:

> "For (use of) Drones and AI, manpower is not reduced but is heavily increased as material resources are strenuously burdened with up-keeping of digital facilities. High energy output, industrial production and mass labor force are crucial for both. Also, the Control Centers are vulnerable and require heavy maintenancc. This situation is akin to the Jevons paradox which postulates that, 'in the long term, increased efficiency of resource 'usage' will generate an increase in resource 'consumption' rather than a decrease'."

India, therefore, must be wary of sudden manpower reductions that could impact the ability of its armed forces to dynamically respond to changing trends in warfare.

Intelligence Upgrade. Recent conflicts have driven home the urgency to upgrade Intelligence, Surveillance and Reconnaissance (ISR) assets. Ukraine has so far managed to hold off the Russian juggernaut that has primarily been through a superior intelligence backbone that disseminates crucial information from the strategic level down to tactical levels in real time. Ukraine has obviously been significantly supported in this endeavour by the Western powers and that has allowed for faster repositioning of war assets in timeframes that are well inside Russia's ISR cycle. This has also permitted Ukraine to preserve large parts of its war assets and prevent these from being targeted. Russians, on the other hand, are affected due to inadequate ISR, leaving many of their assets open to targeting. The complete inactivity of the Russian Black Sea fleet and the shooting down of two Russian AWACS are illustrative of how, in certain domains, the Ukrainians have been able to use ISR assets to degrade Russia's combat effectiveness.

Tactical Level Trends

Battlefield Transparency. With near-total battlefield transparency outside the urban terrain, it is becoming increasingly difficult to assemble forces for massed attacks against any objective. As soon as troops of any size above the platoon level are seen assembling with their support elements, like artillery, engineers, etc., these are subjected to attack by manned and unmanned air weapons, thereby disrupting the build-up for an attack or delaying the planned timelines. Future warfare will have to find solutions to quickly assemble assault troops and their support elements just before an assault on the objective. This may also need changes in training and tactics.

Evolution of Tactical Drones. Drones are becoming ubiquitous on the battlefield. Small-sized drones can target personnel, equipment, tanks, artillery guns, and the like. These can cause serious disruptions to the execution of attack as well as defence plans as these are cheap and disposable and yet can cause damage to far greater scales. In the Ukrainian battlefield, innovations in drone employment are seen to be rising at a very rapid pace. From simple quad-copters, small- sized drones have evolved to First Person View (FPV) drones. Communications between the drone and its controller have been encrypted and multiplexed to reduce the effect of jammers. Drones are also being paired with other weapons in a shooter-killer combination and are being used to relay signals to other drones to increase their range. However, it may not be out of place to mention that despite the proliferation of drones, many of these get neutralised by soft or hard kill systems before reaching their designated targets, and only a small fraction (about 20 per cent) make it. Still, the sheer numbers of these operating on the frontline (in thousands) make drones a potent threat. Small- sized drones also suffer from the disadvantage of low weight of attack and are generally ineffective against concrete targets or vehicles and equipment with drone cages. Anti-drone measures are also evolving rapidly though these have yet to be fully effective across the entire frontages.

Employment of Medium and High-Altitude Drones. In contested airspace, usually the medium and large-sized drones (the Medium Altitude Long Endurance (MALE) and High Altitude Long Endurance (HALE)) are easily detected and shot down. These have, therefore, proved to be largely ineffective in Ukraine. The famed TB-2 Bayraktar that achieved initial success in its operational deployment by the Ukrainian Air Force has disappeared from combat, and its numbers have reportedly dwindled from 50 to single digits. On the other hand, MALE drones are operating with impunity in Gaza as the Hamas does not have the means to shoot them down; otherwise, even in lightly contested airspaces like that over Southern Yemen, the Houthis have brought down no less than six US- made MQ-9 Reapers in a span of just a few months.

Air Power and Air Defence. The effectiveness of air power in an intense air defence environment has come into question. The Russian Air Force did not give a good account of itself during the initial stages of the war. It failed in its task of SEAD/DEAD (Suppression/Destruction of Enemy Air Defence) primarily due to lack of ISR resources. An air campaign, in any operation, has to be tailored to the situation and specifically designed to achieve the desired objectives. Attempts to destroy ground targets in 'Desert Storm'- style without achieving necessary control of the air are doomed to failure. Care must also be taken to employ air assets in ground support role only after the enemy's air defences have been adequately suppressed. Employment of helicopters without frontline deployment of electronic warfare equipment has led to considerable losses. Subsequently, Russia's Aerospace Forces (VKS) has performed better by addressing these issues. But it has still not been able to target Ukraine's Patriot and S-300 air defence batteries that deploy and redeploy rapidly, primarily due to inadequate ISR support available to the Russian forces. This has led to sub-optimal deployment of the Russian forces and their conduct of operations at distances beyond the range of their effective air defences. Nevertheless, their use of 'glide bombs' has turned the tide of the war. The recent Russian successes in Avdivka and Donesk regions would not have been possible without the precision hits scored by heavy duty 1500 kg glide bombs released by the VKS from stand-off distances.

Electronic Warfare. Electronic Warfare (EW) has played a significant role in nullifying the drone factor; otherwise the losses to the troops and equipment would have been unsustainable. EW has caused the small-sized drones to settle harmlessly on the ground due to GPS jamming or to crash due to receiver signal jamming. It is notable for India that EW systems are integral to modern day combat and need to be deployed in substantial numbers to safeguard the battlefield resources. These systems also need to be timely upgraded to counter the enemy's innovations. Qualified and efficient EW personnel are indispensable to any unit, and they should be trained for that purpose. Further, GPS jamming has significantly degraded the accuracy of guided munitions. Excalibur shells have not exhibited the desired accuracy under such conditions and are no longer being used. Joint Direct Attack Munitions (JDAM) and other guided air-launched or ground- launched weapons, with the exception of the Army Tactical Missile Systems (ATACM), have also shown poor accuracy. ATACMs have been fairly accurate as these are launched from far distances and only briefly remain in the jamming area due to their high speed. GPS denial, or in India's case, China's Beidou denial, is a must.

Battlefield Communications. Communications in the battlefield areas will be a challenge to organise. Mobile phones are an absolute 'no-no' as these allow for accurate targeting, particularly the targeting of leading officers. Radio sets need to be secure and of low signature, else these can also reveal position and invite drone attacks. Even communication trenches need to be covered as troops in uncovered trenches can be spotted by drones. The enforcement of innovative solutions and discipline will be the key to minimise battle losses.

Deception. In attrition warfare, little frontline changes occur within shorter time spans. Deployment of decoys, therefore, assumes greater significance. Much of the Ukrainian Air Defence batteries have survived due to the extensive use of decoy launchers. At least a dozen strikes on decoy launchers have been documented, though the confirmation reports come much later because the targeted side wants to continue with the deception. Only when the numbers from the original inventories are tallied with those currently operating does the picture become clear.

Dispersion. In addition to deception, dispersion of assets is also very necessary; air assets are especially vulnerable. Russian air bases have been found to be deficient in hardened aircraft shelters, forcing the Russians to park their aircraft in close lots. As a result, they have suffered heavy attrition in their fighter and transport aircraft assets. The September 23 drone strike on Russia's Pskov area led to the loss of four IL-76 aircraft on ground, and the April 24 strike in the Kursk region led to losses of SU-34 on ground. The recent strike on the Russian depth base of Akhtubinsk has led to the damage of one SU-57 aircraft. In all cases, satellite imagery had shown the aircraft parked in the open and close to each other. Dispersal of assets and use of hardened aircraft shelters are the lessons from the 1967 war. In India's context, there is a need to ensure that its airbases are upgraded with hardened aircraft shelters as well as additional dispersal areas to permit spread-out of its air assets. Besides, more areas need to be allotted to park decoys to deceive the enemy.

Networking Options. In order to make Indian forces' air defence launchers more mobile, there is a need to integrate these directly into the Automated Integrated Command & Control System (AICCS) Network, similar to what the Ukrainians have done with their AD network. This will enable faster redeployment without having to move the accompanying radar groups. Besides, it will also facilitate realistic positioning of decoys.

Security of Logistic Infrastructure. As expected, in the Russia-Ukraine conflict, both sides have very often been targeting each other's fuel stocks, supplies, and power infrastructure. While air defence of vital logistic infrastructure has to be enhanced, additional protection of such facilities against out-of-proportion damages caused by drone attacks has also to be ensured. Vulnerable areas of refineries and oil tanks may need to be protected with ballistic shields to prevent outbreak of large fires due to drone attacks. In future, oil tanks should be constructed in a dispersed manner so as to minimise the chances of having to suffer secondary damages even in cases of single hits.

Underground Structures. Recent wars have highlighted the necessity for underground structures to survive massive aerial destruction and be ready to fight when necessary. For conservation of defence assets, availability of underground structures at air bases and along the defensive lines is a must. It also needs to be accepted that in rapidly developing urban terrain, civil settlements and infrastructure are no longer immune to attacks, and therefore, these need some degree of protection. With civilian population having settled near the air bases and military stations, there is bound to be much collateral damage. Creation of underground infrastructure, such as tunnels, roads, metros, parking, warehousing, etc., should be considered and as a matter of public policy, dovetailed into the overall urban planning process. Underground structures also have to be constructed at a rapid pace so that India's vital assets, including IT infrastructure, are adequately safeguarded against overt and covert attacks.

Conclusion

It might be a bit early to expect conclusive 'lessons' to emerge out of the recent and concurrent wars. Even then, there are enough clearly observable indicators that enjoin the nation's policymakers to take cognisance of the observable 'trends' and adapt to accommodate these into the system in an appropriate manner. In India's case, customised adaptation of the modern trends in warfare is vital. With progressive fructification of military modernisation schemes, the time is ripe for incorporation of the latest warfighting practices into India's defence planning.

6. Air Power: Strategic Inferences for India

Diptendu Choudhury

Introduction

Contemporary conflicts reflect the evolving nature of warfare and especially how the paradigms of air power employment dynamics have evolved apace with the advances in technology. The narrative of the 'reducing appetite for wars amongst nations' has, at best, been a passing one, as shifting geopolitics, transitional polarity, and national interests ensure that use of force remains a most viable instrument in the hands of the state as well as the non-state entities. All that has happened recently is that the type of war, its scale and number of players involved, the duration, and the extent of killings and destruction caused have multiplied.

The blurred lines between conventional, hybrid, grey zone, and the no-war-no-peace conflicts resonate with the quote by two colonels of the People's Liberation Army Air Force (PLAAF): "The war God's face has become indistinct."[1] The quote refers to technology having made the contemporary battlefield less distinct. It also aptly summarises the absence of normative policy norms of the previous century—that of 'declaring' war. Of greater concern is that wars and conflicts are no longer within the state's exclusive domain, having become 'open seasons' for non-state players and armed entities. This situation has placed an enormous burden on the militaries of the world that now have to plan, prepare, equip, and train for the expanded platter of force-application.

The use of the aerial domain and air power has not only remained a constant in most recent conflicts but is also being increasingly used in swift adaptations of technologies that are specifically tailored to the conflict dynamics. Whether it is the extensive employment of conventional kinetics that are underway in the Ukraine war, Israel's aerial pounding of Gaza, air strikes by Myanmar's military or innovative Houthi rebels disrupting Red Sea traffic with drone and missile attacks—inviting retaliatory air attacks by the US and Allied Forces—the list of such operational adaptations is growing. On the other end of the spectrum, use of air power for coercion and political signalling continues to play significant roles in potential conflict zones. China's aggressive and escalating use of the PLAAF by deploying large mixed formations of fighters, bombers, airborne early warning and control aircraft, etc. to transgress Taiwan's airspace has, in effect, erased the sanctity of the Median Line separating the two nations in the Taiwan Strait.

Closer home, air power remains a critical factor in India's ever-present dangers of continental threat from two nuclear-armed adversaries having strong air forces and who share a strategic friendship. Given that India's threat spectrum spans an entire range from nuclear and conventional operations to the more diffused hybrid and grey zone threats, there is much by way of assimilating the recently drawn strategic and tactical inferences from an air power perspective.

Strategic Level Inferences: India's Air Power

Conventional War. From a conventional war perspective, Russia's employment of air power is illustrative of the structural, doctrinal, and organisational shortcomings of its contemporary military strategy and the Cold War-centric approach to the use of defensive air power. In seizing control over the adversarial air space and to facilitate surface campaigns, the Russian military strategy, unlike that of the American and most modern militaries, by and large, limits its Air Force (VKS) to ground support role.[2] Thus, in the absence of a specific counter-air strategy, inadequate coordination and follow-through after the opening air and missile strikes and an inadequately pursued 'suppression of enemy air defence' (SEAD) campaign prevented Russia from establishing full control over the Ukrainian airspace. This cost them the air campaign initiative and stalled the surface campaign at the beginning of the war, when a vastly outnumbered Ukrainian Air Force (PSU) could yet play an effective role in stymieing the VKS air operations with infliction of heavy losses.

Suppression of Enemy Air Defence (SEAD). Ineffective SEAD allowed the PSU to regroup its Air Defence (AD) assets, and with extensive NATO (North Atlantic Treaty Organisation) support, to deny the VKS the freedom to operate over the Ukrainian airspace. Thus, in the efforts to employ their precepts of mass and manoeuvre and to carry out swift offensive operations without having achieved a viable degree of control of airspace, the Russian Army and AF had to suffer higher losses. According to David Deptula, "Russia has never fully appreciated the use of airpower beyond support to ground forces. As a result, Russia, in all its wars, has never conceived of, or run a strategic air campaign."[3] Thus, despite having a powerful air force, inability of a nation to leverage this potent military instrument to the fullest of its capabilities in achievement of its military objectives and national aim is possibly one of the most significant recent time reiterations of the well-established lessons of warfare.

Sub-Conventional Conflict. In the realm of sub-conventional conflict where there is no air opposition from the adversary, control of air enables unfettered employment of air power over the conflict spaces and the option of providing kinetic force without committing boots on the ground. Against the ISIS (Islamic State of Iraq and Syria), the U.S. military and its coalition partners—29 countries that contributed military support—contributed crucial airpower to the combat operations. For example, airpower halted ISIS's 2014 offensive, notably saving Baghdad, Erbil, and Kobani. Strategic air strikes then weakened ISIS finances by targeting the group›s oil business and cash reserves. Iraq and Syria would not have been able to retake their territories from the ISIS without the coalition's airpower, which provided essential intelligence and precision strikes to bolster the partners' troops' confidence and motivation against a fearsome enemy.[4]

Anti-aircraft Capabilities of Non-State Entities. The introduction of Russian air power in Syria has been widely cited as a turning point in the Syrian civil war, as it played a decisive role in reversing the Syrian regime's fortunes. Russia's intervention was designed as a limited-liability expeditionary campaign, with a small theatre footprint predicated on Russian air and naval power supporting the regime's ground forces.[5] Israel's offensive employment of air power against non-state entities like Hamas and Hezbollah and by the US and the UK against the Houthi rebels are more contemporary examples. The caveat here is that while the non-state entities may not have conventional air power assets, they certainly may have anti-aircraft defence capabilities of man-portable surface-to-air missiles and offensive capabilities of their surface-launched rockets, long-range missiles, and drones.

The Aspect of Airspace Control

The salience of control of air has been well underscored in contemporary wars. In case of air opposition, the degree of control of air will depend on the conventional air power capability of the adversary; control of air will be dictated by the size and capability of the adversarial air power. Limited air opposition and adversarial AD capability will lead to benign or low-threat airspaces and create low-intensity contested airspaces. A significant degree of control of air can then be achieved against an adversary with a small air force or limited air power capability.

Adversaries with strong air forces will entail highly-contested air spaces, as in India's case. Thus, for joint operations, control of air over tactical battle areas and corridors, as well as the spaces for depth offensives, will have to be wrested from the adversary. That control, however, will be transient and limited just to the designated spaces and for specific periods. Control of the air is thus no longer just an air force requirement but a crucial joint war-fighting necessity, especially in a continental threat scenario like that faced by India. Briefly put, air power remains a vital instrument of a nation's military power, and its integration into the nation's military strategy, in conventional as well as sub-conventional wars, is an imperative for the contemporary as well as future times.

Aspects related to Weapons of Air War

Combat Aircraft. Fighter and bomber aircraft have been the traditional aerial weapon delivery platforms for offensive application of air power.

While these remain the mainstay instruments for deep strikes, the advanced area denial AD systems and a wide range of tactical surface-to-air missile systems have proliferated to increase the vulnerability of all aerial platforms. Thus, stand-off targeting and aerial weapon delivery with long-range air-launched weapons has increasingly become relevant. To mitigate the increased AD threat in hostile airspaces, advances in self-protection suites of aerial delivery platforms are also evolving at a rapid pace. The goal is to enable manned and unmanned platforms to penetrate the enemy's area denial and AD systems. This goal is to be achieved by using penetration aids, which employ electronic warfare, low observable platforms, sensor technologies, active and passive countermeasures, advanced threat warning and dispensation systems, decoys, and so on.

Long-Range Missiles and Drones. The only alternatives to manned platforms for carrying out deep strikes inside the enemy heartland are air and surface-launched cruise missiles and advanced long-range drones. Typically, long-range missile and stand-off targeting have limitations in accuracy, weapon-to-target matching, over-the-target throw weight needed to create necessary effects, etc. Thus, the enormous employment of rockets as well as cruise and hypersonic missiles has not produced the desired war outcomes for Russia due to two key reasons – weapon accuracy and weight of attack. The first necessitates advanced delivery systems and seeker-heads, which come at a cost—the higher the accuracy, the greater the cost. For a greater weight of attack, more weapons need to be fired against a target to achieve the desired level of destruction. Again, more weapons used means more cost. Cost-effectiveness, therefore, becomes an issue with the expensive modern weapons vis-à-vis the selected target systems being attacked.[6]

Unmanned Aircraft in Support Role. The high and medium-altitude Intelligence Surveillance & Reconnaissance (ISR) drones, which gained credibility in precision targeting during the US global war on terror, are extremely vulnerable to advanced AD systems due to their low speeds and limited manoeuvrability. The simple fact is that most advanced contemporary drones, like the US MQ_9 Reaper, the Chinese Wing Loong II, the Turkish Bayraktar TB 2, etc., are all extremely vulnerable to enemy AD in highly contested airspaces. Advanced large drones are, therefore, increasingly being designated to serve in support role to the fighter jets, relying either on direct control of their manned peers or on-board AI to scout the battlefield, engage the enemy, and sacrifice themselves to shield manned aircraft. The US' Valkyrie XQ_58A and the Sukhoi S-70 types of aircraft are expected to provide cost-effective unmanned team solutions. Being almost as capable as manned fighters but with the advantage of being cheap and easily replaceable, these types allow a military force to produce entire swarms of drones to overwhelm most kinds of enemy defence.[7]At the other end of the spectrum of the ongoing wars, while small drones have delivered some successes in tactical battle areas, these have not produced strategic outcomes. The Royal United Service Institute estimates that Ukraine is losing 10,000 drones per month, indicating both their widespread use and their high loss rate.[8]

Construct of Air Power. Even if vulnerability of the manned fighters has increased, these would still continue to remain relevant in both defensive and offensive avatars, because of their flexibility and wide range of applications, the cost-effectiveness of their multiple reusability as a launch platform, advantage of targeting discrimination, multi-role-multi-tasking and multi-mission capabilities, possibilities of manned-unmanned teaming options, and so on. Recent wars give clear indications that the future of offensive air power has expanded to include advanced hypersonic missiles, cruise missiles, a wide range of drones, and advanced air-launched weapons.

Adaptations of Offensive Air Power

Offensive air power is no longer exclusive to bombers and fighter aircraft. The contemporary and future air power includes a wide range of manned and unmanned combat and weapon delivery platforms as well as increasing ranges of weaponry, whether launched from the domains of air, land, sea, or space for launch and transit. Air forces are already adapting to the future requirements of unmanned systems. Leading nations and groups of nations are investing in advanced generations of manned and unmanned platforms.

In the Indian context, its current offensive capability provides for a degree of asymmetric air power advantage over the Pakistan Air Force (PAF) as well as over the PLAAF. While India's air power will remain dominant over the PAF in the foreseeable future, the margin of asymmetric advantage that the Indian Air Force (IAF) currently enjoys over the PLAAF—due to geography and deployed force ratios—will begin tilting in favour of the latter very soon. Further, any collusive air power threat from these forces would put the IAF on the defensive, much to the detriment of conduct of surface and joint operations. That would exacerbate India's strategic vulnerability by negating its advantage of conventional deterrence and offensive in-depth capability that it currently enjoys against China. India, therefore, must not allow this air power balance to reverse to the detriment of her continental security. Timely prioritisation of India's future air power requirements is a national security imperative.

Imperatives of Airspace Control

The ongoing conflicts in Ukraine and Gaza have yet again underscored the imperative of control of airspace. For India, let there be no doubt that with two strong opposing air forces, any conflict in the future will see extensive use of the aerial medium across the land and sea domains. Battlespaces will be highly contested as the aerial medium will be offensively leveraged by the adversary to further their military objectives. Aside from various kinds of operational employment of manned and unmanned platforms, long-range surface and space-launched vectors will definitively be used in offensive air operations over the tactical battlespaces to strike deep into Indian territory to target military, industry, and strategic assets and infrastructure. Thus, adequate degree of control of air will be mandatory for conduct of joint operations, as the enemy will seek to offensively employ their air power to disrupt India's surface operations. In the current circumstances, while achievement of air superiority over the highly contested spaces is extremely unlikely, securing of favourable air situations over defined tactical spaces for certain periods will remain a critical task for the IAF, not just for air operations but especially so for all joint operations.

Modern warfare today has a very high density of aerial platforms operating in the airspace, especially over battle zones. All air operations in peace and war—fighter, transport, helicopter, remotely piloted aircraft—are strictly governed by air space management norms, as is done the world over. During hostilities, the entire volume of airspace, including the Tactical Battle Areas (TBA) of the Indian Army (IA), would need to be closely managed to enable freedom of own air ops. This airspace is where all our air operations, including Coordinated Air Operations (CAO) missions, operate or transit through; it is where the ISR aircraft operate; it is where the enemy air assets operate to support their forces and attack ours; and finally, it is also the same volume of airspace where all our artillery fire and long-range weapons transit through. In more recent conflicts, long-range rockets, cruise missiles, long-range missiles and stand-off weapons, unmanned aerial systems, etc. have added to the traffic density in the tactical battlespaces.

Battlespaces have become intensely busy, and the dense volume of airspace assets need close surveillance and definitive control to ensure that India can detect, identify, and engage every air threat and permit full freedom of operations for its own forces. All air offensive missions are to be closely integrated within the Airborne Early Warning & Control System (AEWCS) aircraft and surface radar surveillance coverages and closely coordinated with all friendly AD Combat Air Patrol (CAP) and Surface-to-Air Guided Weapon (SAGW) elements. Over and above these, every air movement is to be intricately coordinated and de-conflicted to ensure safe routing of own air forces through the enemy's radar gaps, to be provided protection by our AD aircraft and SAGW systems, and to be kept safe from the IA's own weapon systems and firepower in the tactical battle areas (TBA).

Revealing Observations. Having discussed the recent trends in the application of air power in armed conflicts, it comes clear that in preservation and consolidation of national sovereignty and furtherance of national aspirations in the coming era, there is no relief from commitment to long-term, robust, modern, and continuously advancing defence preparedness. This is true irrespective of the contesting parties' aspirations being found to be inspirational or absurd—idealism is not relevant in this context. This commitment would, of necessity, have to be at the cost of fiscal priorities and dated predispositions in defence planning.

Notes

1. Qiao Liang and Wang Xiangsui, *Unrestricted Warfare*, PLA Literature and Arts Publishing House, Beijing, February 1999, p. 36.
2. https://www.vifindia.org/article/2022/may/23/russia-s-military-understanding-of-air-power
3. Phillips Payson O'Brien and Edward Stringer, *The Overlooked Reason Russia's Invasion Is Floundering*, https://www.theatlantic.com/ideas/archive/2022/05/russian-military-air-force-failure-ukraine/629803
4. Becca Wasser, Stacie L. Pettyjohn, Jeffrey Martini, Alexandra T. Evans, and others, *The Role of Air Power in Defeating ISIS,* Research Brief RAND Corporation, February 12, 2021, https://www.rand.org/pubs/research_briefs/RBA388-1.html
5. Michael Simpson, Adam R. Grissom, Christopher A. Mouton, John P. Godges, and Russell Hanson, *Road to Damascus, The Russian Air Campaign in Syria 2015-2018*, Research Report, RAND Corporation, May 11, 2022, https://www.rand.org/pubs/research_reports/RRA11701.html#:~:text=Russian%20airpower%20played%20a%20decisive,power%20supporting%20regime%20ground%20forces.
6. Air Mshl (Dr) Diptendu Choudhury, "Chariots of Fire: Air War in Ukraine and Gaza-Takeaways for India", *Medals and Ribbons*, April-June 2024, Vol. 4, Issue 2.
7. https://www.aerotime.aero/articles/25712-worlds-best-military-drones
8. https://www.businessinsider.com/tanks-troops-in-the-open-are-hit-within-10-minutes-ukraine-official-2023-9?r=US&IR=T

7. Complementary Inferences from the Recent Trends in Warfare

Diptendu Choudhury

In the preceding chapter, the author has drawn certain valuable inferences from the recent trends in the use of air power. The configuration of air power being a frontier technology and a long-gestation, long-term, and expensive process, it would also be instructive here to look further ahead and consider what should be the follow-up developments towards modernisation of the Indian Air Force (IAF). The purpose is to prepare grounds for such developments at the right time and so avoid getting left behind in the galloping defence advancements.

– Editor

Development of India's Aerospace Power

Integrated Airspace Management. Given India's enormous civil aviation industry and its booming growth, 'One Airspace' is a comprehensive programme projected to span over eight years, including infrastructure development, controller training, and migration to the new systems. Once fully operational, a unified airspace strategy will enable airlines to identify more efficient flight routes to reduce travel time and fuel consumption. By facilitating consistent flight patterns at higher altitudes and smoother descents for landing, the initiative aims to enhance the overall operational efficiency of the aviation industry.[1] But presently, this scheme is limited only to the civil aviation's peacetime traffic management concept, which does not take wartime scenarios into consideration. For example, disruption of civil air traffic over Pakistan due to the post-Balakot closure of airspace has cost India over Rs 8 bn in revenue.[2] Further, while the IAF's operational airspace control has ensured minimal disruption to the civil air traffic, it will not be possible during wartime. At the national level, an appropriately integrated airspace management will warrant a holistic framework for all military and civil aviation assets to ensure comprehensive control of airspace upon the invocation of the Union War Book.

Integration of Civil and Military Airspaces. Future airspace control is vital as it maximises all air operations while ensuring air defence (AD) coverage against enemy air power. Airspace control is equally vital for deconfliction with own artillery fire and friendly air traffic, fratricide and collision avoidance, and finally, to enable combat search and rescue.[3] Integration of advanced Identification Friend or Foe (IFF) feature of all aerial platforms with the modern 'Integrated Aero-Space Defence Architecture' will ensure the safety of the country's all aerial platforms while allowing full freedom of engagement against all types of adversarial aerial and space threats. Holistic integration of the sovereign civil and military airspaces over the mainland, island, and maritime territories would provide for full freedom in application of India's air power and maximise civil aviation operations during war and other kinds of conflicts. That is the way ahead.

Integrated Air and Space Domain Awareness. But will airspace control be enough for the future, given that at least the near-space will be extensively used for military applications? Two areas of paradigm transition and development are critical for India in the future. These are: development of an integrated air and space domain awareness capability; and a transition from integrated air defence to integrated aerospace defence capability. This issue assumes high significance due to China's extensive leveraging of space for its Anti-Access/Area Denial sea-based and land-based space programmes to boost its regional power projection, sub-metric resolution satellite imaging capability, and advanced space-based Command, Control, Communications, Computers Intelligence, Surveillance and Reconnaissance (C4ISR) system. China's space capabilities impact all aspects of conventional and nuclear targeting, ground-air-sea operations, precision conventional strike capacities, missile defence, direct-ascent and co-orbital anti-satellite (ASAT) weapons, directed-energy weapons, cyber-ASAT capabilities, etc.,[4] and all of these would play a driving role in any future conflict with India. China's growing space-based military capabilities are, therefore, a growing concern for India. The current airspace situational awareness system, as provided by the IAF's Integrated Air Command and Control System (IACCS), will no longer be enough, as monitoring of India's sovereign aerospace up to possibly the Karman Line will have to be integrated and enabled to track all aerial vehicles, platforms, and weapons in transit. Thus, in the future, India's airspace control has to expand its scope to 'aerospace' control. For this, there is a fundamental necessity for a considered evaluation of the attributes of the vertical dimension and its future salience in India's national security.

Aerospace Security. Traditionally, India has, with much justification, been focused on its continental security. Very recently, the maritime domain also has assumed higher strategic significance. However, a similar level of focus on aerospace security is yet to be seen, and this does not bode well for India's future. Two aspects need to stand out in India's approach: one, the vertical domain of air is more than just an adjunct to the other two domains as the aerial domain envelopes and impacts both; and two, while the air and space mediums are disparate in characteristics, these are but in a continuum in the nation's security priority. The rapidly increasing military exploitation of that continuum by countries like the US, Russia, and China bears testimony to this development.

Fusion of Aerospace Security. In the context of national security, control of India's vertical aerospace domain is a necessity, not just from a military perspective, but equally importantly, from the civilian one too. Given the immense growth potential of India's civil aviation sector, civil leveraging of space must be a national enterprise. Fundamental to any aerospace control is the necessity of real-time three-dimensional multi-domain aerospace situational awareness. Given the differences between the characteristics of air and space domains, a fusion of awareness across both the domains is not an easy task, but it is still a future-relevant necessity. That is why the US Space Force comes under its Department of Air Force, the Russian Air Force has become the Russian Aerospace Force, and France has converted its Air Force to an Air and Space Force.

The Indian Air Force has sought a similar changeover to 'Indian Air and Space Force'.[5]

Development of Space Monitoring Systems. Artificial Intelligence (AI)- enabled multi-domain integrated sensor fusion of air and space monitoring systems is the way ahead and must be prioritised as an area of research and development. The use of integrated and networked surface, aerial, and space-based sensors, new generation aerial enabling platforms like the Airborne Early Warning and Control System (AEWCS) aircraft, advanced Joint Tactical Information Distribution System platforms, future ISR Targeting (ISTAR) system platforms, future multi-sensor ISR systems, satellites, etc. to produce a three-dimensional aerospace combat situational awareness will be a national security imperative.

Integration of Aerospace Command and Control (IACC). The current combat-tested and proven IACCS of the IAF will have to be upgraded to an Integrated Aerospace Command and Control System to serve as a golden thread, which will network and weave all the elements into a cohesive and integrated system of systems.

Integrated Aerospace Defence Capability. The barrage of firepower in future wars will not be limited to the battlespaces alone but will spill over to in-depth civilian spaces. Both of India's adversaries have strong air forces and have the capability to target its military, strategic, and civilian assets deep inside the nation. Saturation of air and missile strikes on our high population-density rural and urban spaces, resulting in mass civilian collateral destruction, is a reality that needs more attention. The important aspect to consider here is that modern wars and conflicts will inevitably and unavoidably impact the civilian population as the fighting no longer remains limited to border battlespaces. The current conflict trends of mass-scale missile and rocket attacks against high-density population centres to carry the fight beyond the battlespaces deeper into the adversary's heartland has expanded the scope of the aerial dimension in warfare.[6]

Security against Aerial Threats

Looming Threats. Keeping the population safe from enemy air attacks has its limits, especially given India's geographical spread and population density. The state-of-the-art high-tech Iron Dome AD system has undoubtedly saved Israeli lives, but it has also demonstrated that even the best of AD systems cannot assure a cent per cent fail-safe air defence, and that the missiles, rockets, and drones would still manage to get through. But is mere air defence, on its own, adequate for the future? China's military rise and the evident inclusion of space in its geopolitical strategy have serious consequences for India. China's developments of future hypersonic weapons, such as space glide vehicles and fractional orbital bombardment systems, ballistic missile early warning system, anti-satellite capabilities including co-orbital systems, directed energy weapons, high powered lasers, and space-enabled electronic jamming, spoofing, cyber means, etc., pose serious future threats and need to be addressed on priority.

Future Generation Fighters. Even as most air forces are struggling to upgrade their fighter inventories to 4.5 and fifth-generation platforms, sixth-generation fighters are already under development by some nations on their own and by some as joint projects. The US, Russia, China, and India are running their own programmes, while the UK, Italy, and Japan have joint programmes, as do France, Germany, and Spain. There are several commonalities in the platform designs, of which stealth and super-cruise are two important aspects. Advanced skin, airframe, and engine designs are incorporated to reduce sensor observability of the fighters across multiple spectrums, making these stealthy and hard to detect. Super-cruise is made possible by advanced engine designs that greatly enhance both the range and endurance of the platform, which, in turn, expands the matrix of roles-tasks-missions. Future platforms are being designed to make extensive use of AI to incorporate manned and unmanned teaming (MUMT) and the ability to control unmanned wingmen and swarms. Electronic Warfare (EW)-resistant fibre-optics and advanced photonics to replace electronics have greatly enhanced the processes of data acquisition and control, internal power generation for laser and hypersonic weapons, modular system suites for easy maintenance and upgrade options, advanced engines that can operate efficiently across the entire range of subsonic operations to possibly hypersonic speeds in the future, etc. are being incorporated into the design features. Most importantly, these have to be adept at penetrating deep into highly contested battlespaces of the future and undertake a wide range of missions. The list of future-relevant design requirements is long and likely to keep increasing with the rapidly growing warfighting necessities.[7, 8] All these parameters set the key focus areas for future aviation-related technical developments.

Matters of Priority. It is a concern that India's already delayed Advanced Medium Combat Aircraft (AMCA) project is expected to take another decade before the platforms can be inducted into service. By that time, China would be able to alter the air power balance in the region in its favour. This effectively means that by the time India's fifth-generation AMCA arrives, so would China's sixth-generation platform, effectively continuing to leave India well behind the curve. Of equal concern is that in this period, the IAF's mainstay fourth-generation fleet will also have become a decade older despite their upgraded capabilities. That does not bode well from a larger strategic perspective as Beijing's increasing leveraging of its air power capabilities as an instrument of its coercive foreign policy over Taiwan as well as the East and South China Seas is but a harbinger of China's future air dominance over the Indian territory – and beyond. The already visible increase in air activity across the disputed Indo-Tibet borders has made our border issue more complex. Further expansion of the People's Liberation Army (PLA) Air Force's (PLAAF) capabilities against the sanctity and security of India's sovereign airspace is, therefore, a reality. After building extensive infrastructure across the disputed regions, which includes the creation of border villages, increase in aerial violations and coercive air activities across Ladakh, Arunachal Pradesh, and the Indian Ocean could well be expected to become a 'new normal' and bolster Beijing's supercilious narrative of building up a 'push-up' support for its hegemonic ambitions.

Bolstering Combat Air Power. To ride over the turbulent times ahead, urgent fulfillment of the requirement for the Multi Role Combat Aircraft (MRFA), to bolster India's 4.5-generation inventory of its medium-weight category of fighters, is not just an IAF requirement but indeed a national security imperative. Two squadrons of Rafale are nowhere enough, and the urgent necessity of bolstering India's 4.5-generation capability cannot be overemphasised. This is because the upgraded MiG 29, Mirage 2000, and Jaguar fleets would reach obsolescence and would need replacement well before the AMCA squadrons become operational. This will gravely and irretrievably impact the IAF, both in quantum and quality, as even with the best possible bolstering of India's indigenous production capacity over the coming years, it will still not be possible to arrest any further decline in India's combat air power capabilities.

Build-up of Defence Industrial Capacity. With no industrial benchmarks on what exactly constitutes a 'sixth-generation' fighter, the AMCA development must include the actual new-generation capabilities. Given the large numbers involved, bilateral partnership for additional jointly-produced Rafales in India with attendant long-term agreement for joint upgrades and technology transfer for future 4.5- generation-plus variants of the platform and its weapons suites makes sense. It will enable steady induction from a reliable partner, ensure greater platform commonality, assure future upgrades of the platform and weapons, and finally, ensure development of engines for the AMCA. This would balance out India's inventory basket from Russian dependency while obviating reliance over a temperamental US military industry, thereby promoting indigenous defence production in the process.

Investing in Aerospace Technology and Production (ATP). Rapid changes in the operational environment entails that India can no longer afford to develop aerospace systems on the traditional manners of linear acquisition and development timelines. Continuing with the traditional approaches will result in a debilitating technology gap in our critical warfighting capabilities vis-à-vis our technologically superior adversary. Increasing the pace of capability development is critical to narrowing and closing the gap against an adversary whose pace and capacities in the aerospace field are way ahead of us. There is no option but for the Indian aerospace industry to evolve swiftly so that our capability development remains relevant. The ATP has to become adaptable, affordable, and agile to stay ahead of the curve of future needs of aerospace power. In the immediate and near term, collaborative research and developments in science and technology among the academia, the industry, and the military have to be maximised. Simultaneously, agile acquisition processes and time-sensitive acquisition policies, which shrink the development-production-operationalisation lag, have to be brought in. Digital engineering must be leveraged to ensure smart commonality and inter-operability in all fleets and systems across all the Services wherever possible. This includes common support equipment, common system configurations, common interfaces, common architecture, and even common components that simplify logistics and maintenance in the field.[9]

Military-Industry Synergy

The pace of technological advancements can only increase if the IAF and the industry synergistically short-circuit the synapses between the development of future operational concepts, identify operational requirements, cooperate in industrial research, development, and production, and finally, promote operational testing and evaluation. Given the long process and lead times between the drawing board and the field, this matter needs to be addressed at highest priority.

Building Comprehensive Air Power (CAP)

Civil aviation, along with the IAF and aviation elements of the other services, constitutes the nation's comprehensive air power (CAP). Due to inter-operability of capabilities and capacity redundancies, there are vast areas of overlap in matters of national security between civil and military aviation. Aviation also has enormous untapped potential in contributing to economic growth, foreign policy support, diplomacy, political support and signalling, humanitarian assistance, etc. and will certainly have more to offer in the future. The nation has to harness the immense potential of defence and civil aviation industries.

A new approach is needed that embraces public-private partnerships and invests heavily to turn it into a profit-making economic venture. India's aviation industry expects Rs 35,000 cr (US$ 4.99 bn) investments in the next four years, whereas the government plans to invest US$ 1.83 billion for development of airport infrastructure and aviation navigation services and building 220 new airports within a few years.[10] India is already known for cost-competitive space research, development, and production. Expanding this model to an integrated military-civil aviation industry will truly be a strategic investment for the future, given the immense regional necessity for affordable combat platforms, critical enablers, AD radars and weapon systems, aerial weapons, fixed and rotary wing civilian passenger and transport aircraft, unmanned platforms, etc.—the list of possibilities is endless. Investment will not only fill up India's inventory gaps but also generate extensive low-cost competitive exports, expanding India's regional influence by creating technology dependencies in the process.

Given India's future strategic dependencies over a security-contested Indian Ocean Region, the rapidly evolving security construct of the Indo-Pacific as well as the dynamics of existing continental threats, the nation needs an air strategy and an air advisory mechanism to cater for the future requirements of CAP from a security perspective. The growth trajectory of the civil aviation industry and future developmental potential of India's immense aerospace industry calls for synergy in India's future military and civil aviation needs. In its absence, the nation will be bereft of professional inputs on an important instrument of a multi-domain full spectrum military power and would be marginalised against the nation's immense necessity for CAP.

A Strategic Window

There is a strategic window of opportunity for India to create an ecosystem of cooperative development and production with regional partners to our strategic advantage. This will not only enhance India's regional stature as a significant defence industry partner, but it will also foster greater regional air power inter-operability, contribute to multi-domain influence, and create strategic dependency amongst key regional nations.

The need for a comprehensive approach to synergise India's military and civil air and space necessities of the future, in synchronisation with the nation's future security needs of national growth and long-term interests, necessitates the creation of a national air and space advisory body.

Conclusion

The ongoing wars and conflicts are shaped by the contextual political dynamics of the protagonists and their underlying national interests. Since these typically tend to focus all attention on the 'here and now', there is a danger of drawing-up premature and incorrect policies. In India's case, the most important contextual aspect is that unlike most recent and contemporary conflicts and wars, adversarial air power is a serious threat. Drawing relevant operational and tactical lessons from recent wars remains a work in progress. But the strategic inferences drawn so far are most relevant to India's long-term military and national security interests. Given India's current and future threat trajectory, these inferences will not only provide strategic benchmarks for future air and space power developmental imperatives but also vital premises for organisational, doctrinal, and employment strategies. Most importantly, in fulfillment of India's future security needs, these are also the areas of investments in India's swiftly expanding and self-reliant aerospace defence industry.

Notes

1. https://timesofindia.indiatimes.com/business/india-business/india-prepares-for-one-airspace-unified-air-traffic-control-plans-set-in-motion-what-it-means/articleshow/109084063.cms
2. https://economictimes.indiatimes.com/news/international/business/pakistan-suffers-over-8-billion-in-losses-due-to-airspace-closure/articleshow/70290104.cms?from=mdr
3. https://www.vifindia.org/article/2020/july/24/air-defence-is-everywhere
4. Anthony H. Cordesman, *"Chinese Space Strategy and Developments"*, Center for Strategic and International Studies, August 2016, https://www.csis.org/analysis/china-space-strategy-and-developments.
5. https://chanakyaforum.com/the-iafs-transformation-into-the-indian-air-and-space-force/
6. https://www.vifindia.org/article/2024/june/04/Hellfire-from-the-Heavens-A-Perspective-on-Contemporary-Aerial-Strikes
7. Maxwell Goldstein, "Sixth Generation Fighter Programs", Grey Dynamics, February 1, 2024, https://greydynamics.com/sixth-generation-fighter-programs/
8. Joseph Noronha, "Sixth Generation Fighters: Closer Than You Think", *Aero India*, Special Edition, 2021, https://www.sps-aviation.com/story/?id=2884&h=6th-Generation-Fighters-Closer-Than-You-Think
9. Dr Will Roper, "Take the Red Pill: The New Digital Acquisition Reality". Cited by Valerie Insinna, *Defense News*, September 15, 2020. https://www.defensenews.com/breaking-news/2020/09/15/the-us-air-force-has-built-and-flown-a-mysterious-full-scale-prototype-of-its-future-fighter-jet/
10. Aviation Industry Report June 2022, https://www.ibef.org/industry/indian-aviation#:~:text=Market%20Size,airplanes%20operating%20in%20the%20sector.

8. The Russo-Ukraine War: Inferences on Air Combat and Air Defence Aspects

V.K. Saxena

Preamble

February 2014 to June 2024 and counting—that is a decade and more for which a bloody war has been raging between Ukraine and Russia. The current round, starting on February 24, 2022, is 840 days old, with no signs of ebbing in the near future.[1]

Such a long period of catastrophic destruction has thrown up many inferences, both at the tactical as well as strategic levels. Many myths have been broken, many new lessons have been learnt and many old ones unlearnt as this 'global war in a local scenario' chugs its blood-soaked path. This work attempts to study some inferences in the context of air and air defence war.

The Unfinished Job and its Penalty

In the early hours of February 22, 2022, when the Russian offensive was about to be unleashed on Ukraine as a massive pre-emptive strike, a confident President Putin probably imagined it to be a few days for the capitulation of the adversary—*a la* Crimea of sorts. It is no wonder he called it a Special Military Operation—a quick cut and finish job.

Putin's confidence was backed by the punch he packed into the execution of the pre-emptive strike. This included frontline aircrafts (MiG 29s, SU-25, 27, 30, 35s), attack helicopters or AHs (Mi 24, 28, 35 and Kamov 51 and 52s), long- range surface-to-surface missiles (9k720

Iskander, OTR 21 Tochka, Kalibr), an array of multi-barrel rocket launchers (Tornado, BM21, BM30 etc.)[2] and gun power (2S7M Malka guns, Giatsint, Koalistsya, Masta, howitzers, large calibre mortars, etc.).[3]

The said pre-emptive strike, which aimed to kill maximum of the Ukrainian air assets on ground and disable Ukraine's air defence by blinding its eyes and ears (radar systems) and destroying its command, control and communications that control the air defence battle, fell short—very short.[4] With that went the dream of achieving air superiority in providing unstinted support to ground forces to hasten up Ukrainian capitulation.

The inferences lie in the 'why' of the pre-emptive strike falling short - and there are quite a few 'whys'. At the outset, there were reports in some circles that the 'surprise factor', which is the foundational requirement of any pre-emptive strike, was partially compromised (uncorroborated). Whether factual or not, the maximum number of Ukrainian strike aircraft and associated support structures were under concrete and hence, avoided destruction. Similarly, much of the air defence command and control infrastructure was well underground—an exercise that started right after the massacre it suffered in Donbas region in 2014 when Russian air power struck Ukrainian air defences for the first time.[5]

Besides the denial of surprise, Ukrainian successes got a shot in the arm due to many other shortcomings of the Russian war machine that executed the strike. To start with, the very fact that most of the critical targets survived does indicate a certain lack of target information by way of their precise location and the nature of protection each enjoyed. Also, there was sub-optimal targeting, maybe due to the lack of precision guided munitions. There were deficits in communications and connectivity that restricted mobile communications for fire control. Some reports also suggested a lack of airspace control, which cumulatively resulted in air and ground strikes missing their targets.

So, if it ever comes to a scenario of India undertaking a pre-emptive strike, it has to be ensured that: one, the 'surprise' factor is kept intact; two, the targeting information is accurate; three, there is detailed weapon-to-target matching so as to create the right effect at the target-end; and above all, there is a fool-proof airspace control mechanism backed by redundant communications and connectivity. Also, when defending, it will do well to follow the Ukrainian model of ensuring maximum air assets under concrete and saving the air defence infrastructure from the adversary's onslaught through effective camouflage, cover, deception, counter-fire, and more.

Blitzkrieg—A Volley of Tactical Mistakes

With the skies remaining contested, the next phase of the Russian offensive unrolled in some hope that it would anyway force its way to Kiev. Hundreds of tanks (T90s, T80s, T84s, T72s), armoured personnel carriers or APCs (PTS, GTUs, MT-LB), infantry fighting vehicles (YPR 765, BMP 1, 2, 3, 4, BTR 4, etc.), and multi-barrel rocket launchers (9A 52-4, BM21, BM30, etc.)[6] advanced as one 'extended firearm', headed to the heart of the adversary's land. That is where many tactical mistakes happened.

Briefly, understanding the tactical mistakes made by the Russian forces begins with an observation that an offensive machine of such colossal dimensions moved rather un-tactically stretched out for kilometres on end along long winding roads, thus presenting an easy target to the Ukrainian air power.

The worst mistake came with air defence; it, in fact, sat 'out of the battle'. Russians are known worldwide for very strong ground-based air defence weapons. Expectedly, the fire-arm included some deadly air defence weapons. These included guns (ZPU 1 and 2, ZU23, L-70, M-55, ZSU 23-4 Schilka, Gepard), surface- to-air missiles or SAMs (Strmer, Strela 10, OSA–AK, Pechora, Tor, Pantsir), and the mighty PMU series of air and anti-missiles system-PMU 300. But it was ironic to see this deadly arsenal remain undeployed. Rather than advancing tactically and according to the principle of leap-frog (one fire unit deployed, the other moving) and protecting the mechanised columns, it moved as a non-deployed convoy serial! This allowed the Ukrainian air power (that survived to operate another day) to cause many casualties on Russian tanks and APCs.

The most conspicuous were the high Russian casualties due to drone strikes by Ukraine. Ukraine had quite a few of these: the famous Turkish TB2 Bayraktar drone, the US Switchblade kamikaze machines, the Iranian Shahed-136, Germanium-2, etc. and indigenous machines like Aerorovidka R-8.[7] What enabled these machines to achieve disproportionate levels of gains was the conspicuous absence of tailor-made anti-drone weaponry in the Russian inventory. Mighty conventional air defence systems are not suitable to take on these small drones that require sensors optimised to detect them and suitable killing means in soft and hard-kill domains. It was painful to see a small TB2 Bayraktar drone piercing its way through the mighty sensors of the Russian PMU-300 air defence system.

Russian deficiencies in communications, connectivity, and gun-to-target end flow of orders continued unabated as Ukrainian anti-tank missiles (Sweden's RBS-70, US' Javelin and HIMARS, Netherland's NLAW, etc.) and its drone power claimed many casualties against the Russian war machine. A stage was reached (July-Aug 22) where tank casualties in upfront contact battles became untenable. If open sources are to be believed, a whopping 1700 Russian tanks fell to Ukrainian anti-tank weapons in the period from February-July 2022 (Ukrainian data).[8]

Inferences are quite a few. Here was a classic example of how armoured and mechanised columns should not be launched in a blitzkrieg, especially so when the skies above the ground forces are not secured. This was a classic example how air defence weapons must never be used just as convoy serials. This was also a classic example of how lack of tailor-made anti-drone weaponry can make a country's mighty battle systems fall at the hands of the little monsters.

Arising from this end state, there have been some misplaced assessments like writing the obituary of tanks and APCs in modern day combat. Nothing can be further from the truth. Mechanised forces remain very much important. The requirement is to employ these war machines by respecting their foundational strengths—mobility, fire power, surprise, and tactical manoeuvre in battle.

The Magic of Tubes

Another area from where some useful inferences can be drawn is man portable air defence systems or MANPADS. These are the shoulder or pedestal- fired very short-range fire-and-forget missiles that are particularly deadly against the adversary's slower-moving air threat vehicles such as AHs.

The Russian offensive was supported by a considerable fleet of AHs. Initially, these machines went right in and took out targets as much as 50-70 km into the tactical battle area (TBA) in what are called 'hunter-killer missions', providing intimate support to the armour and mechanised forces. Then something changed.

The Ukrainians had a large arsenal of MANPADs (Igla 1, Chiron, Strela 2, Strela 3, Mistral, Marlet, Stinger SAMs from the USA, Star Streak SAMs from the UK and similar weapons from Germany, Denmark, Lithuania, and the Netherlands).[9, 10] They deployed them in large numbers in the TBA. Stuck unobtrusively in every nook and corner of the TBA, these unforgiving tubes overwhelmed the detection and avoidance capability of the Russian AHs. Seeing the twin rotor Kamovs come down in flames upon taking hits from MANPADS became a common everyday sight. Even with measures like missile approach warning sensors, counter-measure dispensing suits etc., the sheer volume of MANPADS proved to be 'far too many' for the AH Fleet.[11] That resulted in disproportionate losses to the Russians. The magnitude can be judged by figures—out of a fleet of nearly 100 Kamov AHs, some 25-30 succumbed to MANPADs.[12] That is a huge number. The loss was not only of the machines but also of trained combat pilots.

In any future combat in the Indian scenario, MANPADs can be great killers. Both our potential adversaries have large MANPAD inventories numbering in thousands. Chinese MANPADS include the HN series (HN5), HQ6, the FN series, and the QW series.[13] Pakistani MANPADS are the indigenous Anza, Swedish RBS 70, US FIM 92 Stinger, Chinese FN 16 etc.[14] It will, therefore, be logical to expect that the MANPADs would proliferate in the TBA, much on the lines of what Ukraine did. These will lie in ambush, marking the most likely avenues of approaches. Our combat aircraft and attack helicopters must be mindful of this threat.

Besides having countermeasures on board, India's aircraft and AHs must also adopt several other ways of countering the MANPAD threat. This includes manned and unmanned teaming or MUMT, where several unmanned platforms accompany the manned air threat vehicles, thus increasing the net outreach, 'look-see' and 'hunt and kill' capability of the mission. Besides this, measures like the use of scouts that precede the mission (to empty out some of the MANPADs) or the 'loyal wingmen' that accompany manned missions are already in practice.

On the flip side, one cannot gloss over India's current deficiencies in terms of MANPADS. Unless and until the Indian forces are able to proliferate their MANPADS in the TBA, they will miss out on a major tactical advantage to overwhelm the adversary's air threat vehicles—especially the AHs. It is heartening that after decades of waiting for MANPADS and living through a trail of failed procurement cases,[15] the Indian Army has finally received the first batch of 24 Igla S MANPADs on April 8, 2024.[16]

Since the requirement is much more than what the imports can address and also in keeping with the resurgent sentiment of *Atmanirbhar Bharat*, it is high time India perfected its indigenous MANPAD. In this context, the open source report of February 2024 about the DRDO testing its latest MANPAD is a welcome development.[17]

Discovering the Chink in the Armour

Early enough in the war and during the faulted Russian armoured thrusts under contested skies, the Ukrainians had discovered a serious chink in the Russian arsenal—lack of tailor-made weaponry to take on the small-drone attacks. Over time, drones became Ukraine's '*bramhastra*'.[18] Having caused disproportionate kills on Russian tanks and mechanised forces, the drones exploded into what later came to be known as the 'Drone Army of Ukraine'. The drones became such effective killers that on February 6, 2024, President Zelensky created an entirely new branch in the Ukrainian Armed Forces dedicated to drones alone. The President then set a target for producing a million drones in 2024.[19]

What did the Drones do?

Besides attacking the advancing fire arm of the Russian forces in conjunction with anti-tank missiles, drones were used to attack many Russian targets on the supply chain. Taking advantage of the fact that the entire Russian ammunition supply was road and rail-based, their ammunition dumps were hit by a combination of drones and missiles in Kherson, Dzhankoi, Belgorod, Khmeinytsky, etc. As per one report, more than 50 ammunition dumps have been struck.[20, 21]

Drone attacks were taken inside Russian territory by taking on civilian targets—logistic hubs, communication facilities, airfields, and even some super stores. A few of such missions even reached the Kremlin. The aim was to cause desperation, nuisance, chaos, and despondency in the minds of ordinary Russians. While most of the drones were shot down, some managed to hit their intended targets. According to one report, the number of drone attacks on Russian territory had crossed 190 by July 2023.[22]

The biggest dividend from drone strikes came from hitting Russian naval targets in the Black Sea. Here, drones, coupled with more specific arsenal of Neptune-Harpoon over-the-horizon anti-ship missiles and Brimstone air-launched ground attack missiles, caused major damage to the Russian vessels.[23]

Deadly Uncrewed Surface Vehicles

Another deadly weapon appeared in the Black Sea battle in August 2022—the Uncrewed Surface Vehicles (USVs). It was a GPS—controlled and remotely piloted small boat laden with explosives and capable of precisely navigating to achieve catastrophic collisions with the target vessel in the Kamikaze mode. Two models of these USVs initially came in—the Sea Baby and the Magura V5.[24] The combined effect of these armaments managed to sink or damage more than 20 Russian naval vessels, a third of the entire Russian Black Sea fleet.[25, 26]

What Happens in the Indian Scenario?

Needless to mention that over a period of time, drones have emerged as potent vehicles for the maximisation of the air threat. Both our potential adversaries are well endowed with their drone arsenals. They hold both versions—the ones that can carry intelligence, surveillance, target acquisition and reconnaissance (ISTAR) machines and the ones that can mount combat missions with a variety of munitions, such as laser-guided rockets and bombs, precision guided munitions, soft kill weapons, and more. These are the Unmanned Combat Aerial Vehicles or UCAVs.

Major Chinese UCAVs include BZK 005, GJs 1 & 2, EA 03, Tianying-Skyhawk, Gongji 1, WZ 7, and more. Another UCAV worthy of mention is the Wing Loong-I & II. This UCAV is actually in the same class as the US MQ9 Reaper, MQ1-C Gray Eagle, etc.[27, 28]

Pakistani machines include the Chinese ASN-105A & 206, Luna from Germany, Snipe Mk II and Streak from the UK, Falco from Italy, Seeker from South Africa, and more.[29, 30] Their indigenous machine is called 'Burraq'. It has a range of 1000 km, a cruising speed of 215 km, and an endurance of 12 hours. Its typical warhead can include guided bombs (YC-200) and AR-1 ASM (a Chinese supersonic anti-tank missile with a range of 10 km and adapted for use by unmanned platforms).

Countering Drone Power

Faced with this kind of drone power, what must be India's strategy? It is to build strong counter-drone muscle and ensure that tailor-made anti-drone arsenal is proliferated in its field force. Notably, the Ministry of Defence (MoD) is making concerted efforts to equip our forces with Anti-Drone Systems (ADS), currently in the soft-kill domain, to jam the electronics and electromagnetics on board hostile drones to render them toothless. Two very effective and indigenous systems are being inducted—the ADS based on DRDO's design[31] and the one made by a private sector company, Zen Technologies Limited, called the Zen ADS.[32] Efforts are on in the industry to realise the ADS in the hard- kill domain as well (i.e., use of high-rate-of-fire small arms like the medium machine guns (MMG) and the air defence guns).

Some 'Turnaround' Tactical Trends

What are the turnaround trends being referred to? They include the following:

a. By around August-September 2022, the scale and quantum of casualties on tanks and mechanised forces in the non-tactically executed headlong thrusts into Ukraine started to become unacceptable to the Russians. In response, a visible change of gear was attempted. In this, the headlong thrusts were given a pass, and instead, massive fire assaults were inflicted on intended targets to pulverise these before the ground forces moved in for mop-up. Tank casualties started to dip.
b. Around this time, in anticipation of a counter-offensive, the Russians executed a kind of strategic pull-back and dug into a strong defensive position around the Kupiansk-Kreminna-Bakhmut-Robotyne-Mariupole line.[33]
c. The counter-offensive by the Ukrainians failed to make a piercing blitzkrieg through these defences. As to the air and air defence battle, the following developments are noteworthy:
   (i) Russian air power and AH power, now operating over their own defended zones, came into full form and effectively countered the Ukrainian air threat. Thus, a local favourable air situation was achieved.
   (ii) By this time (June-August 2023), the Russians had almost made good most of their shortcomings in ADS, both by way of hard as well as soft-kill measures. These started to counter the Ukrainian drone attacks effectively.
d. Supplementing this effort was the coming of age of the Russian Electronic Warfare (EW) arsenal. Russia is a very strong EW power. It has an entire spectrum of EW weapons, consisting of airborne fire control radar jammers (SPN- 2, 3, 4), ground-based radar jammers (Krashuka II & IV), VHF/UHF jammers (RB-341V, Leer-3), GPS and SATCOM jammers (RH-330 ZHITEL), long-range HF jammers (Murmank-BN), anti-drone jammers/repellents, etc. This weapon suit had got stymied in the initial months of war due to being frittered away in penny packets across parallel and mutually interfering thrust lines. In defence lines, these were now deployed as concentrated hubs and wrought havoc on the GPS-guided

weapons, such as the HIMARS, Scalp EG cruise missiles, storm-shadow missiles, M982 Excalibur arty shells, and a large number of drones.[34]

e. Even the deadly arsenal of air defence weapons, on being deployed tactically, showed their might by downing many Ukrainian air threat vehicles.

A turnaround in air and air defence battle had come about—no more disproportional kills of AHs at the hands of Ukrainian MANPADS but a kind of the other way round. The same was the case with drone kills and kills on tanks and mechanised forces.

In this turnaround lie the inferences:

a. For air power to play to its full potential, the minimum requirement is a local favourable air situation (FAS), in case an all-around FAS or air superiority is elusive.
b. Ground- Based AD Weapon Systems (GBADWS) are deadly if they are deployed tactically with their sensors and with the Battle Management Command and Control (BMC2) systems performing to their capability.
c. Drone power is deadly, no doubt. But when pitted against a full spectrum of anti-drone arsenal, the threat can be reduced to insignificance.
d. For the EW arsenal to come into its own, it requires to be given the freedom to operate in the threat domain without mutual interference.

As the war chugs along and Russia continues to make steady gains, its air and air defence power is now performing to its capability.

Notes

1. "Russia-Ukraine war: list of key events," at www.aljazeera.com. Accessed on June 1, 2024.
2. Ibid. Accessed on June 2, 2024.
3. Ibid. Accessed on June 2, 2024.
4. "A year of air and air defence war," at www.vifindia.org. Accessed on June 3, 2024.

5. "Prelude to the Russian invasion of Ukraine," at www. en.m.wikipedia.org. Accessed on June 4, 2024.
6. "List of Russo-Ukrainian war military equipment," at www.en.m.wikipedia.org. Accessed on June 4, 2024.
7 Ibid.
8. "Russia has lost 50,000 troops in Ukraine," at www.rferl.org. Accessed on June 4, 2024.
9. "What are the MANPADS that the west is sending to Ukraine?" at www. thehindu.com. Accessed on June 4, 2024.
10. "List of equipment of the armed forces of Ukraine," at www.en.m.wikipedia.org. Accessed on June 5, 2024.
11. "How the Ukrainians wrecked the Russian best helicopter regiments," at wwwforbes.com. Accessed on June 5, 2024.
12. Ibid.
13. "HY5, HN-5, HQ-5," at www.global security.com. Accessed on June 5, 2024.
14. "List of missiles of Pakistan," at www.en.m.wikipedia.org. Accessed on June 6, 2024.
15. "Critical requirement of VSHORDS – a user's perspective," at www.vifindia.org. Accessed on June 6, 2024.
16. "Indian army receives fresh batch of Igla S hand-held anti-aircraft missiles," at www.wionews.com. Accessed on June 6, 2024.
17. "DRDO's VSORAD gears up for low altitude missile test," at ww.idrw.org. Accessed on June 6, 2024.
18. Drones used.
19. "Ukraine's Zelensky orders creation of a separate military force for drones," at www.reuters.com. Accessed on June 6, 2024.
20. "Russian ammunition depot hit during Ukrainian drone attack on Crimea," at www.reuters.com . Accessed on June 6, 2024.
21. "Ukraine says that it has destroyed 50 ammunition depots," at www.reuters.com. Accessed on June 6, 2024.
22. "What do we know about drone attacks in Russia," at www.bbc.com. Accessed on June 6, 2024.
23. Ibid.
24. "Meet Ukraine's small but lethal weapons," at www.apnews.com. Accessed on June 7, 2024.
25. "Ukraine says it hit two Russian naval vessels in a major attack on Crimea," at www.cnn.com. Accessed on June 7, 2024.
26. "Russia- Ukraine Conflict: The down end of the see- saw," at www.vifindia.org. Accessed on June 7, 2024.
27. Ibid. Accessed on June 7, 2024.
28. Ibid. Accessed on June 7, 2024.
29. Ibid. Accessed on June 7, 2024.
30. Bokhari Farhan, "Pakistan to deploy its own UAVs over FATA," *Janes Defence Weekly*.

31. "DRDO anti-drone technology handed over to BEL," at www.thehindu.com. Accessed on June 7, 2024.
32. "Anti- drone system," at www.zentechnologies.com. Accessed on June 7, 2024.
33. Ibid.
34. "Russian electronic warfare tactics changing on frontlines in Ukraine," at www.businessinsider.com. Accessed on June 7, 2024.

9. Inferences from Recent Conflicts and Implications for the Indian Military

A.K. Chaturvedi

Introduction

Conflicts have always been destructive in more than one way and have a long-term impact not only on the armed forces but also on the nation's civil societies. Wars also throw up many lessons, which need to be taken note of so that mistakes are not repeated in future. If lessons are not taken note of and a country remains ready for only for the 'last war' it has fought, the results are disastrous. In recent times, the Azerbaijan-Armenia war of 2020 substantiates this statement. Although the conflict between Azerbaijan and Armenia over control of Nagorno Karabakh, an Armenian enclave in Azerbaijan, is an old one, the conflict escalated into a full-scale war in the early 1990s after the collapse of the Soviet Union. The war was won by Armenia and the breakaway Republic of Nagorno Karabakh, Artsakh.

However, when Azerbaijan and Armenia again went to war in 2020, Armenia was comprehensively beaten. That was because Armenia was still prepared for its 1990s conflict, which it had won, whereas Azerbaijan had leveraged new technologies of drone and established a new international cooperation mechanism by aligning with Türkiye. Armenia had no answer for that. This clearly brings out that warfare is a very dynamic process, and protagonists need to continuously evolve so that they can surprise their adversaries by leveraging technologies, creating new alliances, and creating a mechanism to sustain during the conflict.

Consequences of Modern-Day War

Wars and other kinds of conflicts are cataclysmic events, which affect not only the armed forces but also the entire country. But the consequences of the past two decades of conflicts are particularly severe. The issue is discussed here in two parts, as follows:

Part 1: Effects of Modern-day War on Human Society;

Part 2: The Recent Trends in Prosecution of Warfare.

Part 1: Effects of Modern-day War on Human Society

In any conflict, more so as seen in recent trends in prosecution of warfare, the overall effect upon the belligerents' civil society is manifested in terms of the debilities, disruptions, and destructions, as described in the succeeding paragraphs.

Casualties. In any conflict that lasts for a long time, the casualties are massive. The worst sufferers, besides the armed forces personnel, are women, children, the elderly, the infirm, and animals. The reported casualties in the recent conflicts so far have been tabulated as below:

Table 1

S. No.	Conflict	Status	Casualties (Services and civilians)	References
1.	Armenia-Azerbaijan War	Lasted from September to November 2020	6916+13193 missing	https://www.primeminister.am/en/statements-and-messages/item/2022/04/13/Nikol-Pashinyan-Speech/ https://mod.gov.az/en/news/list-of-the-servicemen-fallen-shehids-in-the-patriotic-war-38076.html
2.	Russo-Ukraine War	Ongoing since February 2022	500,000+ 100,00 civilians	https://mod.gov.az/en/news/list-of-the-servicemen-fallen-shehids-in-the-patriotic-war-38076.html https://www.aljazeera.com/news/2023/11/21/more-than-10000-civilians-killed-in-ukraine-since-russia-invasion-un-says
3.	HAMAS – Israel Conflict	Ongoing since October 7, 2023	More than 40,000 + 1.9 million displaced	https://www.ochaopt.org/

Impact on Economy. Economies of the adversaries are adversely affected, both during and after the war. In 2012, the economic impact of war and violence was estimated to be 11 per cent of the gross world product, which, in real terms, was $9.46 trillion.[1] In more recent times, Ukraine lost as much as 30-35 per cent of its GDP during the first year of the war.[2] The reason for such a massive impact on economy is that normal economic activities of a society or a country are disrupted, assets are damaged, and people are displaced. As far as the governments of the affected countries are concerned, they are forced to divert funds earmarked for development and boosting their economic activities towards the war effort.

Destruction of Infrastructure. A war can create a catastrophic collapse of infrastructure, with consequences in the education, healthcare, trade, transportation, and almost all domains of civic life. Such damages indirectly impact the social fibre of the society. It is well established that if infrastructure gets damaged or destroyed, it causes serious disruption to the economy because one of the major outcomes of infrastructural damage is the disruption of transportation means. According to a World Bank estimate, the damage inflicted on Gaza is to the tune of $18.5 billion, which is equivalent to 97 per cent of the combined GDP of the West Bank and Gaza in 2022.[3] Likewise, the total war damage in Ukraine till December 2023 has been estimated at approximately $152 billion.[4]

Effect on Labour Force. The labour force is affected in more than one way. Firstly, due to large- scale deaths and migration, the force itself gets shrunk, and this impacts the productivity and cost of labour with attendant issues; secondly, the profile of the labour force also changes from men to women as most of the able-bodied men are required to join the defence forces. Ukraine's annual inflation rate, 10 per cent in January 2022, became 26.6 per cent in October 2022. War leads to reduction in productivity as initially, the female workers do not have the requisite skill sets, and later, when the menfolk return, social tensions arise.

A Perspective on Productivity. The case of Ukraine puts in a perspective of the damages suffered. According to a recent report from the International Rescue Committee (IRC), the explosion of the southern

Nova Kakhkova Dam in June 2023 left 600,000 hectares of arable land without irrigation. This impacted agricultural production. Further, exports and imports had been at similar levels at roughly $7.5 billion in January 2022. But the balance collapsed after the war began, with the trade balance trailing at negative levels. As of December 2023, it was at minus $3.7 billion.[5]

Displacement. Forced migration is a direct consequence of war. Migration could be internal or external. Internally displaced people suffer on two counts. Threat to life is not minimised, while they do not get refugee status and thus are not eligible for protection under the international system. External displacement is detrimental to the home country as well as the country to which these refugees head. The home country suffers lack of manpower, and the host countries suffer from social, ethnic as well as economic problems. It has been reported that around 4.2 million Ukrainians have been given temporary protection in the European Union (EU) member states since February 2022. Also, almost 100,000 Syrians and Afghans have sought asylum in Europe. While these refugees may add to the labour force of the host countries of the EU, social tensions on account of their arrival are being seen as a big problem by the EU countries.[6]

Psychological Impact. Service in combat is a risk factor for development of Post Traumatic Stress Disorder (PTSD). About 25 per cent of military personnel develop delayed PTSD. Refugees are also at an increased risk for PTSD due to their exposure to war, hardships, and traumatic events. The rates for PTSD within refugee populations range from four per cent to 86 per cent. People who are most affected are women and children, particularly those who have been rendered orphans. The longstanding Israel-Palestinian conflict has inflicted a large degree of social and psychological suffering upon those affected. Palestinians, mostly young men and children, have also been impacted as a consequence of this longstanding conflict. Many in the Israeli Defence Forces have also come out and spoken on their mental state after committing acts of violence against the defenceless. In more tangible terms, a survey in Afghanistan in 2023 brought out that around 90.72 per cent of fighters exhibited symptoms of PTSD. The survey even showed that 95 per cent of the parents had experienced more than one traumatic event. This, therefore, is a tragic consequence of a prolonged war.[7]

Impact on the Education System. According to the United Nations Educational Scientific and Cultural Organisation (UNESCO) report, "The groups most negatively affected by conflict were those that suffered from multiple exclusion, for example, based on gender, area of residence, household wealth, language, and ethnicity." One predominantly damaging effect of conflict on education is the proliferation of attacks on school children, teachers, and school buildings. As such, during times of war, teachers and students often suffer fatalities or displacement. For example, in Iraq, school-going boys were pulled out of school to work for their families.

Gender- Based Violence. War impacts women differently as they are more likely to be subjected to violence from indirect as well as direct causes. They are also subjected to sexual violence and exploitation. For example, in the ongoing Ukraine war, at least 3.6 million people inside Ukraine have been subjected to gender- based violence.[8]

Degradation of Environment. War contributes to environmental degradation, with attendant problems of health, in two ways. The first are the direct effects of killing off of the native ecology, and the second is the indirect effects of depriving the species of the resources needed for their survival. For humans, the use of depleted uranium (DU) by the US Armed Forces during the Persian Gulf War drew claims that the deposited DU was the cause of a cancer cluster in Iraq's southern region. Similarly, by an estimate, use of the toxic defoliant, 'Agent Orange', during the Vietnam War by the United States (US) Army resulted in 400,000 Vietnamese citizens either getting killed or maimed by it, 200,000 suffering from cancer and 500,000 born with related birth defects.[9] Even more drastic records are likely to come out as the present mayhem cools.

Collateral Effects of War. Armed conflicts have many other indirect consequences, such as those on health, commerce, education, food, etc.—societal survival, to be precise. Recent armed conflicts have exacerbated these debilitations towards enhanced morbidity, mortality, and destruction of societal and economic fabric of the belligerents.

In Sum

Warfare has always been a function of the following capabilities:

- Leverage of technology (as was done by Azerbaijan against Armenia in 2020 to inflict a comprehensive defeat);
- Geography and weather (as experienced during Napoleon's invasion of Russia in 1812 CE);
- Economics (basically to ensure sustainability of campaigns), geopolitics (especially the interests of bigger powers who manipulate international relations to gain positions of strength and then dictate terms to the vulnerable adversary);
- Capabilities built by the protagonists to exploit doctrinal advantages, which are innovative and are evolved by armed forces over a period of time (like Blitzkrieg of Germany during WW-II or 'Shock and Awe' followed by 'Effect- Based Operations' by the US during 'Desert Storm - II' in Iraq in 2003);
- Demographic dividends of a country to sustain the war effort (Russia is finding it extremely difficult to sustain its war effort in Ukraine due to the average age in Russia being 40.7 years[10] coupled with a birth rate of 1.49 per woman,[11] which is less than the birth rate necessary to maintain its population. This also impacts its industrial productivity, among many other factors).

Suffice to say that today's war can be won only if a 'Whole of Nation's Approach' is taken by a country. War is also impacted by the comparative comprehensive national powers of the conflicting adversaries to sustain high resource drain and absorb large-scale destruction.

Part 2: Recent Trends in Prosecution of Warfare and Inferences therefrom

In General

Warfare remains a function of the following capabilities, but modern wars are conditioned at yet more profound, more devastating scales. Some examples are:

- *Expansion of technological leverages* as was done by Azerbaijan against Armenia in 2020 to inflict a comprehensive defeat, plays a decisive role.
- In high-technology warfare, the effects of geography and weather are more profound, as experienced during the winter rains in Ukrainian plains.
- *Economics plays a decisive role* in ensuring the sustainability of campaigns. Similarly, geopolitics dictates the interests of bigger powers in manipulating international relations to gain positions of strength and then dictate terms to the vulnerable adversary.
- *Frontline capabilities are continuously innovated* by the armed forces over a period of time to exploit doctrinal advantages. Examples are: the 'Effect- Based Operations' by the US during 'Desert Storm - II' in Iraq in 2003, Russia's 'Little Green Men' operations in Eastern Ukraine, drone operations in the Armenian war, tunnel warfare in Gaza, and massive launch of crude rockets and missiles by HAMAS, Hezbollah, and Houthis – all of which have to be countered by high technology and expensive means.
- *Demographic dividend permits a country to sustain its war effort against high casualties.* Russia is finding it extremely difficult to sustain its war effort in Ukraine due to the average age in Russia being 40.7 years[12] coupled with a birth rate of 1.49 per woman,[13] which is less than the birth rate necessary to maintain its population. With migration of unwilling conscripts, Ukraine is in no better position. This factor also impacts the industrial productivity.

Suffice to say that today's war can be won only if a 'Whole of Nation's Approach' is taken by a country. War is also impacted by the comparative comprehensive national powers of the conflicting adversaries to sustain high resource drain and absorb large- scale destruction.

Some Salient Inferences from the Recent Conflicts

Herein, three representative conflicts are analysed, which are listed below. While a longer time perspective might corroborate the lessons in general, it would fail to offer interim lessons that are useful in the immediate conduct of military affairs:

(i) The ongoing Russo-Ukraine war since February 2022

(ii) The ongoing HAMAS-Israel conflict since October 2023

(iii) The Armenia-Azerbaijan war of 2020

I. The Russo-Ukraine War

- **Legacy and New Weapons Complement each other.** Despite the early success of anti-tank weapons in the defence of Kyiv, the hasty proclamations of an 'end of the tank era' have proved to be premature as the battle moves from Ukraine's northern suburbs to its eastern plains. However, the effectiveness of drones as anti-tank and anti-ship weapons has been substantial—the drowning of Moskva was a case in point. Artillery, both in defensive as well as offensive operations, was quite effective while mines have also been very effective in defensive battles. Similarly, manned air attacks packaged with automated flight buddies have proved effective. New weapons have complemented the existing ones, not superseded them.
- **Weaker Force cannot be just an Easy Game.** Although it was never expected that Ukraine would be able to drive away the Russian Navy from the western half of the Black Sea, it did manage to pin the Russian Navy there. Similarly, Ukraine's modest incursion into the Kursk region did check the momentum of the Russian Army's offensive. Indeed, the Russians had committed mistakes similar to those of the Germans during World War II when they fought in the built- up area of Bakhmut. The inference is clear: A weaker force is capable of upsetting, even seriously upturning, the opponent's war plans.
- **Nuclear Deterrence Works but Conditionally.** The Western powers have been deterred from taking ultimate options against the Russian invasion (the so- termed 'Special Operations') no doubt, but only to a point. Putin's nuclear threat has kept the NATO members from sending troops as well as the most potent of the offensive weapons and equipment they possess to Ukraine. The reason for their caution

is not just that Russia has formidable nuclear capabilities; rather, it is that Putin has designated Ukraine as Russia's 'vital national interest', whereas Western governments have not yet done so in respect of Ukraine. Russia has thus, by implication, drawn its 'red line' over Ukraine's membership of the Western power block and qualified any breach of that red line for possible retaliation through its nuclear options. On the other hand, Putin's nuclear sabre- rattling has not prevented the Western powers from extending the range of the weapons they provide to Ukraine to hit Russia. Western allies have, so far, also been able to deter Putin from attacking any of the NATO countries. Deterrence thus remains conditional to the relative stakes and remains restrained by the extent of the adversaries' capabilities.

- **Interdependence does not Prevent War.** Some German policymakers assumed that cutting trade ties with Russia would be so costly that belligerent parties would not opt for open hostilities. But while economic or technological interdependence can raise the cost of war, it does not necessarily prevent it. More to the point, a lopsided interdependence can be 'weaponised' by the less dependent party. Notable is the recent case of delay in supply of GE-404 engines by the US to India, which would impact the operational readiness of the Indian Air Force in short to medium terms.
- **Sanctions can Raise Costs but Do Not Determine Conflict Outcomes in the Short Term.** Oil is a fungible commodity, and sanctions notwithstanding, many countries – not the least, India – are more than happy to import discounted Russian oil transported by an irregular fleet of tankers. Similarly, there have been many instances of circumventing sanctions. China's concerns about getting entangled in secondary sanctions seem to have set some limits on its material support for Russia. Thus, while China has provided important 'dual-use' items (suitable for either military or civilian purposes), it has abstained from sending weapons to Russia. Sanctions notwithstanding, Russia's 'Special Operations' continue - the war goes on.
- **Information Warfare Makes a Reckonable Difference.** Careful disclosure of intelligence by the United States to reveal Russia's invasion plans proved effective in debunking the narrative Putin had

wanted the Europeans to believe. Besides, as predicted, it contributed greatly to the Western allies' solidarity as the invasion occurred. Similarly, Ukrainian President Volodymyr Zelensky has done an extraordinary job of promoting his country's narrative in the West. Modern wars are not only about battlefield wins; these are also about whose 'narrative' wins.

- **Hard Power Matters while Soft Power Influences.** While hard, coercive power trumps the attraction of soft power in the near term, soft power still counts for a lot. Putin failed the soft-power test early on. The highhandedness of Russian fighters in Ukraine caused Germany to finally cancel the Nord Stream 2 gas pipeline – an outcome that years of US pressure had failed to bring about. Zelensky, by contrast, has been relying on soft power from the start. Using his skills as an actor to present an attractive proposition for Ukraine, he has not only won the West's sympathy but also secured large-scale deliveries of military equipment to underwrite his hard power.
- **Decisiveness of Cyber Weapons.** Russia has used cyber means to disrupt Ukraine's power grid since 2015. Many analysts predicted that a cyber blitz against Ukraine's infrastructure and its seat of government would make the Russian invasion a full success. But while there have been many reported cyber attacks during the war, none has proved decisively crippling. When the Ukrainians' Viasat network was hacked, they started communicating through Star Link's many small satellites. With training and battlefield experience, Ukrainian cyber defence and offence have only improved over time. Also, once the war began, kinetic weapons provided higher timeliness, precision and damage assessment to the military commanders than the use of cyber weapons could. That said, electronic warfare can seriously interfere with the linkages that are essential to warfare, including the use of drones.
- **Wars are Unpredictable.** Two years ago, many expected a quick Russian victory, and likewise, just one year ago, there were great expectations of a triumphant Ukrainian summer offensive. The war is still going on, in fact, becoming more destructive with its scope getting enlarged. Putin has managed to sell his war of attrition to the

Russian people as a "great patriotic" struggle against the West. But the probability that the dog he has unleashed could still turn around and bite him cannot be ruled out. Putin certainly never expected to be bogged down by Ukraine's resistance indefinitely. Clearly, with modern options of resistance available to the defender, the promise of a short war is seductive. The most important lesson from the Ukraine war, therefore, remains one of the oldest, that positive correlations of opposing forces are not always a reliable predictor of actual performance.

- Secondary Effects of Modern Era Warfare
  - There is large- scale population displacement (almost every third Ukrainian is displaced). National productivity, so essential in war situations, suffers.
  - Damage to the infrastructure is quite substantial. Water, electricity and fuel infrastructure of Ukraine is damaged to the extent that sustaining life has become difficult. It has also impacted agricultural production as about 6.5-8.5 per cent of the farmland has been abandoned. Damage to Kakhovka Dam over Dnieper River has further reduced food grain production in Ukraine due to damage to the irrigation system.
  - Besides local scarcity, war also has wide-ranging impacts on global supply chains as almost 30 per cent of food grains produced by Russia and Ukraine contributed to the supply chains.
  - War enhances poverty. Presently, nearly a quarter of Ukraine's population lives in poverty. About 1 in 5 families are food insecure.
  - War has an adverse impact over people's mental health (almost 30 per cent of Ukrainians suffer from anxiety and stress).

All these factors directly impact the economy, which also has a bearing on sustaining the war. In the case of Ukraine, the economy has shrunk by almost 30 per cent.

II. The HAMAS-Israel Conflict

The recent Israel-HAMAS (Harakat al-Muqawama al-Islamiyah) conflict has thrown up many lessons in strategic, operational and tactical domains. Some of the important ones are listed below.

Strategic Lessons from Israel-HAMAS War

- Operations against an obdurate adversary as HAMAS have to be a collective endeavour with full cooperation of the allies. With Iran operating in conjoint actions with its non-state actor supporters—like the Houthis of Yemen and the Hezbollah of Lebanon–Israel is leaning to the importance of having allies at different levels and in larger geography.
- As part of geopolitical and political expediency, the USA has historically been igniting hotspots globally with scant regard even for its allies, one example being the deteriorating economies of European nations because of the Ukraine war. The US doesn't prioritise a ceasefire in Ukraine or Gaza, as the wars suit its economy. Political leaders, the world over, do not hesitate to sacrifice their allies' interests for their national benefits as well as to retain or gain power.
- Public support for conflict depends on the perception of success created by the adversaries and their allies. In the instant case, while excessive use of force against Palestinians has galvanised universal consternation, the outrage over hostage- taking by the HAMAS has united Israel as never before. The entire nation wants the Israel Defence Forces (IDF) to teach the perpetrators a lesson. Another lesson that emerges is that if the international laws are violated, the situation becomes quite uncertain and ugly.
- However, stretching of operations against HAMAS over a year with no end in sight puts economic pressure on both Palestine as well as Israel. The economic toll of the war may cost Israel an estimated $400 billion in lost economic activity over the next decade. The war is costing the Israeli economy $ 600M a week due to work absences, according to the Bank of Israel. This is equivalent to about 6 per cent of its weekly GDP. Gaza, on the other hand, experienced a severe financial crisis as a result of Israel's attacks, with access to cash severely limited. Around 85 per cent of the workforce in Gaza is currently without a job, resulting in a significant slowdown in economic activities. As a result, the region is functioning at a mere 16 per cent of its full capacity, resulting in a severe economic downturn, as described by the World Bank.

Lessons at Tactical and Operational Levels

- Preparedness: It needs to be noted that initiative is always with the actor that initiates the action. Choosing of the day of attack by HAMAS, October 7, was a clever move, as it was a Jewish holiday. In fact, it was also the 50th anniversary of the Yom Kippur War. Lowering guard can be hazardous in such a scenario, but Israel's overlooking the Arab behaviour in the past shows that the intelligence network, both technical as well as human, had failed to give indicators of the impending operation. Therefore, it needs to be flagged that underestimating an enemy, however small it may be, will be at one's own peril.
- Regular appreciation of the enemy elements operating within a country's counter-insurgency grid needs to trigger corresponding developments of mechanisms. Such mechanisms help in examining every hostile event, small or big, and prepare the regular forces to respond appropriately in real time. This is a lesson for Indian troops deployed in J&K and also CAPFs deployed against internal security situations.
- Efficacy of Weapons and Tactical Systems:
    - Firepower, even if precision, has limitations in dense urban terrain. Also, airpower alone has failed to deliver the results that the IDF needed. This has caused the scope of operations against the Hezbollah to enlarge into Northern Israel and has allowed the Houthis to thumb their noses at the Western powers in the Red Sea. Meanwhile, Iran and its proxies continue to operate in Syria/Golan Heights while the HAMAS and its allies continue to operate in Gaza and the West Bank.
    - Air/Missile defence has potential. It is felt within the IDF as well across Israel that the Iron Dome and its various versions of air defence have worked well; these have saved lives and limited property damages.
    - Operational values of conventional fighting and active protective systems like infantry, armour, etc. remain central to prosecution of war. These are of great value even in built-up areas, against sniper fire and to clear the terrain of rocket/missile launch pads.

- Excessive dependence on technology turns counter-productive. Technology is subject to operating limitations, weather and the enemy's capability to employ tactical as well as electronic counter-measures—to avoid detection across the fence or in congested areas, for example. Fences need to be backed-up with manning and multiple means of echeloned surveillance.
- Intelligence Cycle: Despite an earlier input about a likely attack by the HAMAS, the IDF did not react. This reiterates that besides intelligence acquisition, it is equally important to get it corroborated, processed and disseminated to the troops in contact, and finally, to have a force ready to respond to it. Thus, the system for collaboration among intelligence agencies, both internal and external, needs to be kept ticking. It is further reiterated that advancement in intelligence acquisition technology has not reduced the relevance of human intelligence - more so in anti-terrorist operations in which it always pays high dividends.
- Tunnel Warfare: The HAMAS used the tactics of fighting through tunnels, a task that has always been formidable even for the technologically most advanced countries. Thus, despite all their might, the IDF have not been able to finish off the HAMAS in Gaza. The HAMAS has also been able to sustain its logistic system despite a very strong presence of the IDF in Gaza, besides Egypt closing its border to the Palestinians and the US Navy blocking Gaza from the sea side. Tunnelling is not a new concept. The Chinese used it in the Korean War, and in the Vietnam War, the US was unable to subdue the Vietnamese, despite using defoliants and chemicals, when the latter used Sochi Tunnels as defence works. The concept has again picked up momentum, and it is now reported that Pakistan is using tunnels in Pakistan Occupied Kashmir while the People's Liberation Army (PLA) is digging tunnels and caves east of Depsang Plains in Ladakh. India needs to develop her own doctrine of tunnel warfare in defensive as well as offensive operations. Leveraging corresponding technology (use of robotics, AI and drones) would be a way ahead.

III. The Armenia-Azerbaijan War of 2020

- A classical case of leveraging technology was noticed in the Azerbaijan-Armenia War of 2020. Azerbaijan had developed an impressive arsenal of drones composed of Turkish and Israeli Unmanned Combat Aerial Vehicles (UCAVs), including the Israeli loitering munitions, also known as 'suicide' or 'kamikaze' drones. In that conflict, Azerbaijan also had reportedly modified its Soviet-era An-2 Colt biplanes with remote-control systems, flying them to the frontlines to draw out Armenian air defences. Azerbaijan had likewise invested heavily in rocket artillery having the ability to target up to 120 and 200 km away.
- Although Armenia, too, had deployed some of its indigenously produced drones, and later, more sophisticated Russian-made Orlan-10 UCAV, it was Azerbaijan that took control of the skies. The effects of these weapons were game-changing. These enabled the Azerbaijani forces to find, fix, track, and kill targets with precise strikes far beyond the frontlines. No wonder, drones contributed to disabling a huge number of Armenian tanks, fighting vehicles, artillery units and air defences. Azerbaijan also used the high-definition cameras fitted to Türkiye's TB2s drones to produce many propaganda videos.
- Yet, while drones played an important role in this conflict, their capabilities need not be exaggerated. These platforms are very vulnerable to air defences (AD) that are designed to counter them. However, Armenia was ill-prepared to deal with the onslaught of drone warfare as it had not built an arsenal of modern AD Systems to counter the drones. The bulk of Armenia's air defences consisted of obsolete Soviet-era systems. This reiterates the need to remain contemporary to the evolving military technologies.
- It is also true that both sides saved their smaller holding of ballistic missiles, probably apprehending that their early use might leave them bereft of these systems when needed the most. Armenia did have some Iskandar Missiles but used these only towards the end when it was already too late. As against this hesitation, use of the most lethal

weapon in one's arsenal could be a game- changer—the Houthi rebels used missiles against Saudi Arabia very effectively as they had assured supply of missiles from Iran. An assured system of supply can happen only if either an indigenous capability exists or international tie- ups are such that the supply chain does not get disrupted.

- The above situation also flags the importance of full-spectrum AD systems. Azerbaijan was able to exploit this gap with its large fleet of sophisticated drones. No wonder, major powers like the USA, China, and Russia are in the process of developing and deploying their own drone countermeasures, including kinetic interceptors, electronic jammers, and even counter-drone drones. While these technologies exist today, there are difficulties in developing these at an affordable cost and rate to provide defence at multiple echelons, including at the tactical levels, in the desired timeframe. Armour and other heavy ground units are likely to remain vulnerable until mobile Short Range Air Defence (SHORAD) systems improve and proliferate. It is indeed an important lesson for India to work harder to develop this capability indigenously.
- Both the Azerbaijan-Armenia conflict and the ongoing Russo-Ukraine War highlight the importance of passive defence. With the proliferation of sensors and shooters, armed forces will have to think afresh about camouflage and deception. Probably, the tested battle craft of dispersal and concealment ought to be reinvigorated. Soldiers should train to limit their electronic and thermal signatures for longer durations and distances.
- The Armenia-Azerbaijan conflict-2020 brings out the important lesson that competent synchronisation of new weapons and equipment with the existing ones renders the modern battlefield capabilities much more lethal. Azerbaijan's combination of drones and artillery effectively targeted Armenia's high-value military assets—most notably the attacks on Armenian T-72 tanks and S-300 air defence systems. Indeed, the most complex threats are the integrated attacks incorporating multiple threat capabilities in a well-coordinated and synchronised attack.

Conclusion

It is important to note that countries and societies that learn lessons from their previous experience of conflicts and also from the experience of others while remaining contemporary to evolutions in technology have a fair chance to come out with successful strategies to subdue their adversaries, provided they invest in following:

- Indigenous production of military equipment;
- Research and development of dual- use technologies;
- Efficient harness of human capital; and
- Reliable international collaborations, like Azerbaijan has established with Türkiye.

The above analysis concludes that India needs to work to enhance its comprehensive national power. In this respect, some of the important elements which need to be addressed are:

- The need to work out a National Security Doctrine;
- Thrust on boosting the economy to enhance sustainability of military power;
- Management of defence budget to modernise the Armed Forces to be at par with our adversaries;
- Investment in defence research and development (R&D) to remain contemporary with the technological strides;
- Modernisation of the nation's nuclear capability to achieve more effective deterrence capability;
- Investment in professional human capital to develop military-industrial complex; enhance self-reliance with a view to reduce vulnerability to international pressures; go for international collaboration/interdependence with a view to build capacity to withstand threats from adversaries; harness the demographic dividend with better scientific and technological training; and finally, build up the nation's intrinsic strengths to keep fissiparous tendencies under check.

Notes

1. "The Economic Costs of Violence and Containment". The Institute for Economics and Peace (2012).

2. https://www.economicsobservatory.com/ukraine-whats-the-global-economic-impact-of-russias-invasion.
3. https://www.worldbank.org/en/news/press-release/2024/04/02/joint-world-bank-un-report-assesses-damage-to-gaza-s-infrastructure.
4. https://www.statista.com/statistics/1303344/ukraine-infrastructure-war-damage.
5. https://www.aa.com.tr/en/economy/2-years-of-war-russia-ukraine-conflict-exacts-stinging-economic-costs/3146218
6. https://www.euronews.com/business/2024/01/22/the-economic-impact-of-migration-on-europe
7. https://www.nature.com/articles/s41598-023-31228-0
8. https://www.plan.ie/blog/gender-based-violence-and-the-ukraine-war.
9. https://www.chronogram.com/news-politics/damage-plan-2169376?show FullText=true
10. https://www.statista.com/statistics/1090520/russia-mean-population-age.
11. https://datacommons.org/place/country/RUS?utm_medium=explore&mprop=fertilityRate&popt=Person&cpv=gender,Female&hl=en
12 https://www.statista.com/statistics/1090520/russia-mean-population-age
13 https://datacommons.org/place/country/RUS?utmmedium=explore&mprop=fertilityRate&popt=Person&cpv=gender,Female&hl=en

Additional References

1. Joseph S. Nye, Jr., "Old and New Lessons from the Ukraine War". Uploaded on https://www.project-syndicate.org/commentary/ukraine-war-eight-lessons-for-military-tactics-grand-strategy-sanctions-by-joseph-s-nye-2024-06#:~:text=Another percent20lesson percent2C percent20then percent2C percent20 is percent20that, Finally percent2C percent20war percent20is percent20unpredictable dated June 4, 2024.
2. "Three lessons for the West from Russia's war in Ukraine", *The Looking Glass.* Uploaded on https://www.defence.gov.au/defence-activities/research-innovation/research-publications/three-lessons-west-russias-war-ukraine#:~:text=Lesson percent20one percent3A percent20successful percent20deterrence percent20relies,strategically percent20about percent20Russia percent20and percent20Ukraine.
3. https://www.wfpusa.org/articles/ukraine-after-2-years-war-how-conflict-has-affected-civilians/#:~:text=Immediate percent20Effects percent20of percent20the percent20War percent20in percent20 Ukraine&text=6 percent20million percent20people percent20

displaced percent20were,a percent20third percent20of percent20the percent20population.

4. Shaan Shaikh and Wes Rumbaugh, "The Air and Missile War in Nagorno-Karabakh: Lessons for the Future of Strike and Défense", Pub. by CSIS dated December 8, 2020. Uploaded on https://www.csis.org/analysis/air-and-missile-war-nagorno-karabakh-lessons-future-strike-and-defense.
5. Raphael S. Cohen et al., "Lessons from Israel's war in Gaza", pub. by Rand Corporation, pub. on October 18, 2017. Uploaded on https://www.rand.org/pubs/research_briefs/RB9975.html
6. "Lessons from the Israel-HAMAS War: Unravelling the Complex Lessons from the Israel-HAMAS Conflict", pub. by SP's Land Forces during July 2024. Uploaded on https://www.spslandforces.com/

10. Emerging Technologies in Recent Conflicts and Implications for India

P.K. Mallick and Gautam Banerjee

Preamble

The ongoing Russo-Ukraine War has been named by the defence analysts as a full–scale drone war, first Artificial Intelligence (AI) war and the first war into the commercial space, qualifying it as "a significant, fundamental change in the character of war as recorded in the history."[1] It is further stated that "the country that masters those technologies, combines those with their doctrine and develops its leadership to take maximum operational advantages from such technologies is likely going to have significant—perhaps even decisive—advantage in the next war."[2]

The fundamental 'nature' of warfare remains more or less the same. But the 'character' of war is ever-evolving. Influx of new technologies into the military institutions has been happening since the earliest forms of formal warfare, and this has increased in frequency since the First Industrial Revolution. In recent years, the difference manifests in the faster rates of the upgrades in technology. Military technologies in the new era are thus triggering fast changes in the methods of warfare. Emerging and disruptive technologies in autonomous and hypersonic weaponry, Unmanned Weapon Systems (UAS) (e.g. drones), electromagnetic detection and signal interception, cyber operations, space weaponisation and access to extensive sources of intelligence, all customised to the Artificial Intelligence (AI) algorithms to integrate all such means with the operational concepts in innovative and unanticipated ways, are creating new ways to apply the military forces. At the other end, while technology has imparted unprecedented transparency in the battlefield, it has also thickened the inevitable 'fog of war' by the role played by modern camouflage and deception measures.

Unlike when the military had been the source of technological developments, most of the modern-day technologies that drive changes in methods of prosecution of war are from the commercial sector. Today, private firms control the bulk of investments in AI, satellite surveillance, drone development and advanced manufacturing of military hardware. Most of such technologies are also dual-use. For example, commercial drones turn into armaments when explosives and military-specific fitments are strapped onto these. Armed forces have to innovate to adapt to such technological developments.

This chapter delves into the observed roles of the 'Emerging Technologies' in prosecution of the recent armed conflicts, to draw military inferences from these developments and the major implications for India. Notably, more time, authenticated data and professional analyses would be needed before these inferences can be crystallised into formal military lessons.

Even then, in defending Indian interests in a hostile neighbourhood, it would be helpful to adopt empowering mid-course measures into India's military institution.

Transmuting Character of Modern Warfare

Emerging technologies are qualitatively changing the way people perceive the environment, communicate and make decisions. These have far-reaching military implications. Major indicators of modern-day characterisation of warfare are:

- Wars could turn into prolonged contests that place high premium on strengths of the industrial base, ecosystem of innovations and political resolve.
- Critical societal infrastructures are viewed as legitimised targets for destruction. So is the case with collateral destruction of non-military assets.

- Threat of use of nuclear weaponry is brazenly flouted as retaliation against an all-out aggression.
- Proletariatisation of armed conflicts raises the risk of escalation into outbreak of war between states.
- There are trends of repudiating ethical moderations and international obligations while unleashing the emerging and disruptive technological power.
- Accelerating adaptations to modern software and its connectivity into military operations.
- Proliferation of sensors, analytical tools, precision guided munitions, and non-kinetic payloads, like cyber and directed energy weaponry, are in the process of fundamentally altering the 'hider–detector' contest.

Today, software is integral to every component of the military decision-making tree as well as its 'kill chain'. The increasing importance of software and connectivity will hasten the adaptation of latest military technologies into the realms of military tactics. Accordingly, the national armed forces are developing their future systems, capabilities, and operational methods with software-centric orientation in mind.

Universal usability of unmanned aerial vehicles (UAV), unmanned surface vehicles (USV), smartphones, satellite imagery, commercial data links, sensor-based technologies, and the vast array of open-source intelligence are fundamentally changing the way armed forces would fight. These systems, coupled with emerging AI platforms, can dramatically accelerate the pace and extent of modern-day warfare. These new technologies, therefore, necessitate updating of past ideas, strategies, and the manner of preparing the people for war.

Emerging Technologies of Warfare

'Emerging Technologies' are a range of scientific and technical developments that, when applied to military applications, are likely to have a transformative impact on the future of warfare. Thus, factors like superior data collection and assimilation, connectivity, computing power, algorithms, and system security would be the modern sources of battlefield advantage.[3] 'Disruptive Technologies' mean new or enhanced technologies that bring about a radical, not just incremental, shift that might change how the world operates, thus disrupting the pre-existing notions of affairs. Smartphones and AI are some examples of such technologies. Thus, the emergent disruptive technologies are increasingly assisting militaries in chartering unexplored domains, while maximising their effectiveness, cost efficiency, sustainability, and resilience.

Realising the potential of the emergent disruptive technologies in revolutionising the military capabilities, advanced countries have started to invest heavily in research and development (R&D) of such technologies. Collaborations with private institutions and innovators are being explored to seek the possibilities and applications of such technologies, many of these being of dual-use. Accordingly, the NATO, in its 2021 Summit, launched its '2030 Agenda' to focus on nine priority defence technology areas. The focus is more or less universally accepted[4]:

- Artificial intelligence (AI)
- Autonomous systems
- Quantum technologies
- Biotechnology and human enhancement technologies
- Space
- Hypersonic systems
- Novel materials and manufacturing
- Energy and propulsion
- Next-generation communications networks

Drones, satellites, artificial intelligence and cyber capabilities have already assumed significance in all the recent military conflicts. Herein, new technologies have been employed in concert with traditional military hardware. Some of such technologies, which have had an immediate impact on warfare, are:

- *Software and connectivity* accelerate the adaptation of tactics and military technology.
- *Proliferation of collection platforms, analytical tools and precision-guided munitions* are altering the hider-finder contest.

- *Relatively inexpensive drones and loitering munitions* are changing how militaries conceive of combined arms warfare.
- *Starlink low-speed data transmissions* have given Ukraine an incredible advantage in terms of transmitting high-quality video.
- *Technology companies, including drone manufacturers, AI companies, commercial cyber-security companies, social media companies and space actors* act as force multipliers.
- Further, the emerging technologies have also prompted the following changes:
- New actors, excluded so far, are exerting influence on the information ecosystem and the course of the war.
- New vectors for information diffusion, including social media platforms, have generated owners who find themselves in a content moderation role.
- The compound effect of sustained information operations could create a polluted information environment with long-term adverse effects.
- With the increasing tempo of conflicts, there is an information overload. There is less time for decision-makers to choose their option.
- New capabilities are liable to expose new vulnerabilities, cause indefinite effects and introduce new actors operating in unfamiliar ways. Uncertainty during conflicts would increase.
- Overwhelmed by information overload, political and military decision-makers may choose to depend, with reducing human intervention, on employing AI-enabled capabilities to collect and process information across the battlefield domains, assess various courses of action, and determine the best possible outcome, thus recommending particular choices and executing that response. Results, however, of that kind of 'out-sourcing' to the machines could be but anything!

Recent Wars: Observable Trends and Inferences

Future wars will not just be about which side can get the most combatants or field the best aircraft, ships and tanks. Autonomous weapons systems and powerful algorithms will also make reckonable differences. Accordingly, the armed forces will have to reform their structure, tactics, leadership development, and training and procurement processes.

The observable trends and related inferences from recent wars may be listed as follows:

- Besides relying primarily on concentration of forces and tempo of combat operations, armed forces are also creating wider operational opportunities by using long-range, precision fires to destroy higher echelon headquarters and disrupt enemy logistics. In complex battlefield environments, the forces with the shortest response time from detection to destruction will win.
- Drones are changing battle procedures for fire and manoeuvre. They are used for expendable intelligence, surveillance, and reconnaissance (ISR) systems, munitions or to correct long-range artillery fires to pinpoint accuracy. Cheap, expendable drones play important roles in degrading costly, advanced air defence systems by forcing the latter to expend expensive and limited missile stocks while exposing themselves to follow-on attacks by cheaper drones, aircraft and missiles. However, drones are also vulnerable to air defences and electronic warfare countermeasures.
- From sensing targets to decision-making, attacking and making battle damage assessment, software is now integral to every part of combat. The quality of the software will determine who will have the edge on the battlefield. The wars in Ukraine and Gaza have shown that in any next major conflict, artificial intelligence (AI) will be integrated into every aspect of military planning and execution. Ukraine has used AI in conjunction with satellite imagery to create software that helps the artillery locate, aim, and destroy targets in the most efficient and lethal manner possible.[5]
- Intelligence can be searched for and gathered quickly. Open-Source Intelligence (OSINT) is very useful to provide immediate information. Beyond the need for updated intelligence, AI- integrated intelligence management systems would be critical for disseminating information across the domains of a future conflict.

Notably however, the paradox of the war is that mass and technology arc intimately bound together. Jack Watling of the Royal United Services

Institute stated, "What blunted the Russians north of Kyiv, was two brigades of artillery firing all their barrels every day."[6] Excalibur shells with a small, rugged chip fitted inside could receive GPS signals from America's navigation satellites to turn precise and effective in pinpointing target locations. This reduces the number of shells required, thereby lowering the logistical loads.

Contrarily, in a glimpse of things to come, even the chips inside the Excalibur shells have been tampered with; these are not always landing on the designated targets. Similar counter-response mechanisms would continue to develop in this cat-and-mouse game.

Advantages of Defensive Operations

The assimilation of new technologies brings the following advantages in the effectiveness of defence in recent wars:

- Using local knowledge with advanced machinery, defenders are able to rapidly prepare alternate positions to redeploy after fire and manoeuvre drills.
- Force signatures are minimised by deliberate adoption of modern camouflage techniques, use of overhead cover, and by remaining stationary.
- Long-range weapons enable the defender to concentrate fire on the bottlenecks while remaining dispersed.
- The movement of attackers generates multiple give away signatures. Under ubiquitous surveillance, attacking forces have to seek cover and move quickly and frequently to avoid being targeted by the increasing variety of drones, missiles, and smart artillery and mortar munitions.
- Attacking force-elements have to assemble without the benefits of secured 'firm bases' or the so-called 'iron mountains'. Spilling out of their 'hides', force-elements have to form-up on the move under an air-defence umbrella.

Ruling Observations

The days of operations launched from large garrisons and massed columns of vehicles are fading away. The transition will require considerable efforts in revising the force-composition, grouping, tactics, techniques, procedures, and equipment profile. Correspondingly, the armed forces would need to focus on those platform-agnostic, semi-autonomous weapons, which offer greater ranges and lesser costs. In that respect, the ruling observations may be listed as follows:

Ground Operations. Emerging technologies affect the ground operations in the following ways:

- Armour continues to rule the Ukrainian War, providing shock action on the battlefield, facilitating the forces to penetrate the enemy front, and supporting the infantry operations.
- Infantry remains the 'Queen of Battle'. However, personnel protective gear and use of armour-protected infantry fighting vehicles are key to battlefield survivability.
- Artillery remains a decisive factor on the battlefield. Mobile, precision and long-range rocket artillery has proved to be most effective in defensive as well as offensive operations.
- Man-portable anti-tank, anti-aircraft missiles and ground-based air defence weapons, backed by drones, counter-drones and modern electronic warfare systems have proved extremely effective for the soldiers engaged in ground operations.
- For effective command and control, communication systems have to be able to withstand the adversary's modern countermeasures.

The Naval Domain. Notable developments are as follows:

- Ukraine, a country essentially without a navy, could yet limit the Russian Navy's monopoly of the Black Sea and threaten its traditional home base in Crimea. The Russian Fleet had to move out of the range of Ukraine's cruise missiles and airborne and sea-based drones.
- Low-cost drones and cruise missiles have destroyed about a third of Russia's Black Sea surface fleet, or 20-odd warships, including a submarine. Ukraine has even destroyed the Russian Navy's Black Sea Flagship, the cruiser, Moskva.
- Reportedly, Ukraine has been able to severely restrain the Russian Black Sea Fleet's amphibious capability from the southern waters, which is viewed as a 'Russian lake'. It has thus considerably reduced Russia's ability to carry out precision sea-based strikes.

- In the world-wide perspective, carrier-based groups, attack submarines, frigates, support ships, and corvettes continue to be the fundamental constituents of naval power projection. Naval fleets can also be boosted up with grouping of uncrewed support ships.

Air War. Technological advancements have enhanced the effectiveness of air weapons in the following ways:

- Airborne and space-borne assets are playing crucial roles in the recent wars. Tactically designed mixes of crewed and uncrewed air weaponry are being experimented with for optimal grouping of air task forces.[7]
- Air superiority has assumed added criticality in conduct of all types of operations. The value of space assets as well as the multi-role fighters, ground attack aircraft, bombers and Unmanned Aerial Vehicles (UAV), armed or as well as in ISR role, has increased manifold.
- Ground-based missiles and drones have proved to be vital instruments of air power.
- As a prerequisite for sustaining its operations against the Russian invasion, Ukraine is consistently raising demands from its Western allies for more and more of the fourth-generation fighter planes, like the F-16, along with training and maintenance support.
- Ukraine is also demanding longer range weaponry to target Russia's depth areas, a demand the allies are reluctant to concede to against Russia's threat of massive retaliation and a consequent war-escalation. This vexing situation has added to the complexities in war management. It has also opened up new options for aggression as well as defence.
- Passive defensive measures like painted decoys on runways, camouflage on aircraft, screens and barrage-type balloons to intercept drones have proved to be helpful and cheaply deployed.
- Some analysts believe that modern air defence systems can create an area of air denial where crewed aircraft would be reluctant to operate. Russian and Ukrainian crewed aircraft rarely attempt to penetrate the multilayered air defence systems of the other side.[8]

Non-state Forces' Use of Emerging Technologies.[9] Violent non-state actors and terrorists can pose significant threats to societies by exploiting low-cost, commercially available technologies and automated systems like AI, drones and digital platforms. The inferences from militarisation of the digital age are clear:

- Unaccountable entities like the IS, Hezbollah and Houthis, even the state-hired mercenaries, exploit emerging technologies to conduct attacks at low costs as well as to avoid detection.
- Technological advances, including AI, bio-technology and the Internet of Things, offer opportunities for the terrorists to develop cross border collaborations and remote methods to conduct high-profile attacks.
- Autonomous delivery vehicles guided by AI systems could enable a terrorist group to strike dozens of targets in simultaneity. These outlaws could come to possess the weapons of mass destruction to conduct spectacular mass casualty attacks.
- Augmented reality environments could organise virtual terrorist training camps to connect experienced plotters, protected by their distant sanctuaries, with the terror operatives.
- Entities like insurgent groups and terrorist organisations can collect crypto-currency donations to sustain operations, purchase weapons and recruit new members and train them. Exploiting the relative obscurity and insufficiency of regulatory frameworks, these outlaws can increasingly leverage crypto-currencies and new 'fintech' tools to finance their nefarious activities. In fact, the non-state forces do not seem to have any dearth of black funds.
- As state, non-state and hybrid actors continue to exploit disruptive technologies to undermine the established rules of reason and law, the international community, in order to promote peace and security, has to remain vigilant, adaptable and united in adapting to the counter-measures.

Role of the Private Sector. The commercial sector, by out-investing the government in critical areas of satellite surveillance, drone development, autonomous systems, AI, quantum computing, space, biotech and other emerging technologies as well as advanced manufacturing, leads the direction and pace of modern innovations. Most of such technologies in use on the modern-era battlefield are derived from commercial developments and are likely to advance more rapidly than most government projects. Militaries, therefore, have to engage the private sector as a prominent source of technology and innovations, forge public-private partnerships with the commercial sector and harness the accruing technological advantages towards military purposes. They would need to create appropriate organisational structures to experiment, customise and integrate these commercial ventures at a rate faster than their adversaries.

Effects of Technological Developments on Warfare

The ongoing conflicts in Ukraine, Gaza and the Red Sea have thrown open several technological phenomena to characterise the future conduct of warfare:

- Conventional air and missile defence systems have been used to counter massive and repeated barrages of drones and cruise as well as ballistic missiles.
- There has been mass use of drones and First Person View (FPV) loitering munitions for reconnaissance and strike.
- There has been galloping and dynamic evolution of Electronic Warfare (EW) measures and countermeasures, including GPS jamming and counter-drone EW.
- Maritime drones have been used to cripple major surface combatants at sea and in ports.
- Drones and cruise missiles have been used to breach the advanced layered air defence systems.
- Recent wars have shown that defensive works, anti-tank ditches, camouflage, mines, booby-traps, dragon's teeth, barbed wire and other obstacles in depth can render the battlefields as killing grounds and absorb the heaviest of offensives. Defeating these measures takes feats of combat engineering and a will to acquire innovative technologies.
- High-intensity destructive powers available among the contestants have forced both sides to go underground in deep trenches, bunkers and cellars to survive.

- The proliferation of information collection platforms and sensors, AI-enabled analytical tools and precision-guided munitions is changing the 'hider finder' contest. In every contested domain, including in space and under-sea, it has become increasingly difficult to hide military assets as well as their tactical manoeuvres, thus rendering the battlefield somewhat more transparent.
- An extremely capable central hub of command is required to organise competent control over the plethora of system networks operating on the battlefield. So far, command posts have mostly been stationary, larger and relatively safer in their electromagnetic emissions to control military operations. These hubs are now highly vulnerable to electronic warfare, satellite imagery, electromagnetic signal detection and surveillance UAVs. Such inherent vulnerabilities would be exploited in any future conflict.
- In contrast, with expanding options of effective deception and other active and passive measures, it could be difficult to gain operational surprise and apply successful tactics to gain the upper hand. Combat forces have to adapt to dispersal-concentration-forming-up tactics that lower their overall signature across multiple domains. Junior officers have to be active in directing the distribution and movement of forces. This has major implications for leadership, training, equipment and tactics.
- 'Proletariatisation' of higher-quality information and its spread right up to the edges of the chains of command require the systems of command and control of forces to be upgraded. This recourse would be a sophisticated version of the German concept of 'Auftragstaktik' (mission-type orders) that stressed on considerable freedom of action to the tactical commanders in achievement of the force commanders' intent.
- The war in Ukraine has also been labelled as the "smartphone war". Civilians and observers, including soldiers on the ground, contribute to this narrative of 'fighting via social media'.

The current wars in Ukraine and elsewhere have been pronounced as a "super laboratory of inventions". Technological companies as well as sundry entrepreneurs can test their newly developed weapons and equipment directly on the battlefield. Besides, the integrated battle-management systems offer up-to-the-minute transparency about troop movements and locations down to the basic unit levels. A senior official in Ukraine's military intelligence service warns, "Today, a column of tanks or a column of advancing troops can be discovered in three to five minutes and hit in another three minutes. The survivability on the move is no more than 10 minutes."[10] Dispersal and deception have thus assumed added importance in defensive as well as offensive operations.

Cautionary Thoughts

Innovation is an inherently risky process. Private developers are unlikely to have the necessary training and experience to evaluate all such risks due to lack of access to classified data and specific analytic expertise that is held by the armed forces or intelligence agencies. The process, therefore, could go wrong if the armed forces prematurely disassemble their existing capabilities to create new ones, ignore the associated risks, or rush into the standard vetting processes just to speed up deployment.

Emerging technologies, by themselves, might not significantly change the outcome of any conflict—there are many decisive factors, both military and political. Russia, for the first time, used new Kinzhal hypersonic air-launched ballistic missiles in Ukraine in March 2022. But multiple uses of Kinzhal missiles did not lead to any significant shift in the war in Russia's favour. Similarly, many nations are pursuing Directed Energy Weapons, like laser and microwave systems, to improve their air defences and to defeat drone swarms. However, to be lethal, these weapon systems require massive power sources to operate. The ability to move and deploy such power- generating systems by land, sea or air imposes severe limitations over the use of such weaponry, whereas the defenders are better placed to tap power directly from their national grid or to deploy as many generators as needed to supply practically unlimited power.

Presently, AI is still far away from becoming a matured military technology. Its use in the current conflicts is limited; neither Russia nor Ukraine has deployed AI-enabled weapons that autonomously select and engage targets. AI applications in coordination of drone swarms or in assisting human pilots in carrying out air operations are still on the drawing boards. Military AI applications are, therefore, unreliable yet for combat operations or for trustworthy use by the professionals. Conversely, such considerations do not matter to the irregular and unaccountable forces like Iran's Revolutionary Guard Corps (IRGC), the Houthis, the Hamas and their ilk, who might use AI rather loosely and irrespective of the results.

It is too early to conclude as to how and whether emerging technologies would impact the nature of warfare with due consistency. Most of these technologies remain under development, and their future applications and implications are not yet fully understood. But it is a foregone conclusion that increased use of AI, cyber space, drones, hypersonic missiles, and autonomous weaponry on future battlefields will increase the pace and complexity of combat operations. Rightful developments of these might enjoin the military decision-makers to rely on machines to help out with the processes of data processing, battlefield management and decision-making, hopefully without any potentially catastrophic consequences.[11]

Realities of Professional Insights

Harder realities emerge when the above- discussed 'Ruling Observations' and 'Cautionary Thoughts' are tested against professional insights. Accordingly, the inferences from recent wars lead to the following considerations:

- **Use of Autonomous Systems and Nascent AI.** New technologies of simpler designs have been in limited use before the currently raging conflicts. In 2020, in perhaps the first autonomous drone attack, a Turkish-made drone was used by the Libyan government troops to hit the retreating rebel forces. In the same year, Azerbaijan's military used Turkish and Israeli-made drones along with loitering munitions in Nagorno-Karabakh. In Gaza, Israel has been using hundreds of drones linked to AI algorithms. As the rebel forces and the governments in Myanmar and Sudan fight, they both have been using unmanned vehicles and related algorithms. The emerging technologies, as discussed above, have indicated the feasibility of finding wider and more debilitating military applications.

- **Centrality of Regular Military Hardware.** For regular militaries, sole reliance on sophisticated systems cannot be enough. The Ukraine War is not all about newly emerging or disruptive technologies of AI, apps, drones, automated systems and more. As General Sir Patrick Sanders, Head of the British Army, said, "You can't cyber your way across a river." Indeed, Ukraine has been frantic in its demands of tanks, artillery, munitions and fighter jets. Consequently, as the battlefield gets saturated with enormous quantities of artillery and continuous swarms of ISR drones, replenishment against spent munitions and battle losses of weapons and equipment becomes extremely crucial.[12]
- **Logistic Sustainability.** As General Omar Bradley said, "Amateurs talk strategy; professionals talk logistics." Often underestimated, logistics functions have proven crucial in the Russia-Ukraine War. Both Ukraine and Russia have struggled in their sustainment of munitions, equipment and manpower supplies. As their built-up stocks of crude rockets, etc. deplete and their sources of production and supply are strained, irregular forces like the Hamas and the Houthis, too, could be severely weakened.
- **Digital Vulnerabilities.** Digital capabilities are susceptible to the following kinds of effective countermeasures:
  - Pre-emptive electromagnetic assaults and cyber attacks could disable digital networks, if temporarily.
  - Early warning satellites could be duped or hijacked.
  - Digital technologies can be undone for longer periods with strikes on basic physical infrastructure, such as the transmitter stations, cables and database facilities that present lucrative targets for precision munitions and sabotage.
  - Reliance on high-tech components exposes the forces to supply-chain risks. For example, states with large arsenals of smart munitions depend on access to microchips. Their militaries can be paralysed if that supply dries up.
- **Use of Commercial, Low-cost, Maverick Products in Conflicts.** Terrorists and non-state actors can pose significant threats by exploiting low technology, low-cost, commercially available technologies such as open-use AI, commercial digital platforms and

unmanned systems to build their maverick, remote attack systems. Some examples are:

- Groups like the Islamic State (ISIS), the Houthis and the Hezbollah exploit commercially available, lesser cost technologies to conduct stray yet injurious attacks and thereafter, to evade detection. In 2016, IS terrorists used elementary, unadorned drones to interfere with the U.S.-supported advances in the Syrian city of Raqqa and are presently using such drones to strike at U.S. air bases in Iraq, with limited results but disproportionate threats.
- The Houthis are launching such relatively coarse drones and missiles to attack civilian shipping in the Red Sea. Even if the strikes are intermittent and cause limited damages, the risks imposed remain rather formidable. Similarly, the Hezbollah has been extensively using their rough and ready missiles to strike at Israeli settlements. Possibly, the Boko Haram in Nigeria and the al-Shabab elsewhere in Africa could be expected to adopt this practice.[13]
- Terrorists' AI arsenal includes technologies like ChatGPT, drones and biometrics. Terror groups are using these tools for recruitment, hacking into high-value civil systems and triggering stray attacks just to inflict casualties. Malicious use of AI, including creating deepfake videos to sow disinformation, to polarise societies and to stoke grievances could grow in the future.

All stated, the recently emerging battlefield realities show that the advantages of technological sophistications are considerably high. However, such advantages are liable to last as long as the opponent has not adapted to them. Success, therefore, lies in integrating the new systems and technologies into regular operations and tactics rather than relying on technologics alone. The stakeholders in this endeavour are academic researchers, innovative company laboratories, investors and entrepreneurs. As a corollary, a nation's security industrial base would need to be extended beyond the traditional bounds of the defence sector to customise and incorporate the beacon of breakthrough high-technology developments.

National militaries need to examine the current conflicts to derive lessons learned as related to their existing doctrines, organisations, training, war-like inventories, and their curricula of professional military education and leadership development programmes. They have to assimilate the recently gathered inferences and lessons into structuring, training and equipping a force that is able to dominate future conflicts all along their expanded spectrum contests.

Overview of the Inferences in the Indian Context

Modern-era conflicts have many dimensions. There is violent fighting on land, sea and air, while information warfare, the electromagnetic domain, space and cyber space are marshalled to play vital roles. However, recent conflicts have been centred on either defending or conquering ideologies and capturing territories in which the ground forces have to take the lead role. The main task of all the other means of India's state power is to support that kind of decisive ground battle.

Technology cannot be the end of the story. War is a human endeavour, and the recent wars in Ukraine and elsewhere have highlighted the importance of soldierly skills in wielding new technology. Modern warfare demands militaries that can optimally use modern technology while operating in a dispersal-manoeuvre-battle-dispersal cycle.

Modern-era warfare is not just about emerging or disruptive new technologies. Notwithstanding the ability of technology to create more robust systems that extend the capacities of conventional weaponry and war-like equipment, quantity still matters. As former Estonian president, Kersti Kaljulaid, succinctly put it: "There is no point in having one fancy weapon if the enemy has 10,000 non-fancy ones." In warfare of these days, weapons and munitions of war are expended at an incredible rate, and therefore, the stocks need to be continuously recouped. Most of Ukraine's urgent demands have been for tanks, artillery, air defence, fighter aircraft and various munitions. Israel, too, is veering towards that situation where its dependence on American supplies keeps rising. Therefore, the scales of India's War Wastage Reserves of weaponry and other inventories of war-like equipment, particularly artillery ammunition, missiles, etc. will require an express review. Most importantly, India's indigenous defence production capacity needs to be matched to that scale. The corresponding balancing between budget, stocking, expenditure and end-of-life discard is going to be a difficult regulatory exercise.

In contemporary times, the Indian military's operational concepts and its fighting elements will have to remain resilient and adaptable to risk-taking, accelerate their decision-making and seek to optimise the life-cycle costs of their war wherewithal. Besides assimilating the relevant issues, as discussed in relatively general terms in the preceding parts, the Indian defence planners have to be proactive in considering the following thrust areas:

- India has immense strength in software. This asset needs to be actively harnessed in comprehensive modernisation of command and control functions, as well as the activities in respect of all its weapons and services.
- Correspondingly, in view of the rapid development of emerging technologies, India needs to update the structure of its armed forces, aimed at the absorption of the latest military technologies. Concurrently, the armed forces have also to update their tactics and leadership development programmes.
- While essential off-the-shelf procurements of latest military hardware have to be resorted to, new designs of defence weaponry and equipment have to be developed indigenously at a brisk pace. Accordingly, flexible procedures for defence acquisitions, both internal and external, need to be devised. Meanwhile, the current pace of defence industrialisation needs to be sustained.
- Training of personnel has to be upgraded, including contemporising of remote operations, air defence measures, camouflage, concealment and deception—all supported by appropriate application of emerging technologies, including AI.[14]

Concluding Comments

In the ongoing conflicts, brisk integration of cutting-edge technologies with regular processes of battle-craft and war-fighting is taking place. Key integrations among these relate to the arrays of modern sensors, precisely networked high-performance weaponry and war equipment, smart and loitering munitions, AI-enabled analytical tools as well as deceptive measures, and space-based imaging and communication facilities. Battlegrounds have thus become increasingly intense and cripplingly destructive against the military as well as civil infrastructure. It is extremely difficult to assemble or move massed formations and yet remain undetected on land, air, underwater or in space, just as it has become extremely difficult to find effective protection from remotely delivered attacks.

In order to protect its sovereign concerns in the face of relentlessly aggressive powers, India would do well to act on the inferences drawn from the recent wars.

Notes

1. Jim Garamone, "Milley Makes Case for Deterrence in New Era". https://www.defense.gov/News/News-Stories/Article/Article/ 3446709/ milley-makes-case-for-rules-based-order-deterrence-in-new-era.
2. Maj. Gen. P.K. Mullick, VSM, a former Directing Staff at the National Defence College, is one of the leading authorities and analysts of modern-era military technology. His expert lectures and volumes of professional writings on military matters are highly rated among the strategic fraternity.
3. Final Report (March 2021) of the US National Security Commission on Artificial Intelligence (NSCAI).
4. "Emerging and disruptive technologies", NATO, Aug. 8, 2024. https://www.nato.int/cps/en/natohq/topics_184303.htm
5. "Ukrainian Innovation in a War of Attrition". https://www.csis.org/analysis/ukrainian-innovation-war-attrition?ref=readthemaple.com
6. "Disruptive Technologies in Security and Defence: Preparing for 'Known Unknowns'". https://directionsblog.eu/disruptive-technologies-security-defence/
7. "Human-machine teams driven by AI are about to reshape warfare", *The Frontier Post*. https://thefrontierpost.com/human-machine-teams-driven-by-ai-are-about-to-reshape-warfare/
8 "How Ukraine Is Remaking War: Technological Advancements Are Helping Kyiv Succeed". https://www.foreignaffairs.com/ukraine/how-ukraine-remaking-war?mod=djemCapitalJournalDaybreak
9. "Global Trends 2040". Report of the U.S.National Intelligence Council.
10. "Tanks, Troops in the Open Are Hit Within 10 Minutes". https://www.businessinsider.com/tanks-troops-in-the-open-are-hit-within-10-minutes-ukraine-official-2023-9?_

11. "Star tech enterprise: Emerging technologies in Russia's war on Ukraine", | ECFR. https://ecfr.eu/publication/star-tech-enterprise-emerging-technologies-in-russias-war-on-ukraine/
12. "What Western armour gives Ukraine in the next round of the war", Royal United Services Institute. https://www.rusi.org/news-and-comment/in-the-news/what-western-armour-gives-ukraine-next-round-war/
13. "The Future of Conflict and the New Requirements of Defence". https://www.scsp.ai/reports/mid-decade-challenges-for-national-competitiveness/chapter-5/
14. "Human-machine teams driven by AI are about to reshape warfare", *The Frontier Post*. https://thefrontierpost.com/human-machine-teams-driven-by-ai-are-about-to-reshape-warfare/

11. Role of Open-Source Intelligence (OSINT) in the Ukraine War

P.K. Mallick

The Russia-Ukraine War has highlighted the importance and impact of Open- Source Intelligence (OSINT) within the broader ambit of intelligence and security analysis. It has highlighted the benefits of weaponising intelligence to wage information warfare (IW) and the salience of multi-sensor intelligence processing, exploitation and dissemination (PED) supported by Artificial Intelligence (AI).

OSINT's relevance to the Ukraine War is not a coincidence; it is a result of OSINT's steady development in recent years that has been helped by advancements in data tools, including geolocation and chronolocation software. Geolocation refers to pinpointing the exact location where an image was captured, whereas chronolocation deals with identifying the time the image had been captured. Together, these techniques offer the right context and assist in validating the authenticity of images.

By supporting conflict- tracking, intelligence-gathering and de-mining efforts, OSINT has been a pivotal measure in the Russia-Ukraine War. Before the invasion, investigators used OSINT to monitor Russian military build-up, and since then, it has been vital in mapping the conflict and identifying the online information operations. Ukraine has effectively leveraged social media platforms like Instagram and TikTok, aided by civilian as well as designated groups, to locate Russian forces, track naval deployments and assess hardware losses. Crowd-sourced reporting, commercial satellite imagery and computer vision models have enabled near real-time situational awareness to its forces. Geographic Information

System (GIS) software has guided demining by identifying unexploded ordnance zones.

Satellite imagery, including SAR technology, has been instrumental in observing Russian activities during the Kherson retreat, the pontoon bridges and new defensive positions, along the M14 highway, for example. High-resolution images also exposed the damages inflicted by Ukrainian drone strikes inside Russia. These technologies continue to play a crucial role for both sides in enhancing their intelligence as well as operational capabilities.

Information Operations

Online Media. Ukraine used OSINT to develop anticipatory intelligence, shift public sentiment and counter Russian propaganda. This provided a platform on which the people could participate actively in passing battlefield information, offer alternative views through the crowdsourcing of information, and deliver missing pieces, likely corroborating intelligence collected from sensitive sources.

Before the war, Ukrainian President Volodymyr Zelenskyy was a relatively obscure figure with limited domestic support, polling at just 23 per cent. His lack of global influence and Ukraine's political instability likely led Vladimir Putin to believe that a quick push could topple his regime. However, Zelenskyy turned the tide by leveraging social media to masterfully communicate Ukraine's plight. Through personal displays of courage, relatable humour and viral messaging, he inspired Ukrainians and the world.

Zelenskyy's online campaign had tangible effects. His approval rating soared to 91 per cent, and 70 per cent of Ukrainians believed in their military's ability to win despite overwhelming disadvantages. The Ukrainian state defied Russian expectations of a collapse, highlighting the critical role of morale and digital communication in modern warfare.

Beyond mobilising Ukrainians, Zelenskyy's digital strategy also reached the global audience, transforming Ukraine into a symbol of resistance. This global sympathy reshaped political priorities worldwide, influencing policy shifts even in distant nations like Japan and Australia. Germany's decision to send tanks to Ukraine, breaking 75 years of foreign policy tradition, underscores the profound international impact of Ukraine's narrative.

Telegram App. The single most important repository of data during the war has been the 'Telegram' app. In early 2022, Telegram experienced a significant user surge due to Russia's restrictions on Western-owned social media platforms following the onset of the Ukraine conflict. User numbers in Russia grew from 25 million in January to 41.5 million by July, with 13 million joining between February and March. Its functionality, including rapid bandwidth-heavy content sharing via channels, groups and super-groups, made it an effective communication and information dissemination tool. This growth positioned Telegram as one of Russia's dominant platforms. Telegram's rise created a valuable OSINT resource, with numerous supporter-run channels providing insights into Russian sentiment and attitudes toward the war.

OSINT analysts search Telegram channels, such as 'Rybar', an account with over one million followers, to harvest images of the battle, testimony from the frontline and the mood among the troops. Rybar is not neutral, but it offers relatively timely and accurate accounts of movements in the battlefield, including Ukraine's blitz through Kharkiv. It is often critical of Russian policy.[1]

OSINT has been pivotal in countering Russian narratives and aiding Ukraine's defence. It debunked Putin's invasion claims and enabled Ukraine to track Russian military movements through data from civilians' and soldiers' posts. The value of intelligence led to the creation of the 'Diia', an app managing contributions from external OSINT volunteers and analysts, thereby showcasing its critical role in modern conflict.

Rise of Democratised Intelligence

The afore-stated democratisation of intelligence is reshaping the modern battlespace, making it more transparent and turning virtually anyone into a potential sensor or intelligence contributor. As individuals increasingly volunteer their skills informally to influence conflicts, this trend of communication is blurring the line between combatants and non-combatants. Such civilian involvement hints at future conflicts when these capabilities may further challenge the Service members' ability to differentiate between combatants and non-combatants. This could possibly raise concerns under the framework of the Geneva Conventions.

The Russian Army has had significant breaches of security. In December 2022, a Russian volunteer posted photos of Russian forces stationed at a country club in Sahy, an occupied area of Kherson province. The volunteer's post included a geo-tag to reveal the precise location. Subsequently, Ukrainian missiles targeted the site. Following the strike, the volunteer shared another post, this time uploading a video that showcased the destruction, thus effectively providing Ukraine with a ground-level damage assessment.

This incident underscores the importance of operational security in modern warfare, where persistent surveillance makes it crucial for ground forces to adopt tactics like dispersion, deep concealment, or rapid movement to minimise vulnerability.[2]

The rise of democratised intelligence in 21st century warfare presents new challenges:

- **Increased Transparency**. Democratised intelligence, where anyone can potentially contribute to intelligence gathering, makes the battlefield more transparent.
- **Blurring Combatant/Non-Combatant Lines**. Civilian communicators can now readily volunteer their services to influence a conflict, making it harder to distinguish between those directly involved in hostilities and those who are not.
- **Geneva Convention Concerns.** The Geneva Conventions aim to protect non-combatants. However, the increased civilian involvement in intelligence gathering challenges this principle. Service members may face difficulty in determining who is a legitimate target or a protected civilian.[3]

Marking an early use of commercial technology in a foreign war, the U.S.-based Maxar Technologies used commercial satellites to inform Ukrainians about the effects of Russian munitions. Despite having secure communication tools, Russian forces, due to poor discipline and operational failures, often relied on unencrypted radios and commercial cell phones. This allowed Ukraine to intercept calls, geo-locate personnel and target Russian forces effectively, resulting in significant losses among Russia's senior leaders.

'Planet Labs', 'BlackSky Technology', and Maxar Technologies continuously produce satellite imagery of the conflict. Based on requests by Ukraine, some of this data is shared almost instantly with the Ukrainian government and defence forces.

The Ukraine War is the First Open- Source War, in which OSINT is the dominant source. Application of OSINT in the Ukraine War can be summarised as under:

- Cloud-connected smartphones with extensive capabilities across Ukraine provided direct tactical insights into the conduct of the war. Ukrainian-developed software has transformed widely accessible tablets and smartphones into advanced targeting systems, now extensively utilised by the Ukrainian military. This innovation takes the form of a mobile app that integrates satellite and other intelligence imagery into a real-time targeting algorithm, enabling frontline units to accurately direct fire onto designated targets. Being software-based rather than hardware-dependent, the app is easy to update, upgrade, and distribute to a broad range of personnel.
- Cybersecurity analysts and cyber threat intelligence companies are sharing indicators of incidents faster than ever and before any tipping and queuing by government sources.
- The targeting app is among dozens of battlefield innovations that Ukraine has developed during the conflict, frequently devising cost-effective solutions to address costly challenges. The movement of units from the hinterland to operational areas is tracked in the social media used by troops and their families to give out the details. Tools like 'Flightradar' and 'MarineTraffic' have allowed analysts to track military and civilian aircraft and naval vessels, thus providing insights into logistical operations. Analysts and hobbyists have established methods of using freely available ship tracking information (AIS data) to provide foundational data on shipping situational awareness, including showing ships carrying oil and coal. The status of shipping in the Black Sea was analysed and found useful.

- Open- source analysts are eavesdropping into and translating military communications. Commercial imagery showed troop deployment locations, field hospitals, and other proofs of the invasion. 'Tiktok' provided direct evidence of the nature of troop and equipment movements. 'Twitter' has provided a platform for highly skilled and deeply experienced open-source analysts to provide military insights.

There, therefore, is a strong case for OSINT to be integrated into the holistic efforts of all- source intelligence.

Countering Disinformation

With both Russia and Ukraine employing propaganda to shape their narratives, the Ukraine War has become a battleground for information warfare (IW). In that context, OSINT has played a critical role in debunking false claims and exposing disinformation:

- **Fact-Checking.** Organisations like 'Bellingcat' have used OSINT to verify or debunk viral contents. For instance, geolocation techniques have been employed to confirm the authenticity of images and videos shared online.
- **Narrative Analysis.** OSINT tools have analysed the trends on social media to identify coordinated campaigns, such as amplifying pro-Russian hashtags or bot-driven misinformation.
- **Exposure of False Flags.** OSINT analysts have uncovered instances where fabricated evidence was used to justify military actions, thus undermining the credibility of such narratives.

Humanitarian Applications of OSINT

OSINT has also been instrumental in addressing humanitarian concerns. Key applications of OSINT include the following aspects:

- **Tracking Civilian Casualties.** By analysing social media posts, satellite imagery and local news reports, OSINT has helped document attacks on civilian infrastructure, such as hospitals and schools, providing evidence for Russia's wartime excesses.
- **Mapping Refugee Movements.** OSINT tools have mapped the displacement of millions of Ukrainians to aid the humanitarian organisations in resource allocation and response planning.

- **Monitoring War Crimes.** Civilian analysts have used OSINT to gather evidence of war crimes, such as the massacre in Bucha, providing data for international courts and human rights organisations.

Challenges in OSINT Utilisation

Despite its effectiveness, OSINT has faced several challenges in the Ukraine War on the following counts:

Verification and Reliability. The sheer volume of information makes verification difficult. Analysts must cross-reference sources and use advanced techniques to authenticate data.

Ethical Considerations. Using OSINT raises questions about privacy and the unintended consequences of sharing sensitive information, such as revealing troop movements.

Adversarial Countermeasures. Both state and non-state actors have attempted to flood information channels with false data to create noise, thus complicating analysis.

Skewed Accessibility. While OSINT democratises intelligence, the users have to address the disparities between those having advanced analytical tools and those who have to be reliant on basic methods.

OSINT: Lessons

Collaborative Analyses. The Ukraine War has shown the power of collaborative OSINT efforts, with professional analysts, journalists and civilians working together to uncover truths.

Real-Time Utility. The ability of OSINT to provide near-instantaneous updates has proven invaluable in dynamic conflict environments.

Transparency and Accountability. OSINT has enhanced conflict transparency by exposing war crimes and countering disinformation.

Increasing Adoption. Military and intelligence agencies will likely integrate OSINT more deeply into their operations.

An Improving Tool. AI and machine learning will further improve OSINT capabilities, enabling faster analysis and better pattern recognition.

Conclusion

OSINT is fast assuming the role of a regular source of information input for operational intelligence assessment. There may be a case for framing regulatory frameworks for international guidelines to govern ethical use of OSINT, particularly in conflicts.

Note

1. "Open-source intelligence is piercing the fog of war in Ukraine", *The Economist*, August 22, 2024. https://www.economist.com/interactive/international/2023/01/13/open-source-intelligence-is-piercing-the-fog-of-war-in-ukraine 4/11
2. AMY ZEGART, "Open Secrets: Ukraine and the Next Intelligence Revolution", *Foreign Affairs*, Volume 102, Number 1, January/February 2023. https://www.foreignaffairs.com/world/open-secrets-ukraine-intelligence-revolution-amy-zegart 2/17
3. "Open-source intelligence is piercing the fog of war in Ukraine", *The Economist*, August 22, 2024. https://www.economist.com/interactive/international/2023/01/13/open-source-intelligence-is-piercing-the-fog-of-war-in-ukraine

12. New-Era Trajectories of Conflict Management

Gautam Banerjee

The Purpose

In the era of an unprecedented rise in global tumult, nations cannot have the choice of prioritising between economic development and national security—both are equally significant factors for a sovereign existence. Towards that end, besides taking cognisance of the trends and inferences from the recent wars, we also have to take note of the conflict- generating matters that are shaping up in the horizon.

This note lists out some such matters, which need to be considered in dealing with new chapters of armed conflicts that could possibly break-out in the coming days.

Coalescence of Collective Defence

In a techno-industry-driven course of defence preparedness, sharing and coordinating military innovations among allies is a necessity in building-up their collective defence mechanisms. The European Union's lead in coordinating the continental defence mechanism, America's inclination towards sharing selective defence knowhow with the NATO members in the Russian backyard, and enhancement of the trilateral security partnership between Australia, the UK and the US (the AUKUS)—that includes easing of defence technology exports and equipping Australia with nuclear submarines—are some examples of this emerging feature of collective defence.

There are also hints of budding coalescence of political-defence resistance among the nations having modest military capabilities and who stand arrogated by aggressive powers like China, Russia, Iran, etc. Thus, there are reckonable, albeit faint yet, signals of the underdogs' rejection of the regional strong man's arbitrary impositions. Such signals have started emanating from the China Seas littorals that stand victimised by China's military highhandedness. These contenders are the Philippines, Vietnam, Japan and some of the region's relatively reticent stakeholders, besides the stake-holding members of the Western power block as well. Ukraine's resistance against Russia is another example of the same.

No doubt, extending support of high-effect weaponry, military technology and intelligence systems to selected strategic partners will bolster the collective defence posture of the peace-loving members of the global community and cool the revisionist contenders' territorial cravings. The 'Global Combat Air Programme', jointly launched by the UK, Japan and Italy in the margins of the G20 Summit in Brazil in November 2024, is one such recent initiative. This indicates the importance of international collaboration in technology development and defence production.

Conversely, supply of weaponry and munitions to some of the intransient regimes from their collaborating partners—mainly Iran, China, North Korea and Türkiye—is also a serious matter to reckon with.

Influencing Observations from Recent Wars

Warfare stands influenced by the following recent events:

Air War

- Recent evolutions in aerial threats have necessitated upgrades of military strategies and technologies. Packaging of manned and unmanned systems, extensive radar coverage, aerial engagements and electronic warfare capabilities are now the key elements of defence planning.
- Integrated and layered air defence create effective defensive networks against wide-ranging threats. Integrated Air/Missile Defence (IAMD) Systems, layered down to the Man-Portable Air-Defence Systems (MANPADS), have prevented either of the contestants from

severely crippling their opponent by massed air and missile attacks. Air and missile strikes, therefore, have to be packaged exclusively to be able to beat the opponent's air defence systems.

- High-technology and costly intercepting weapons to neutralise air and missile attacks require their design features to be graded according to the value of the targets to be defended. Production capacity, cost-effectiveness and expense rates also need to be factored into the mission plans of the defenders as well as the attackers. Reportedly, in 2024 alone, above three million drones have been used in the Russia-Ukraine War.
- Ukrainian forces have deployed various combinations of missiles as well as maritime and aerial drones to destroy nearly a third of the Russian Black Sea Fleet, thus driving it out of its home base at Sevastopol to nearly 300 kilometres to the east. In doing so, Ukraine has crippled much of Russia's maritime power. Elsewhere, the Ukrainian drones have forced the Russians to adopt extensive tactical and technical restrictions to protect their forces in the combat zones.
- Subsequently, the warring forces have organised many versions of their Integrated Tactical Reconnaissance-Strike Complex (TRSC). These complexes comprise their conventional fire power systems, communication systems, UAVs, and drones of varying degrees of lethality and ranges. Indeed, Ukraine's multi-layered defence networks have redefined the concept of air superiority.

Electronic Warfare

- Electronic Warfare (EW) systems of the warring forces have been regularly disrupting their adversary's drone operations at varying ranges. Russia's EW capability was a major element in disrupting Ukraine's counter-offensive in 2023.
- EW systems have also triggered extremely high rates of drone fratricides.

Ground Warfare

- Developments in air warfare have imposed new conditions in the conduct of military operations on ground. As a corollary, significant move and manoeuvre operations have become extremely hazardous to undertake, adding much to the attackers' difficulties. Russia adapted to these tactical developments with emphasis on radar coverage and air defence capabilities, particularly against low-altitude drones. The evolving nature of aerial threats to ground operations is reflected thus.

- Ukraine's integration of advanced technologies in the use of mobile air defence as well as the ground combat units has redefined modern warfare in terms of concealment, mobility, stand-off, and precision fire and force re-deployment. These innovations have allowed the Ukrainian forces to remain effective in both defensive and offensive operations despite being outmatched in terms of sheer numbers and firepower.
- A notable feature of the Israel-Hamas War is that the Israeli forces are forced, much reluctantly, to deploy ground troops in close-quarter fighting through the thickly built-up areas with civilian façade and through the Hamas' extensive tunnel networks.

War Reserves

- Maintenance of full-flow production and supply of various types of precision munitions is a necessity in the new-era military engagements. Stocking scales of war reserves as well as targets of surge productivities may have to be revised upwards.
- The conflicts in Ukraine and West Asia highlight the importance of international collaborations in defence strategising and technology sharing.

An Age of Unmanned Aerial Vehicles (UAVs)

Modern UAVs have found wide-ranging utilities in new- era battlefields. Various categories of UAVs are designed and equipped for tasks, such as surveillance and intelligence gathering, communication relay, delivery of logistic loads, and engagement of designated targets with lethal and precision-guided strikes—all in long-range remote mode. As the UAVs are integrated with latest software of autonomous capabilities and are mass produced for expendable use, development of counter-UAV capabilities becomes a priority for engaging in battle.

The ability to disrupt or destroy enemy UAVs before these can carry out their missions is increasingly seen as a prime need for any modern military force. The organisation of an efficient array of cost-effective ground-based air defence systems to engage regular UAVs, drone swarms, and modern missile threats has, therefore, become mandatory. Russia has expanded its deployment of radars and advanced air defence systems, such as the *Tor*, *Buk* and the *S-series*. It has also designed more effective EW measures to disrupt the communication links between the Ukrainian UAVs and drones with their ground controllers.

Besides, finding the right equation between the cost of attack weapons and ammunitions versus the potential damage that an UAV or any drone swarm can inflict has to be reckoned with.

Upgrade of Military Training

Changes in the operational environment necessitate corresponding upgrades of the military's training curricula. Besides small-unit tactics in the new-era battlefields, the upgrades include scientific education, technical competence, and battle procedures of combined arms as well as joint services combat. The training curricula would include functioning and exercise of leadership under the pervasive networks of electro-magnetic emissions, disruptive techniques, operations in remote and unmanned modes, and innovative fieldcraft with the military's latest devices of protection, movement and firepower.

Logistic Realities

That future wars would be short (and intense) has been a welcome notion among the middle-power nations. This notion stands vindicated by many actual and observable patterns of armed conflicts that have taken place over the past decades. Apparently, the notion gains wide political acceptance as it assuages the classical three-dimensional dilemma that the middle-level powers have to contend with: one, threats to national security; two, the pulls of 'defence vs. development'; and three, finding affordable and sustainable war-waging capabilities. Taking a cue from this, professional military hierarchies, too, have found satisfaction with the idea of engaging in short wars as that allows them to manage their extremely excruciating mandate with limited war wherewithal, particularly in terms of modern military hardware, including arms and munitions. Notably, the attractiveness of this notion has caused India to drastically cut down her war wastage reserves.

The US, with its status of a global superpower, strong military alliances, and huge industrial capacity is the only country that is ready for a relatively long war.

Russia, in spite of its hoary military traditions, fell for the notion of short wars to launch its 'Special Military Operation'. In this, the lack of military preparedness in terms of manpower, tactical upgrades and war-sustaining stocks came to haunt the Russian military during the first phase of its aggressive manoeuvres. Even if somewhat controlled later after two years of the campaign, these long gestation debilities continue to impinge on the Russian forces' operational deployment, depth, and duration.

The recourses adopted by both Russia and Ukraine to address their logistic debilities are listed as follows:

- Stocks of training munitions and expired lots of munitions, including missiles, were refurbished and fed into the supply chain. The resultant safety hazards were accepted.
- Stocks of mothballed arms and equipment, including dated versions of armour, artillery pieces, ancillaries of combat, etc., were pulled out, serviced, and released to units deployed in the war zone.
- The defence industry was revived to its surge, multi-shift production capacity. The shortage of an experienced and skilled workforce was gradually overcome.
- The civil industry was activated to supply dual-use items into the war stocks. Russia even resorted to diversion of certain civil-use items, like semi-conductors and computer chips, to circumvent the regime of sanctions.
- Both Russia and Ukraine have sought, and are receiving, weapons and munitions from their allied partners. While China, Iran, and North Korea have come to the assistance of the Russians, the 'Ukraine Defence Contact Group (UDCG)' has been formed among the Western powers/NATO to build-up Ukraine's defence. Of particular interest is the Czech Republic's initiative in procuring artillery

ammunition for Ukraine from the global market and fund that by contributions from the Western nations.

Exploitation of the enemy's vulnerability is a classical principle of warfare. Therefore, having prepared to engage in short- period warfare, nations under threat of war have to find innovative solutions to build-up sustenance when warfare goes on longer than expected.

Mercenaries in War

Most powerful nations have, at times and in various forms, hired non-state, mercenary fighters in war. Unlike the regular forces who are expected to operate within the rules of war, the mercenary forces—Russia's 'Little Green Men' in Crimea and Donbas (Ukraine), for example—remain unaccountable in crossing the 'red lines' of warfare. These forces are, therefore, conveniently hired to do the warring state's dirty jobs, even if they are liable to go loose against the sponsoring states' control.

In recent years, Wagner's mercenary forces have come to gain considerable notoriety. Russia's strategy of offering quasi-military services to the authoritarian governments in African Sahel—Mali, Burkina Faso and Niger being the latest examples—had subsequently been further extended to the offensives against Ukraine. But on both counts, after some successes, the throwbacks against the sponsor power have been serious. The lesson is stark. Mercenaries have their selfish priorities as distinct from those of the sponsoring state. Many times, interests clash when the situation turns embarrassing and dangerous for the sponsoring power.

Rise of Genocidal Civil Wars and Humanitarian Strife

The traditional global order is not new to vicious, violent and debilitating civil strife and the resulting bloodbath and famine. But in recent times, in many of the African and West Asian countries, the incidents of outbreak of civil wars of varying forms, scales and intensities have been rising, Myanmar being another example in South Asia. The surge in outbreak of such conflicts comes by the rise in the peoples' awareness as well as their rather tall aspirational levels. Much of such aspirations being partisan and unachievable, the seeds of socio-political friction are sown thus. This is manifested in humanitarian strife—societal frictions, mob attacks, famine, mass migration, etc.—that upsets the domestic as well as cross-border harmony.

Powerful and affluent nations understand that they cannot escape the spillover effects of this kind of tumult. It prompts serious concerns regarding the well-being of their privileged internal politico-social-economic systems. Peaceful resolution of such tumult by means of political intervention, humanitarian assistance, and economic settlement has thus become a necessity for global stability. The burden of ameliorating such tumult through socio-political inducements as well as military action is likely to grow in the coming days. Leading members of the global community have to prepare accordingly.

Afflicted with one of the deadliest civil wars for over three decades, the **Democratic Republic of the Congo** (DRC) suffers from relentless violence perpetrated by the Hutu extremists who were also responsible for the genocide in Rwanda. UN peacekeeping missions as well as the US-sponsored diplomacy with the stake-holding neighbouring nations in 2023 have so far failed to secure a durable truce between the army and Rwanda-backed rebel forces in this bloody ethnic strife.

Meanwhile, according to the U.N. Sanctions Monitoring Team, the Islamic State terror group's **Somalia** affiliate has been gaining strength by the influx of foreign fighters from the Middle East countries—Syria, Yemen, Ethiopia, Sudan, Morocco, and Tanzania.

South Sudan is facing a spiralling humanitarian crisis with hunger and cholera cases escalating in several parts of the country. The World Food Programme has warned that the food situation in South Sudan has reached critical levels, with more than half of the population already facing "crisis-level" hunger. The country's hunger crisis is compounded by several factors, including economic breakdown, soaring food prices, the turmoil of conflict, limited road networks for transportation of food, severe floods, and influx of refugees from the neighbouring Sudan, where conflict between government troops and a powerful rival militia is raging. To top all these, an outbreak of cholera has exacerbated the crisis.

Sudan stands devastated since April 2023 by a violent conflict between the Sudanese Armed Forces (SAF) and its paramilitary cousin, the Rapid Support Force (RSF). Amid reports of mass killings and gender violence, this conflict has, so far, internally displaced 11 million people. So far, the international response to this violence has been grossly inadequate. This collective failure cries out for international intervention to prevent further destabilisation of the region.

The long-simmering civil war in Syria turned active in November 2024 when the Islamist extremist movement, the Hayat Tahrir al-Sham (HTS), first took control of parts of the city of Aleppo and then forced the Assad regime to collapse. The decades-old conflict involves an Assad-headed Syrian Government backed by Russia and Iran against the Syrian-Kurdish rebel forces supported by the United States and some Turkey-sponsored rebel groups. Notably, the HTS is the successor of the Jabhat al-Nusrah and the Al-Nusrah Front. With its multifaceted cross-alliances among the aggressively fixated and heavily armed rebel groups, violence in Syria presents a complicated order of terror and humanitarian crisis. Half a dozen intra—as well as inter-regional powers are the participants in this struggle, each for their distinctly partisan political and religious supremacy. The Sham region is likely to remain in turmoil for long and may lead to the outbreak of more vicious conflicts. In the future, the situation might necessitate organised international involvement to control it.

The above examples apart, there are many more such instances around the world that could classify as genocide and humanitarian crises. The violence in Gaza, Syria, and Lebanon are some of such reckonable cases. These situations require to be attended to by the global community through the various options of crisis management and backed with military interventions. In the coming years, these responsibilities would add to the burden of military responsibilities of the prominent members of the global community. This situation calls for corresponding defence preparedness.

PART-II
Emerging Military Technologies in Recent Conflicts and Implications for India

P.K. Mallick & P.K. Chakraborty

13. Uncrewed Aerial Systems (UASs), Unmanned Aerial Vehicles (UAVs), and Drones

'Uncrewed Aerial Systems (UASs)', 'Unmanned Aerial Vehicles (UAVs)', and 'Drones', and these have been used interchangeably.

Introduction

Uncrewed Aerial Systems (UASs) have great utility on the modern battlefield. During the late 1990s, a remotely piloted vehicle, the MQ-1 Predator, was used exclusively in intelligence, surveillance, and reconnaissance (ISR) operations. From 2001, it was equipped with Hellfire missiles, allowing it to fly armed hunter-killer missions. Over the next decade, Predator and its successor, the MQ-9 Reaper, carried out a variety of US military operations, including counterterrorism operations in regions, such as Iraq, Syria, Afghanistan, Pakistan, and Yemen, highlighting their capability to execute precise strikes with reduced risk to friendly personnel.

Drones have crucial advantages over manned weapons. They can stay airborne for over 14 hours, compared to under four hours for manned aircraft like the F-16, allowing for continuous surveillance without risking pilot safety. Drones offer near-instant responsiveness, with missiles striking targets within seconds.

Long-range precision strikes have provided a substantial military advantage to the United States and other Western powers for decades. These capabilities remained out of reach of governments and other forces that could not afford the resources to employ these systems. The introduction of a new generation of UAVs has given precision long-range strike capability in the hands of smaller, less developed forces, including those employing irregular warfare tactics and terrorists. Not only are these weapons effective long-range strike systems, but they are also relatively low cost and can be manufactured in quantity by non-state actors.

From the battlefields of Libya to those of Nagorno-Karabakh and Ukraine, combatants have used uncrewed aerial vehicles (UAVs), or drones, to great effect. In the 2020 war over Nagorno-Karabakh, Azerbaijan's fleet of Turkish TB2s and Israeli drones destroyed Armenian air defences and precisely attacked rear echelon forces. In the ongoing Ukraine war that began in 2022, drones are playing an unprecedented role. Both Russia and Ukraine have used military-grade as well as commercial drones for surveillance, artillery fire targeting and strike missions. Kamikaze drones were employed to conduct battlefield precision strikes and attack enemy targets deep behind the frontlines.

In the contemporary security environment, small UASs have already proven to be a potent tool in the current war between Ukraine and Russia, between Hamas and Israel, in Syria, and during the Second Libyan Civil War from 2014 to 2020.

The Second Drone Age has been defined by the spread of weaponised commercial drones and the spread of state-manufactured military technologies to more than 65 non-state actors. At least 113 nation-states have a military drone programme now[1] China has become a global leader in the export of combat UASs. At least 17 countries own inventories of Chinese-made combat UASs. These systems have been employed in conflicts worldwide.

The UASs will play a critical role in conducting several types of missions as part of combined arms warfare, including:-

- Domain awareness and early warning;
- Battlefield awareness;
- Targeting for stand-off attacks;
- Strike;
- Electronic warfare;
- Information operations.

Advancements in engines, energy-saving technologies such as high-energy solar arrays made from silicon, lithium, iron and phosphate technologies, batteries, and lightweight material will increase the speed, range, and payload capacities of UASs.

It was suggested that drones are difficult to defend against cost-effectiveness as the defending missile will typically cost much more than the inbound uninhabited vehicle. However, Iran's massive air attack against Israel in April 2024 consisted of hundreds of these UAVs, as well as cruise and ballistic missiles. Nearly all were shot down or ignored if they did not have a lethal trajectory.

Types of Drones

Today, hundreds of different drone systems are in use in the ongoing conflicts, an assortment of military, commercial, hobbyist, makeshift and other systems flown by soldiers, volunteers, and civilians. NATO classifies drones into three widely accepted types based on their maximum take-off weight:

- Class I drones of less than 150 kilograms, including small mini and micro drones;
- Class II tactical drones of between 150 and 600 kg;
- Class III drones of more than 600 kg.

For land forces, UASs could be divided into three broad categories:

- Rotary-type UAS, able to manoeuvre close to the ground and in complex terrain and used for reconnaissance, situational awareness, target acquisition, fire correction and a wide range of other tasks;
- Fixed-wing UAS, able to fly at medium altitude into operational depth and perform a single task, which may be target acquisition or direct effects;
- Platforms carrying higher echelon sensors. This includes the TB-2, Watchkeeper, and Protector.

The first and second categories of UAS must be cheap and available in quantity. The third category is costly.

Kamikaze drones, or loitering munitions, are non-recoverable one-way attack drones that detonate on impact. Functionally, they are in-between a drone and a missile. They behave like disposable ammunition and offer an offensive capability that can loiter in the target zone before impact. Loitering munitions made appearances in Libya (Turkish Kargu drone) and Nagorno-Karabakh (Israeli Harop drone).

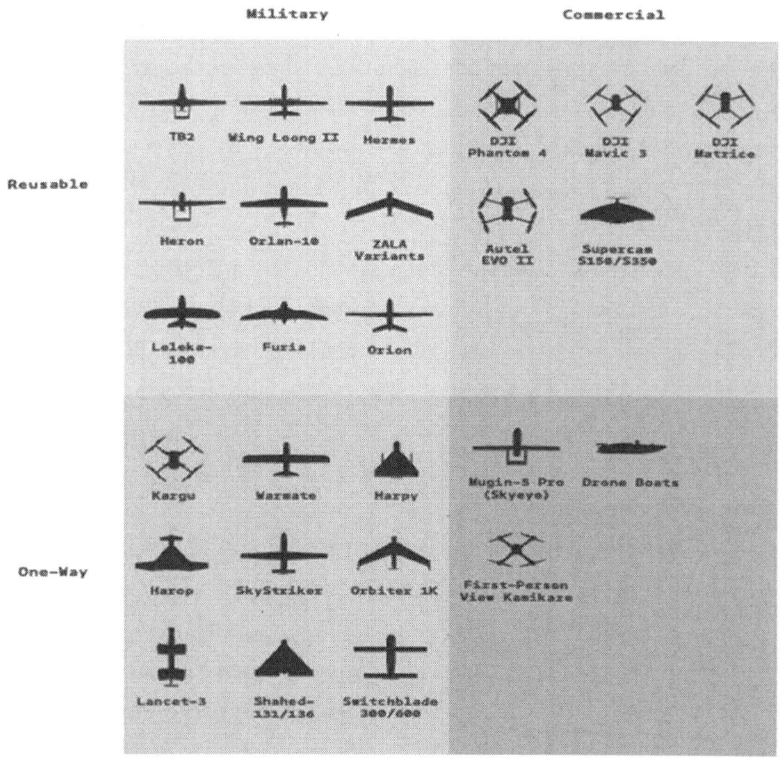

Source: Stacie Pettyjohn, "Evolution Not Revolution: Drone Warfare in Russia's 2022 Invasion of Ukraine" (Washington, DC: Center for a New American Security, February 2024). https://www.cnas.org/publications/reports/evolution-not-revolution. @CNASDC 1

Drones in War

The U.S.

As of January 2023, the U.S. has donated more than 1,800 Aevex Phoenix Ghost tactical UASs and more than 700 AeroVironment Huffman Switchblade UASs to the Ukrainian military. These tactical UASs link sensors to shooters in a small platform, can be carried in a backpack, and are relatively inexpensive to replace if destroyed by an adversary on the battlefield. The U.S. Department of Defence and the defence industry are working on such unmanned systems as collaborative combat aircraft, including the Gambit, X-62 Vista and XQ-58 Valkyrie, MQ-28 Ghost Bat, MQ-25 Stingray, and MQ-1C Gray Eagle Extended Range. These efforts also include the development of AI so that unmanned systems can be entirely autonomous.

The more sophisticated Israeli Harop kamikaze, with these sensors and seeker, can only fly about 124 miles and costs approximately $ 800,000 each.

Ukraine

In the current conflicts, a variety of combat UAVs are employed extensively. Ukrainian forces use a variety of military drones. Ukraine has become a testing bed for new producers in direct contact with troops, who are refining their products as the fighting drags on. Some of these are categorised below:

- US-supplied Switchblade, a kamikaze drone, is the smaller variant, a warhead of only a few kilogrammes. Switchblade drones can eliminate various targets, ranging from small targets six miles away to tanks twenty-five miles away.
- Used U.S. Phoenix Ghost Drones with advanced optical systems to destroy targets have been deployed.
- The Turkish Bayraktar TB2 drone was used effectively to destroy Russian equipment in the initial stage of the battle. Russia adjusted its air defence systems, significantly reducing the effectiveness of these drones.
- An Australian company has provided cardboard drones.
- A British firm offered 3D-printed suicide drones.
- A German company delivered over 100 AI-supported surveillance drones.
- Norwegian–produced Black Hornets were the smallest available military surveillance drones.

Ukraine developed the AQ-400 Scythe UAS, which entered service in December 2023. It is a long-range kamikaze drone with an ability to carry 42 kg of munitions. It flies autonomously with a range up to 900 km and can use visual positioning techniques to overcome jamming of satellite navigation. The majority of Ukraine's drones are open-market commercial products that have been purchased and assembled by volunteers. These systems are then sent forward to Ukrainian units for deployment. Ukraine's creative engineers are making them on a simple plastic frame with a Foxeer Razer video camera, costing about $14, a Diatone Mamba MK4 flight controller ($44), and a Lollipop 4 antenna ($20). These homemade drones are fixed rather than with rotary wings and can be equipped with handmade anti-personnel bombs that are more powerful than the standard grenades dropped by quadcopters.[2]

The First-Person View (FPV) Drones. In addition to homemade and modified drones, Ukraine is deploying first-person view (FPV) drones in thousands. The characteristics of FPV drones are:[3]

- Launched from improvised platforms, they can fly between 5 and 20 kilometres, depending on their size, battery, and payload.
- They are controlled by a soldier using a headset for a first-person view, with another providing guidance via maps on a tablet.
- They are used to target vulnerable points, such as tank hatches or engines.
- Their real-time video feed, transmitted through goggles or a headset similar to VR gaming, gives the operator precise control, especially in complex environments like urban warfare or dense terrain.
- They are effective for reconnaissance, targeted strikes, and even suicide missions, where they carry explosives and fly directly into a target.
- These are not hindered by anti-aircraft systems near the frontlines unlike planes or helicopters.
- They can cost around $500 USD each. A $500 FPV drone can target the open hatch of a Russian tank worth millions of dollars, demonstrating their cost-effectiveness in modern warfare.

Ukraine is deploying these drones at a rate of 100,000 per month, with plans to produce one million FPV drones in 2024.

Russia

Russian forces have used Iran-supplied Shahed 131/136 Attack Drones extensively and are now manufacturing thousands of its improved variants. The characteristics of Shahed include:

- It is a kamikaze, which costs $50,000 and is constructed from inexpensive materials and mass-produced commercial electronic components, making it much cheaper than reusable military-grade drones.
- It has a take-off weight of 200 kg, an eight-foot wingspan and 11-foot length.
- It has a range of 2,500 km, flies autonomously using satellite-based navigation and travels at 185 km/h, carrying a 50 kg warhead.
- It can be launched from ground sites or the back of trucks using a boost rocket.
- It is being employed to strike at strategic Ukrainian targets well beyond the frontlines of the conflict.
- Russia has also made EW hardening standard to their production variant of the Shahed-136, known as the Geran-2 (Geranium).

The Orlan-10, a medium-range UAS used for reconnaissance, jamming, and other missions, has been in the Russian inventory since the early 2010s and has been employed extensively in the Ukraine conflict:

- Russian manufacturer *Kronshtadt* developed it and it has also been used for strikes in Syria.
- It is a system built to military specifications with anti-jam data links and a maximum altitude of 5,000 m, reducing the platform's acoustic and visual signature.
- It has a 10-foot wingspan, six-foot length, and top range of 370 miles.
- Various payloads can be carried on the Orlan-10, including imaging sensors, electronic intelligence sensors, and EW emitters.
- It is quite capable but is relatively expensive at a cost of roughly $150,000 per system.

The Lancet is typically employed in conjunction with an Orlan-10 as a spotter and has proven to be very effective:

- The Lancet ranges from 40 to 70 km and a 1 to 3 kg warhead, depending on the variant.
- Early versions of the Lancet required operator guidance to a target up to impact; a new version of the weapon may allow for autonomous target selection via pattern-matching algorithms.
- The new version may allow multiple Lancets to collaborate to deconflict targets during cooperative attacks. If implemented in combat, this system software enables swarming, a new military capability.

Russian forces have also used Chinese-made drones, most notably, DJI products.

Both sides in the Russia-Ukraine War, especially Ukraine, have increasingly been using small, cheap commercial models of drones, such as the DJI Mavic 3, which costs about £ 1,700. These can be fitted with small bombs but are mainly used to spot enemy troops and to direct attacks. However, commercial drones are much less capable than military ones. For example, the DJI Mavic's total flying distance is only 30 km, and it can only fly for a maximum of 46 minutes. Russia is using electronic devices to counter them. Russian forces have the Stupor rifle, which shoots electromagnetic pulses. This stops commercial drones from being able to navigate using GPS. Russian forces have also used online systems, such as Aeroscope, to detect and interrupt communications between commercial drones and their operators. These systems can cause a drone to crash or return to base and can stop it from sending back information.

The Russo-Ukraine conflict is not only demonstrating the value of drones but also the requirement for vast numbers of them. The quadcopters survive an average of only three missions, and fixed-wing drones survive for only six missions. To sustain the roughly five hundred drones that the Ukrainians use to support a major operation requires a very large number of surveillance drones.[4]

Bayraktar TB2 drone

Max altitude: 25,000 ft (7,600 m)
Max range: 186 miles (300km)
Max speed: 140 mph (220 kmph)
Weapons: 4 MAM-L laser-guided bombs
Wingspan: 39 ft (12 m)

Source: BBC Research, Getty Images

Shahed-136 drone

Max range: 1,550 miles (2,500km)
Max speed: 115 mph (185 kmph)
Wingspan: 8.2 ft (2.5m)
Warhead weight: 66-110 lb (30-50kg)

Source: Defence Express, Getty Images

DJI Mavic 3

Max altitude: 19,685 ft (6,000m)
Max flying distance: 18.6 miles (30 km)
Max speed: 42.5 mph (68.4 kmph)
Wingspan: 11.1 inches (28.3cm)

Source: DJI, Getty Images

China

China has become the leading exporter of military drones in the world. DJI and Autcl, both Chinese companies, control over 90 per cent of the global drone market. Subsidised pricing allowed the Shenzhen manufacturer, DJI, to penetrate international markets rapidly, including within the U.S. and NATO countries. Since its first quadcopter was launched in 2013, the company has remained firmly ahead of the competition in both features and sales. At least 17 countries own inventories of Chinese-made combat UASs, and these systems have been employed in conflicts worldwide.

The PLA has integrated UAVs in the following manner:

- UAV battalions are integral to the PLA's army brigade combat team. The VT-5U light tank in the tank battalion is equipped with a vehicle-mounted UAV, which can take off independently, ensuring the tank's aerial vision and enhancing its battlefield situational awareness. The VT-5U has the capability of "manned-unmanned conversion". In high-risk combat situations, VT-5U crews can get out of the vehicle, if necessary, and fight with a remotely controlled tank. This would turn the tank into an unmanned combat vehicle. Doctrinal changes are in the making.[5]
- UACV units are part of the PLA Air Force. The latest FH-97A with stealth design is a new autonomous UAV formation system that can form a dense formation. It can efficiently coordinate with manned combat aircraft and provide them with intelligence, information, and firepower support to perform air superiority operations, air defence suppression and air escort missions.

Rapid Proliferations of UAS Employment on Contemporary Battlefields

There has been an increase in the production, employment, and success of UAS in the current conflicts. The low acquisition cost and wide availability of the technology required to build UAS means that smaller, resource-constrained state and non-state actors may be able to challenge powerful states with large defence budgets and robust manned air forces. The next evolution of UAS, first-person view (FPV) and one- way-attack systems

(OWA) are proving critical in the ongoing Russia-Ukraine and Israel-Hamas wars.

Both the private industry and governments are developing families of more capable surveillance drones. These drones range from small, hand-launched platforms to aircraft with wingspans over 100 feet. These companies have developed multispectral, Synthetic Aperture Radars (SAR) and electromagnetic sensors (EMS) for every drone size. Ukraine has as many as 500 drones in the air for a relatively standard military operation.[6] However, their most important function is to provide critical intelligence and artillery spotting for tactical units in contact with enemy forces.

Ukraine has already trained 10,000 drone operators. The government has allocated $ 867m to create 60 "drone army" strike companies. Fedorov has specifically advertised the initiative as "a great opportunity for drone manufacturers to test their equipment in harsh conditions". The head of Ukraine's special communications service, Yurii Shchyhol, announced in August 2023 that "Ukraine plans to produce and purchase approximately 200,000 combat UAVs during the year."

Drone attrition on the battlefield has been extremely high. Ukraine is losing an estimated 5,000 to 10,000 drones a month, which means over 160 drones daily. Most are downed by Russian jamming that causes the operators to lose the radio control signal or scrambles their GPS signal. In the bitter fighting for Bakhmut, the Russian EW operations were so intense that drones could fly only a few hundred yards from their operators before they lost the link.

Battlefield deployment of drones at scale is a disruptive capability and challenges traditional concepts of air-delivered precision strikes being delivered by costly, logistics-heavy, high-end platforms. Fixed-wing aircraft require airfields and major logistic support bases. In an era of persistent surveillance, these will be targeted. New drones outrange many crewed fighters/bombers. Cheaper than crewed aircraft, these missiles and drones provide even small states with the ability to strike airbases and parked aircraft. The effectiveness of drones has become evident as we can see examples of Ukrainian drones striking deep into Russian air bases and logistics nodes.

Rapid, sustained improvements in the range, payload, and speed of drones open an entirely new field of massed, precision attack. The density of such attacks will be further enhanced by the evolving cruise missiles that can be launched from air, sea, and ground platforms, including transport aircraft, commercial ships, and ground vehicles. The ongoing exchange of fire between Israel and Hezbollah is an example of things to come.

For land forces, tactical sub-units must have a means of detecting the presence of hostile UASs. Frontages should be covered by the means of defeating enemy UASs. Defeating UASs does not mean kinetically destroying them. It means that the UAS is denied the ability to achieve its mission. This could be done through the dazzling of sensors or denial of navigation or control. The most efficient protection against UAS is EW, ensuring that electronic attacks and protection are available at all echelons.

It is essential to understand that Electromagnetic Spectrum (EMS) fratricide and Command and Control (C2) are significant challenges of widespread EW employment. Both the Ukrainian and the Russian military have suffered. The recent downing of a Ukrainian F-16 aircraft is an example of fratricide.

Drone Swarms

As automation continues to be developed and implemented at higher levels for UAS operations, humans will no longer be required to direct flight one-to-one. This will lead to large-scale simultaneous use of UAVs, known as Swarming. Swarming technologies may enable large numbers of relatively low-cost UASs, which are not very capable individually, to work together to accomplish missions that would be far more challenging for expensive airborne platforms.

A swarm can leverage the sensors, weapons, communications, and autonomy of the entire UAS fleet deployed in an area. It allows many UAVs to operate in the same airspace in a coordinated fashion to prevent collisions and fratricide. Mass can be generated partly by well-trained UAS pilots, but automated technology to enable UAS swarms would be more effective. Countering a swarming threat will require new thinking around sensors and effectors. Swarming creates the following challenges for defenders:

- Swarm tactics can overwhelm a defender's systems, creating significant challenges.
- Autonomous UASs that do not require a link back to a control station will become invulnerable to several contemporary control detection and jamming techniques.
- Because of their numbers and the use of autonomous coordinated tactics, swarming UASs could overwhelm or outsmart much of today's Counter Unmanned Aerial System (CUAS) technology.

Battlefield swarming is in its infancy, despite its widespread use in the civil industry, particularly for light shows and replacing fireworks. As of date, there has not been any deployment of UASs designed to achieve automated swarming. Ukrainian forces have typically coordinated attacks using multiple remotely piloted assets to create simultaneous time on target to confuse Russian air defences. However, employing multiple UASs using coordinated tactics is quite a different method of warfare from employing automation to achieve a 'system-of-systems' swarm attack.

On September 10, 2024, Ukrainian forces launched the largest drone attack of the war to date, targeting Moscow with 144 drones. The assault resulted in 20 drones being shot down, with several multi-story residential buildings near Moscow being set ablaze. Flights from Russia's most important airports were temporarily suspended. In response, Russia launched a retaliatory strike using 46 drones.[7] Swarm is here to stay.

AI-controlled swarms are still some time away. Using AI for swarm display and military purposes are two different things. UASs operating in a group can have a similar effect. UASs can be designed in groups that allow for the division of labour between the individual systems. A few of them can carry sophisticated payloads like advanced sensors to gather actionable information and share it or EW payloads. In contrast, most can carry relatively simple payloads like munitions and decoys. The loss of a few of these systems would not seriously harm the formation, but it could impose significant costs on an adversary who employs expensive weapons against inexpensive drones.

Use of Drones by Non-State Entities

Deployment of Iranian-manufactured military drones by non-state actors like Houthi rebels and Iraqi militias for almost five years indicates what these future high-tech drone wars may look like. Non-state actors were able to use increasingly advanced commercial drone elements, which were easy to purchase, hard to track, and difficult to place under arms control measures, to turn the drone shells into effective robotic killing machines. Non-state actors across the Middle East can now manufacture, deploy, and even supply weaponised drones to other terrorist and militant groups.

Non-state actors have utilised drone systems in novel ways, including rudimentary swarm attacks as multi-drone deployments, frequently alongside missiles and rockets. The objective of these attacks is to overwhelm enemy defences in a tactically and technically sophisticated manner. As more advanced drones fall into the hands of non-state actors, the number of drones connected in a single attack will increase, making it difficult to counter.[8] In 2016, the Islamic State in Iraq and the Levant (ISIL) terrorists used cheap drones to counter U.S.-supported advances on the Syrian city of Raqqa and the Iraqi city of Mosul, dropping grenade-sized munitions from the sky. In the spring of 2017, at the peak of its drone operations, ISIL was conducting between 60 and 100 drone bombing attacks against anti-ISIL forces in Syria and Iraq per month.

A detailed examination of ISIL's drone programme exhibited that the group required little technical sophistication to develop an effective military capability. Low-cost commercial drones were imported into the operational theatre and could be used immediately for surveillance and reconnaissance. For kinetic attacks, Commercial Off-the-Shelf (COTS) systems were modified with a bomb-drop mechanism consisting of plastic tubes and a release mechanism that was described as something a sophisticated high schooler could put together.

In Operation 'Guardian of the Walls' in 2021, Hamas fired 4,300 rockets and drones towards Tel Aviv and central and southern Israel. Between 10 and 20 per cent of the strikes broke through the existing, world-leading Iron Dome defences. This proves that even the world's most advanced air defence system can be overwhelmed at points by the current generation of drone-assisted saturation strikes. Hamas has effectively employed UAVs to compete with the far more capable Israel Defence Forces (IDF) in the current Israel-Hamas War that started on October 7, 2023.

Israel has one of the best air forces in the world, possesses the vaunted Iron Dome air defence system and has excellent surveillance and early warning systems. Nevertheless, Hamas has effectively eluded these expensive technological defensive systems to attack targets in Israel. Israel's Iron Dome defence system was overwhelmed as Hamas saturated the airspace with thousands of crude rockets and missiles, which allowed many missiles to bypass its air defences. Hamas also used small FPV drones carrying specialised explosive munitions to sow chaos by striking vulnerable IDF communications and logistics sites. It assisted in the destruction of Israel's formidable Merkava main battle tanks.

Before the arrival of cheap drones, Israel would have had complete air superiority and never worried about suffering an attack from the air, except through missiles and other indirect fires. But the proliferation of cheap, easily obtained UASs allows Hamas to compete in the air domain, whereas Hamas previously would have ceded this domain to the far stronger Israeli Air Force.

Today, Iranian-backed insurgents are using drones to strike U.S. air bases in Iraq. The military group, the Houthis, that controls much of Yemen, are sending drones to strike ships in the Red Sea. Their attacks have tripled the cost of shipping from Asia to Europe. Hezbollah and Al Qaeda in the Middle East might engage in more regional attacks, as could Boko Haram in Nigeria and al Shabab elsewhere in Africa. Drones are also helping rebel groups beyond the Middle East and Africa. A rag-tag coalition of pro-democracy and ethnic militias in Myanmar is using repurposed commercial drones to fight off the military junta's once-feared Air Force. Now, it controls over half the country's territory.

Non-state actors will capitalise on the vulnerabilities of more powerful state militaries by adopting the latest technologies to help improve the effectiveness of their locally produced, augmented or state-supplied weapons systems.[9]

Counter-Drone Defences[10]

Proliferation of cheap, expendable drones has created an unfavourable interception curve for traditional air defence platforms. Larger drones with a distinct radar cross-section are easy, slow-moving targets for air defence interceptors and artillery, while conventional air defence systems have some limitations against small systems. The challenge of counter-drone defence is its cost-effectiveness, where the counter-drone system must be cheaper than its target. Greater investments in EW will be a crucial part of any counter against the threat of drones.

Counter- Drone Technology

Globally, counter- drone technologies have converged to focus on three specific aspects:

- Detection and Identification Technologies;
- Disruption Technologies;
- Counter- Drone Defence Networks.

Detection and Identification Technologies

- Command and Control (C2) Systems;
- Radar-Based Systems;
- Radio Frequency (RF) Detection;
- Electro-Optical/Infrared (EO/IR) Sensors;
- Acoustic Sensors;
- Multispectral Sensors and Data Fusion.

Disruption Technologies

- RF Jammers;
- GPS Spoofing;
- Directed-Energy Weapons (DEWs);
- Kinetic Interception;
- Electromagnetic Pulse (EMP) Devices.

Counter-Drone Defence Networks

The moment the UAS was used, the counter-UAS systems emerged. The tactics, techniques, and procedures (TTPs) that worked for the first six months of the war no longer work today. The initial success of the Turkish Bayraktar TB2 drone and its subsequent neutralisation is an example.

To prevent drones from reaching their target, a crucial counter-measure is the Electronic Warfare (EW) Networks. EW activities to control the electromagnetic spectrum include jammers, spoofers, and deception of enemy communication systems, radars, and other electronic devices. Jamming is conducted by directing high energy towards the UAV to mask the radio frequency control or data signals. It causes the target drone to fall, veer off course or turn around and attack its operator. In Bakhmut, Ukrainian drone operators could not fly drones further than 500 metres due to Russian jamming.

Counter-uncrewed aerial systems (C-UASs) are specifically designed to detect, track, and neutralise UAVs. This can be achieved through:-

- Detection systems (radar, electro-optical/infrared sensors and acoustic sensors that identify UAVs in the airspace);
- Jamming devices (portable or fixed);
- Missile weapons (anti-missile systems, air-to-air weapons);
- Kinetic weapons (shotguns, anti-air machine guns, and cannons);
- Directed energy weapons (high-energy lasers or microwave beams can disable UAVs by damaging their electronics or propulsion systems);
- Nets and drone-on-drone technologies (physically intercepting or capturing UAVs).

UAS relies on links, such as launch and recovery units, ground control stations, communications equipment, logistics, and supporting systems. Disrupting or neutralising any of these links can hinder the UAS's operational capabilities. Electronic jamming devices work on specific frequencies, and drone pilots are adapting by switching to less commonly used ones. To counter this, new technologies like pocket-sized "tenchies" and backpack EW systems have emerged, jamming signals across a broader 720-1,050 MHz range, making them more effective against Russian drones. Notwithstanding Ukraine's deployment of these newer jammers, Russia's use of hunter-killer drone systems like the Orlan-10 for spotting and the Lancet for strikes, along with missile-equipped Orion drones, continue to challenge Ukraine's drone defences.[11]

Both sides in Ukraine, along with other nations, are heavily investing in counter-drone technologies and have begun deploying various systems, including:

- Advanced EW to jam drone communications, forcing them into autonomous modes;
- EW systems designed to damage or destroy drones not sufficiently hardened against such attacks;
- Vehicle-mounted counter-drone systems, such as directed-energy weapons;
- Reactive armour or other physical defences adapted to protect vehicles;
- Dispersion tactics using decoys and military deception to mislead adversaries;
- Disrupting enemy logistics to prevent drone resupply, with effects similar to HIMARS strikes on artillery depots. Dispersing drone movement creates a detectable footprint, making it a target;
- Autonomous kinetic interceptors capable of identifying and destroying enemy drones..

Additionally, investments are being made in lethal autonomous drones, equipped with AI algorithms that allow them to operate independently of real-time communications. While drones are crucial for transforming modern warfare, they are not a standalone solution. Success depends on their effective integration with traditional combat systems, modernised and adapted for dynamic use.

Cost Benefit Analysis

In any conflict, cost is critical—the fewer resources used to destroy a target, the better it is. Defeating a $ 500 drone with a $ 3M missile may be effective but not sustainable. A Patriot missile can shoot down a Shahed-136, but a Patriot missile costs 4 million dollars, and the Shahed-136 costs a mere 1 to 3 per cent of that price. The high cost of the detection systems and launchers related to these sophisticated air defence systems limits the number of such capabilities available to counter UASs on any battlefield.

Affordability of cheap drones could allow states to send swarms of drones without worrying about attrition. These swarms could overwhelm legacy air defence systems, which are not designed to shoot down hundreds of objects simultaneously. Even when defence systems prevail, the cost of defending against swarms will far exceed the price of the attack for the enemy. Iran's mass drone and missile strike against Israel in April 2024 cost at most $100 million. However, the U.S. and Israeli interception efforts cost more than $2 billion.

Ukrainian forces have used 3D printers to add tail fins to anti-tank grenades. When dropped from a commercial drone, these inexpensive and simple munitions can pierce the relatively weak top armour of Russian tanks and troop carrying vehicles (BMP). This innovative combination has been used for carrying out stealthy, short-range precision attacks to destroy Russian tanks and BMPs, costing millions of dollars, for the price of a $100 grenade and a $1,000 drone.

Increasing capabilities of commercial drones are changing how militaries will use this technology. Major corporations are aggressively pursuing drone package delivery. The requirements for delivery are basically the same as for military platforms: vertical take-off and landing, Global Positioning System- independent navigation, electronic hardening reliability, and low cost with ever-increasing endurance and payloads.

Some of the most well-known American military drones cost hundreds of millions of dollars. These military systems can carry heavier, higher-performing payloads and can operate over longer ranges and periods than commercial drones. These systems are so expensive that military leaders are often reluctant to use them in contested environments. Large drones like the MQ-9 Reaper have been successful in counterterrorism operations in Afghanistan, Iraq, Pakistan, Somalia, Syria, and beyond. Due to their long endurance in performing surveillance and remote strikes, they were most effective in uncontested airspaces. However, these large aerial systems do not appear to be suitable for the current conflict in Ukraine or Somalia, as they become fragile in active shooting wars when no side controls the skies. In contrast, smaller drones operated by land forces are transforming the dynamics of the lower airspace in Ukraine by their size and sheer number. Small drones provide eyes in the sky and empower individual soldiers to spot enemy units and navigate artillery fire, which increases ground forces' pace precision and keeps troops out of harm's way.

A case in point is the U.S. MQ-9B Predator drone. Its average unit cost is estimated at $32 million in 2023. Since the onset of the Israel-Hamas war in Gaza in October 2023, five U.S. drones have been shot down by the Houthis, with the first incident occurring in November 2023, followed by subsequent incidents in February, April, and now twice in May 2024. In addition to the five drones shot down by the Houthis since October, these drones have previously been downed by the group in 2019 and 2017. Yemen's Houthi rebels shot down two American MQ-9 Reaper drones in under a week. The U.S. military acknowledged that the Houthis shot down the first Reaper on September 10 and the second on September 16, 2024. The U.S. also lost two more MQ-9 Reapers in the past year: one shot down over Iraq in January and another forced to crash into the Black Sea after a collision with a Russian fighter jet in March 2023. MQ-9B Predator drones have relatively low speed and lack a robust defensive mechanism. Their survivability in contested airspace is suspect as the rag-tag force of Houthi rebels using low-grade technology have successfully shot down so many Predator drones. The Russians, too, have shown the vulnerability of drones against fighter aircraft. Notably, India has almost finalised a deal with the U.S. for 31 MQ-9B Predator drones at an estimated cost of $ 3.99 billion (Rs 33,060 crore).

In the global civilian drone industry, Chinese companies are the leaders. More than 90 per cent of civilian drones are made by the Chinese companies, DJI and Autel. The People's Liberation Army (PLA) has a considerable arsenal of strategic, operational, and tactical UAVs with sound capabilities. It has been reported that China has collaborated with Russia to enhance Russian FPV drone production capabilities. China displayed some of its unmanned platforms for the first time at a military parade in its capital on October 1, 2017, to mark the 70th anniversary of its founding. The parade also saw the debut of the HSU001 large unmanned underwater vehicle. Each is powered by two propellers and appears to be able to mount a variety of payloads.

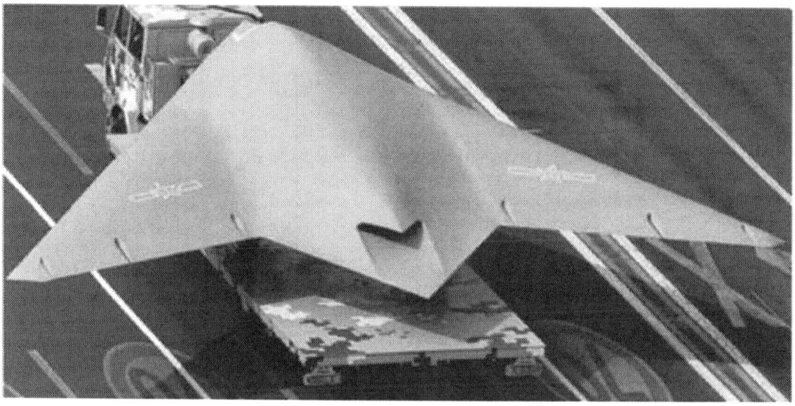

Source: https://asiatimes.com/2019/10/china-unveils-its-military-might-in-beijing-parade/

Analysis

The ongoing conflicts have made one thing clear: drones play an important role on the battlefield. Drones have transformed battlefields in Libya, Nagorno-Karabakh, Gaza, Israel, Ukraine, and the Red Sea. These recent conflicts have led to a range of conclusions about drones and the future of warfare. There are two distinct schools of thought:[12]

a. Drones are causing a revolution in warfare:
   - Drones are fundamentally changing the character of war. The war in Ukraine is spurring a revolution in drone warfare using Artificial Intelligence (AI).
   - Both Russia and Ukraine had deployed small drones that used artificial intelligence to identify and home- in on targets. They wouldn't need a human operator to guide them to impact.
   - Drones allow actors to field a relatively cheap, disposable air force, yet are able to deliver firepower through mass and resiliency.
   - Drones render tanks obsolete or replace existing weapons, such as artillery.

b. Drones are evolutionary:
   - Drones are an evolutionary improvement to existing technology.
   - Air defences can easily counter drones.
   - UASs are valuable for countering terrorists and non-state actors, but they are not effective against nations with modern militaries.

- Even large numbers of small drones cannot match the potency or volume of artillery fire and thus cannot substitute for howitzers.
- While drones provide affordable airpower, they have not replaced traditional air forces or obtained air superiority.

There is a third school of thought in-between these two extremes:

- Drones have been most effective when used with other capabilities, such as artillery, to rapidly close kill chains.
- Drones allow defenders to detect an attacking force quickly and concentrate fires on it, making offensive manoeuvres prohibitively costly.
- The effects remain localised. Most drones are piloted by humans who control and coordinate their actions.
- Drones are not substitutes for aircraft, artillery or missiles but complement existing weapons. Drones have not reduced the importance of legacy systems, such as artillery, armoured vehicles, and tanks.
- As drones share real-time information, become more autonomous, and shape doctrine and organisational structures, they may revolutionise warfare. But that day is yet to come.
- Drones have not eliminated close combat. These can only be effective if they are operated by skilled military personnel and integrated with other multilayered and conventional systems.
- Drones cannot achieve the ultimate goal of war: they cannot seize and hold terrain.

Lessons Learned from the Second Nagorno-Karabakh War (September 27–November 10, 2020) are:

- Drones can be used in a preplanned attack to take enemy forces by surprise.
- Medium Altitude Long Endurance (MALE) and kamikaze drones supported by EW systems can be very effective at Suppression of Enemy Air Defences and Destruction of Enemy Air Defences (SEAD/DEAD) operations.

- Innovative use of improvised or unsophisticated drones can have outsized effects.
- If one side has air superiority, MALE drones can conduct dynamic air-to-ground operations and acquire targeting information to enable precise ground-based fires.
- In a one-sided drone fight, military and kamikaze drones integrated with artillery can enable manoeuvre.
- Drones allow riskier missions and are seen as less escalatory than the use of crewed aircraft.

Practicalities of Drone Usage

Drones are collecting massive amounts of video footage. They cannot send it all back—the existing bandwidth is insufficient, and communications links are often jammed. The analysis must be done "on the edge", meaning on the drone itself.

In Ukraine, Israel, and elsewhere, we see an accelerating adaptation battle between UAS used for attack and the tactics, technologies, and techniques to disrupt or destroy these systems, their communications links, their navigation subsystems and the people operating them. The adaptation battle currently favours attackers. When confronted with large numbers of minimally capable UAS, the defenders face a difficult choice. They can spend expensive weapons to shoot at low-cost systems, knowing well that more waves may be coming. Or, they can hold onto their costly weapons and suffer the consequences of the attack. Thus, in order to protect deployed conventional forces, the cost-of-intercept curve has to be turned in favour of the defenders.

Armed forces undertake a series of actions, called 'kill chains', with a variety of sensors like video cameras, thermal imagers, radio antennae, etc., which collect information on the environment to detect targets, send data to the best-placed shooter, whether a gun, missile or warship, decide what to do, and then act. Typically, kill chains refer to a targeting cycle involving finding potential targets, confirming the target, precisely locating it, engaging it with a weapon, and assessing whether the attack had the desired effect. Armed drones can perform all the steps in the kill chain themselves. However, unarmed drones that perform the front-end tasks (find, fix, track, and target) in the kill chain and then share this information with shooters like artillery units or other drones that fire on or engage the target have had the most significant impact on the battlefield.

An increasing number of drones now have certain rudimentary AI capability aboard. Small, low-powered chips can find out whether an object seen below is a T-80 or a T-90 tank, a task that could once have been done on a distant cloud server. The drone then can transmit a few kilobytes of essential information, say, the type of target and its coordinates, even if its communications are irregular. Even then, the AI-augmented drones do not seem to have made any measurable impact. The 'Centre for a New American Security' has dismissed the AI drones, saying, "Both parties claim to be using artificial intelligence to improve the drone's ability to hit its target, but likely its use is limited."

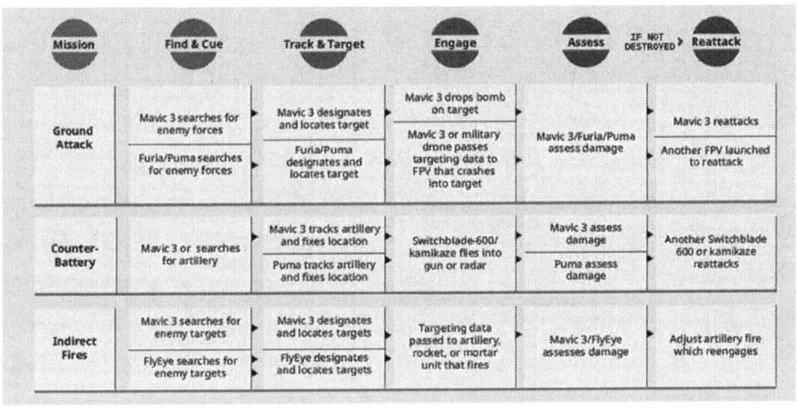

Kill Chains in the Ukraine War

It follows that despite the disruptive nature of UASs, these are not, just by themselves, transforming war *per se*. Transformational change will occur only when drones are combined with digitised command and control systems and new-era meshed networks of civilian and military sensors. One can learn the importance of EW in negating these systems. Russian forces have instituted an integrated system that employs a mix of electronic warfare, missile systems, and connected sensors to degrade Ukrainian use of drones and loitering munitions. This Russian EW system not only interferes with Ukrainian drones but also with critical communications links. Russian forces were able to pinpoint Ukrainian headquarters, cut the link between drones and their operators, find drone operator stations, and jam or degrade the effectiveness of Ukraine's drones and precision weapons.

Practical inferences from two years of the war in Ukraine include:[13]

- Drones are slow-moving electronics that can, in principle, be detected and disabled, unlike artillery rounds.
- Tactical drone payloads are limited. Limited drone payloads drive trade-offs between sensors and weapons.
- Larger drones with longer ranges and larger payloads require more infrastructure to operate as well as specifically launching areas and can be more easily detected and downed.
- Current drones are more impacted by weather effects than artillery.
- Drones operating in stacks and connected to artillery create resilient kill chains. In Ukraine, drones have operated in stacks rather than swarms.
- Long-range kamikaze drones can support penetrating strikes to complement or substitute for strategic missile strikes.
- Drones and their operators are vulnerable to counter-drone operations, ranging from sophisticated EW to simple nets.
- Surveillance and targeting missions continue to remain more important than drone strikes.
- Drones make it more challenging to concentrate forces, achieve surprise, and conduct offensive operations.
- Kamikaze FPV drones provide cheap precision strike capabilities, but the tactical beyond-line-of-sight weapons primarily extend the reach of ground forces.
- Even large numbers of small drones cannot compete with the power of artillery fire.
- Drones provide reasonable air power, but they have not substituted traditional air forces or been able to obtain air superiority.
- If drones are cheap and plentiful, they do not have to be survivable because one can have resiliency through reconstitution.

Observable Trends

- While drones provided critical capabilities in the battle for Tripoli in the Libyan civil war, the war over Nagorno-Karabakh and in Ukraine, their importance to battlefield outcomes has been exaggerated.
- Drones alone did not determine who won or lost in these cases.
- Across the three case studies, there was a decreasing emphasis on large military drones and an increasing use of small military and commercial drones and kamikaze drones.
- There are many ways to counter all types of drones, but a layered system of defences is needed to protect against the full spectrum of threats.
- Drones can be helpful to ground, air, and maritime forces and are needed at all echelons.
- Drones enable riskier missions and are particularly well-suited for SEAD/DEAD operations.
- Because most drones are not survivable, large drone fleets are required, and the ability to rapidly produce additional drones is critical in a protracted fight.
- Drones are more effective when used in pairs or groups, but these tactics are not actual swarms.
- Drones have removed humans from some of the most dangerous ground and air force missions, such as spotting or SEAD/DEAD, but many human drone operators are still needed.
- The drones used in these wars were remotely piloted and had little autonomy.
- Drones complement other weapons and can partially offset capability gaps, but they have not replaced crewed aircraft, artillery units, or missiles.

PLA's India-specific Operational Options[14]

In a hypothetical conflict scenario between China and India, Chinese forces will try to establish a lodgement on Indian soil. To achieve this goal, China must find, fix, track, and neutralise Indian fire units and air defences and defeat incoming Indian attacks.

China has a large and growing fleet of aerial drones. It could employ long-range systems, such as the Soaring Dragons, BZK-005, TB-001, or Wing Loong IIs. China is also developing several very high-end drones for long-range operations in defended airspace, such as the supersonic WZ-8 and the stealthy GJ-11, which may be used to find high-value mobile targets, such as Army hypersonic missile batteries or aircraft carriers. Long-range military drones could find the initial targets. Armed drones, such as the Wing Loongs, could engage them directly or pass targeting information to PLA Rocket Force (PLARF) missile batteries, or truck-launched kamikaze drones, such as the Harpy or CH-901, if high-value targets are found. These can engage Indian air defence radars.

Many of the PLA's long-range drones would be shot down by Indian air defences. However, the PLA will likely have enough reserve to absorb substantial losses and take out high-value targets. Alternatively, the PLA might focus the opening missile salvos of its joint firepower campaign on suppressing Indian ground-based air defences, which could thin them out and make it easier for follow-on long-range PLA drone attacks. After destroying Indian air defences, PLA medium and some short-range drones could be used to find targets, which could then be engaged from Tibet by China's WS-2 multiple-launch rocket systems.

Since China has deep inventories of ballistic and cruise missiles, it may choose to use drones as decoys or to perform supporting missions instead of strikes. PLA drones thus could be decoys, interceptor sponges, or bait that tricks air defenders into revealing their location. PLA rocket launchers could deploy swarms of tiny drones into their own airspace that would operate as a collaborative autonomous swarm. In this concept, some drones would emulate Chinese fighter aircraft while kamikaze drones would target SAM radars. These Chinese drone swarms would help locate India's air defences and force it to waste SAM interceptors on small drone decoys.

Autonomous long-endurance drones, such as balloons, equipped with multiple different passive sensors to collect intelligence, could also bolster China's kill chain. These balloons could serve as communications relays and be armed with air-to-air missiles to shoot down adversary drones. These balloon drones could certainly be shot down but would require devoting fighters to the mission. They could still serve their purpose by providing redundancy during the key opening phases of the war.

Imperatives for India

The Indian Armed Forces have been alive to the rapid developments in drones and their employment in current conflicts. Drones have been procured from the U.S., Israel, and India's own industrial base to operate at strategic, operational, and tactical levels. The Defence Research and Development Organisation (DRDO) is providing the research and development inputs. The Ministry of Defence (MoD) and the Armed Forces have included all categories of UAVs in the negative list for imports. This means that UAVs have to be indigenously produced under the various categories of the Make in India initiative. A lot is being done for anti-drone systems. The MoD's initiative, Innovation for Defence Excellence (iDeX), is also paying rich dividends.

The Indian Army has inducted indigenous integrated drone detection and interdiction systems in the northern border. Developed by DRDO and Bharat Electronics, the Army Air Defence had got seven of these systems, five of which were inducted for deployment close to the northern borders. These systems, too, had both soft and hard kill options.

Apart from these indigenous systems, other improvised systems with different counter-UAS capabilities have been deployed by the armed forces. This includes prototypes of laser-based systems developed indigenously with Army Air Defence, improvised versions of ZU-23 and L/70 guns for drone detection and killing, ad-hoc handled jammers, and low-level lightweight radars, among others. The armed forces have inducted anti-drone systems from Indian private firms and the Israeli SMASH 2000 plus systems to tackle enemy drone threats.

The Indian Army has been hosting various events in Ladakh's high-altitude areas to revolutionise drone operations in one of the world's most challenging terrains. In collaboration with the Federation of Indian Chambers of Commerce and Industry (FICCI), the Army has hosted the HIM-DRONE-A-THON 2 event in Ladakh's Wari La Pass where 20-odd domestic makers were invited to showcase drone solutions for high-altitude applications. The Wari La Pass is located at over 15,000 feet, and operating drones here is comparatively difficult. A diverse array of technologies was on display, like surveillance, logistic, loitering, swarm and first-person view (FPV) capabilities with specialised payloads, such as EW and Communication Intelligence. Such events serve as platforms for identifying promising home-grown products and suggest the necessary technological advancements and indigenous procurement.

The Indian military is learning from the experiences of current conflicts. Smaller, cheaper, lighter, faster, disposable, reconfigurable on a table and readily accessible in electronic stores, this new drone threat poses a challenge to all conventional armies. In modern conflicts, units that consolidate or operate in anything other than very small groups create a prime target for enemy drone pilots. Large combat tactical operations centres are likely to be things of the past.

Disruptive technologies that help with sensing, sense-making, and decision-making are improving rapidly. The capabilities of UASs have increased dramatically over the last two years. The quantity of fielded systems has increased, and the cost has decreased. These trends will continue.

The Indian military has to reconfigure, either on its own or by the force of circumstances. We must modify our thinking about war in the air and on the surface through the lens of doctrine, organisation, training, material, leadership and education, personnel and facilities (DOTMLPF) since everything from doctrine to organisations and training will need to change. Military doctrine will need to continue to evolve to include new tactics, techniques, and procedures for UAS-supported fire and manoeuvre. We must develop and refine operational concepts and tactics for drone employment specific to our environment. New tactics, such as swarms and stacks, will need to be introduced into tactics, techniques, procedures manuals, and the units' training schedules. These would require speedy implementation to gain an edge over adversaries.

Today, UASs are being tightly integrated into infantry tactics, used in new and creative ways for reconnaissance, leveraged for forward operating base defence to provide critical intelligence and deployed for data collection. The same applies to artillery and other combat arms. As the persistent spell and sound of drones may cause psychological effects on the troops on the ground, Indian troops have to get used to operating under the threat of drones on the scale seen in Ukraine. UASs' threat can no longer be a concern only for the air defence units. All units, at home or deployed, may find themselves targeted by UASs and, therefore, need to understand methods to mitigate and defeat the threat. Because of the thickening of air traffic, all services, their arms, and units will require UAS operation and counter-UAS operational capabilities. That would necessitate innovative joint doctrinal, technical, and tactical solutions to meet the new challenge. It would require the services leaders to assign responsibilities for various aspects of conjoined air defence. This could involve certain integration of command posts or through a coordination mechanism like altitude separation. Besides the armed forces, the border guard forces, too, have a major role in counter-drone operations. All these organisations have to be brought under a common umbrella. MoD should take the lead in this.

The traditional procurement models for equipment and their various modifications would not be successful in procuring fast-changing technology like drones. Some factors which need serious consideration are:[15]

- Numbers will be high as there is a very high attrition rate. A recent report from the Royal United Service Institute described an attrition rate for the Ukrainian armed forces of approximately 10,000 per month.
- There is a trade-off between sophistication, including electronic hardening and capability, cost and quantity.
- There is no 'one size fits all' mission approach available.
- A wide variety of systems will be needed, from low-end, cheap tactical systems to more high-end, expensive ones. Some will require longer endurance, faster speeds, and more advanced capabilities.
- Not all of these UASs can be sourced commercially or rapidly acquired.
- Additional testing and a tolerance of some failure to learn lessons about the trade-offs between capability and capacity in UAS will be required.

- Optimal levels of existing inventory vs. just-in-time production as part of national mobilisation will be required.
- A right balance will have to be struck between internally developed versus commercially sourced systems.
- Key enabling technologies like micro-electronics, advanced manufacturing and alternative fuels are advancing rapidly. It is extremely difficult to publish optimal requirements for UASs and their hard and soft kill counter systems.

The long timeframe connected to developing a new system delays the ability to incorporate advances in commercial technology. Procurement trade-offs may include:-

- Weight, speed, range, endurance, materials, and signature against key threats;
- Power and cooling for modular components;
- Ease of manufacture and assembly;
- Complexity of operation;
- Sustainability in the field including possibly repairing systems with parts produced near the edge;
- Degrees of autonomy;
- Flexibility in updating software;
- Safety considerations;
- Built-in redundancy.

To sum up, the Indian Armed Forces might-

- Need a diverse fleet of aerial drones that includes a mix of higher-end and cheaper systems;
- Invest in autonomous kamikaze drones for offensive operations;
- Consider pre-positioning short and medium-range drones at selected locations;
- Develop and refine operational concepts and tactics for drone employment specific to Indian requirements;
- Invest in training drone pilots to be skilled in operating closely with crewed systems;

- Invest urgently in various counter-drone capabilities, including layered, high-capacity air defences and EW systems;
- Build both the commercial and military drone industrial base to scale up production and create surge capacity;
- Equip the army with first-person view (FPV) kamikaze drones to provide additional cost-effective short-range precision fires;
- Integrate short and medium-range drones with ground-based fire units and stockpile large amounts of artillery shells, mortars, rockets, and missiles. In Nagorno-Karabakh and Ukraine, drones were most effective as part of a ground-based fire complex and helped to convert unguided artillery into precision weapons;
- Develop battle management software to integrate drones with ground-based fire units;
- Develop operational concepts and tactics and focus on integrating and sharing information between drones and fire units of the Army and the Air Force;
- Train on commercial, military, and especially FPV drones at the earliest.

Notes

1. "The Third Drone Age: Visions Out to 2040," Centre for International Governance Innovation. https://www.cigionline.org/articles/the-third-drone-age-visions-out-to-2040/
2. David Hambling, "Bargain Basement Bombers: Ukraine's Homemade Drones Hit Russian Forces," Forbes, January 24, 2023. https://www.forbes.com/sites/davidhambling/2023/01/24/bargain-basement-bombers--ukraines-homemade-drones-hit-russian-forces/
3. Antonio Graceffo, "From Ukraine to Myanmar, Drone Warfare Marks a Paradigm Shift," September 11, 2024. https://www.geopoliticalmonitor.com/from-ukraine-to-myanmar-drone-warfare-marks-a-paradigm-shift/
4. "How are 'kamikaze' drones being used by Russia and Ukraine?" *BBC*, December 29, 2023. https://www.bbc.com/news/world-62225830
5. Chinese arms firm offers army brigade combat team solution - Global Times. https://www.globaltimes.cn/page/202211/1279138.shtml
6. Mark Bowden, "The Tiny and Nightmarishly Efficient Future of Drone Warfare," *Atlantic*, November 22, 2022. https://www.bbc.com/news/videos/cw4y2mrp4jwo
7. Antonio Graceffo, "From Ukraine to Myanmar, Drone Warfare Marks a Paradigm Shift", | *Geopolitical Monitor*, September 11, 2024. https://www.geopoliticalmonitor.com/from-ukraine-to-myanmar-drone-warfare-marks-a-paradigm-shift/

8. "The Third Drone Age: Visions Out to 2040", Centre for International Governance Innovation. https://www.cigionline.org/articles/the-third-drone-age-visions-out-to-2040/
9. Global Emerging Technology Summit 2022 - 2-2-2. https://scsp222.substack.com/p/global-emerging-technology-summit 9/15
10. Zachary Kallenborn & Marcel Plichta, "Breaking the Shield: Countering Drone Defenses," *Joint Force Quarterly* 113 (2nd Quarter 2024). https://digitalcommons.ndu.edu/joint-force-quarterly/vol113/iss1/7.
11. Antonio Graceffo, "From Ukraine to Myanmar, Drone Warfare Marks a Paradigm Shift," September 11, 2024. https://www.geopoliticalmonitor.com/from-ukraine-to-myanmar-drone-warfare-marks-a-paradigm-shift/
12. "Evolution Not Revolution", | Center for a New American Security (en-US). https://www.cnas.org/publications/reports/evolution-not-revolution
13 Ibid.
14. Stacie Pettyjohn, Hannah Dennis, and Molly Campbell, "Swarms over the Strait: Drone Warfare in a Future Fight to Defend Taiwan," Center for a New American Security (CNAS), June 2024. https://www.cnas.org/publications/reports/swarms-over-the-strait
15. Jake Epstein, "A Ukrainian Donation Drive built an 'Army of Drones' and Picked Up an Unusual System Called a 'Shahed Hunter' for Kyiv's Forces," *Business Insider* (2023). https://www.businessinsider.in/international/news/a-ukrainian-donation-drive-built-an-army-of-drones-and-picked-up-an-unusual-weapon-called-a-shahed-hunter-for-kyivs-forces/articleshow/100143731.cms

14. Artificial Intelligence (AI)

Introduction

Artificial Intelligence (AI) has been transforming the way modern warfare is conducted. The integration of AI in military operations has the potential to enhance the capabilities and efficiency of military organisations greatly, but it also raises important ethical and security concerns. The current conflicts have shown that artificial intelligence is already changing warfare. The next major conflict will likely see the wholesale integration of AI into every aspect of military planning and execution.

Armed forces around the world are closely watching the current conflicts, taking stock of what works and what does not where opposing sides adapt their methods and systems daily, and old military equipment is paired with the latest technologies in innovative ways. AI is being incorporated into many applications like Intelligence, Surveillance and Reconnaissance (ISR), logistics, cyber space operations, information operations, command and control, semi-autonomous and autonomous vehicles and Lethal Autonomous Weapon System (LAWS), AI-assisted decision-making, AI-assisted Common Operating Picture (COP), drones and swarms.[1]

Advantages of Military Application of AI

Some of the benefits observed in the current conflicts are:

- The ubiquitous employment of drones and loitering munitions by both sides offers AI-enhanced autonomous capabilities in flight, targeting, and firing.

- AI is used to analyse satellite images and open-source data, such as social media photos, in geopolitically sensitive locations. Neural networks are used to combine ground-level photos, drone video footage, and satellite imagery to enhance intelligence and produce strategic and tactical intelligence advantages.
- AI is increasingly and structurally used in conflicts to analyse vast amounts of data to produce battlefield intelligence. Most AI will be deployed in systems far removed from the battlefield, such as cloud computing and data analysis systems related to planning, logistics, and preventive maintenance.
- AI is enhanced by the convergence of other developments, including the growing availability of Low-Earth Orbit Satellites and the unprecedented availability of Big Data from open sources.
- Foreign geospatial intelligence companies willingly assist in using AI-enhanced systems to convert satellite imagery into intelligence, surveillance and reconnaissance advantages. In the Ukraine War, U.S. companies like Palantir Technologies have provided AI software to analyse how the war has been unfolding, understand troop movements, and conduct battlefield damage assessments. Another U.S. company, 'Primer', has deployed AI tools to analyse unencrypted Russian radio communications.
- AI is playing an important role in EW and encryption in cyber warfare due to the advances in AI-enhanced threat intelligence and the quick distribution of protective software to cloud services and other computer networks. AI-enhanced facial recognition software has been used on a substantial scale.

Military Applications and Implementation of AI.[2] The challenges here are in terms of:

- *Ethical Concerns.* There is potential for autonomous weapons systems to make life-or-death decisions without human oversight. We need to ensure that the use of AI in military applications aligns with ethical standards and principles.
- *Reliability.* Accuracy of AI models heavily depends on the quantity and quality of data used for training. There is always a risk of errors

and bias in the data. Any inaccuracies in the output of an AI system could have severe consequences, particularly in military operations. Adversarial attacks can cause AI systems to produce incorrect results by manipulating input data and cause an AI system to misidentify targets or provide misleading information.

- *Cyber security*. AI systems in the military are often interconnected with other systems and vulnerable to cyber attacks. Malicious use of AI can cause significant harm to the military's infrastructure, personnel, and operations. AI-powered cyber attacks could be difficult to detect and prevent.
- *Training*. Developing and training AI systems requires significant resources and expertise. The quality and quantity of data available for training can be limited, making it tough to create accurate and reliable AI models.
- *Integration*. Integrating AI systems with existing military infrastructure and processes can be challenging. This requires significant changes to existing systems and processes, which can be time-consuming and expensive.
- *Public Perception*. It raises concerns among the public about the potential for AI machines to replace human soldiers, reduce accountability, and increase the risk of harm to civilians.

Although the military applications of AI are expected to yield a wide range of benefits, they also present significant risks. Some of the risks are:

- Decisions might be made too fast. This could result in increased escalation. Systems might be fielded before full safety testing.
- AI could be less accurate/precise than human interventions. Data might be dirty, resulting in error. Behaviour might not be explainable and may exhibit emergent behaviour.
- It may be hard to distinguish combatant from non-combatant. It may also be hard to differentiate between anomaly and threat. It reduces attribution, thereby encouraging bad behaviour.
- It cannot adapt to programming. It might result in automation bias and cause arms racing and proliferation. It may also be vulnerable to spoofing/hacking.

- Humans could lose essential skills.

Opportunities and Challenges for AI in the Armed Forces

AI and digital capabilities are a double-edged sword. They present a multitude of opportunities to improve defence and security functions. They also provide a variety of new ways for criminals and terrorists to advance their methods of operation.

Opportunities. The main advantages of military application of AI are:-

- AI technology solves well-defined, narrow problems where the necessary data and feedback are fully available to the system. AI-powered intelligence systems provide the capability to integrate and sort through big troves of data from different sources and geographic locations to identify patterns and highlight useful information, significantly improving intelligence analysis.
- AI technology can facilitate autonomous operations, which lead to more informed military decision-making and will increase the speed and scale of military action.
- AI technology can be used in military scenario planning at all levels of command to determine the requirements for a mission. AI ensures the most advantageous use of resources during a mission.
- AI technology provides improved situational awareness, enhanced targeting and reconnaissance. AI can analyse large amounts of data from numerous sources, such as satellite imagery, unmanned aerial vehicles, and sensors, in real time. It could provide military leaders with a more comprehensive and up-to-date picture of the battlefield and identify potential targets and gather intelligence on enemy forces.
- Although humans will be present, their role will be less upfront. The judgments of autonomous weapons systems will not be affected by emotions like fear or hysteria. The systems will be capable of processing more incoming sensory information than soldiers without discarding or distorting it to fit preconceived notions.
- AI technology will make combat less uncertain and more controllable, as machines are not subject to the frailties that cloud human judgment, like being tired, frightened, bored, or angry.

- AI is far superior at solving multiple control problems very quickly due to its ability to process massive amounts of information to detect patterns without suffering fatigue, recognition error, bias, or emotional interference.
- Non-lethal activities, such as logistics, maintenance, base operations, veterans' healthcare, life-saving battlefield medical assistance and casualty evacuation, personnel management, navigation, communication, cyber defence, and intelligence analysis can benefit from AI. It may play essential roles in new systems for protecting people and high-value fixed assets and deterring attacks through non-lethal means.
- Lethal autonomous robots have the exceptional potential to function at a tempo faster than humans can achieve and to strike even when communication links have been severed.
- Between human and robot soldiers, the latter could be more trusted to report ethical infractions they observed than a team of soldiers who might close ranks. There are ethical advantages to removing humans from high-stress combat zones in favour of robots.

Challenges. Some of the disadvantages of AI systems in the military are challenging:

- The armed forces lag far behind the private sector in integrating innovative and disruptive technologies, such as AI, into their operations. They largely remain hindered by antiquated technology, cumbersome processes, and incentive structures designed for outdated or competing aims.
- Notwithstanding that, the commitment and reliability of the private sector in the serious matter of national defence, unless strictly regulated, remains uncertain.
- Reliance on AI systems in military operations increases the dependence on technology and can reduce the decision-making ability of military leaders.
- The data required for machine learning is currently isolated, disorganised, or frequently discarded, and the platforms are not well connected. The methods for acquiring, developing, and implementing

AI are rigid sequential processes that hinder early and ongoing experimentation and testing, which is essential for AI.

- AI systems can struggle to function reliably or correctly if the data inputs change or encounter uncertain or novel situations. AI systems can be designed and trained on biased data, leading to biased and discriminatory decision-making in military operations.
- Adversarial attacks on Machine Learning (ML) systems can target the algorithms or data the system uses. Even minor modifications can lead to malfunction, incorrect conclusions, or other unforeseen issues.
- AI/ML systems cannot typically explain the reasoning behind their decisions, recommendations, and actions. The lack of explainability significantly hampers building trust between human and AI teams.
- The complexity of AI algorithms and the black-box nature of many AI systems make it difficult to understand and predict their behaviour, leading to concerns about accountability and transparency in military operations.
- AI technology is unpredictable, vulnerable to unique forms of manipulation, and challenging to human-machine interaction.
- There is an enduring necessity for human presence on the battlefield alongside AI systems in some capacity as the principal restraining factor that will keep the technology from upending warfare.
- Lethal Autonomous Weapon Systems (LAWS) will inevitably produce errors. These errors will be problematic to correct or prevent from reoccurring. Taking corrective action without understanding how the weapon system behaves and why is complex. Automation bias could create denial that an error has even occurred.
- AI systems used in military operations are vulnerable to cyber attacks and hacking, which could compromise the security of military assets and put troops at risk.
- The deployment of LAWS might result in accidental and collateral damage risk, causing mass fratricide, with large numbers of weapons turning on friendly forces and civilians. This could be because of hacking, enemy behavioural manipulation, simple malfunctions, unexpected interactions with the environment, or software errors.

- LAWS' errors would likely repeat with a consistent level of force until some external agent intervenes. Human error tends to be idiosyncratic and one-off, given a human operator's common sense, moral agency, and capacity for near real-time consequence management.
- Waging war via robots is unethical. Robot warfare has serious strategic disadvantages because it spurs so much moral outrage among the population from whom the country needs support.
- Service members at every level may lack the technical education and experience to employ AI.
- Current capabilities in the military sphere are far from perfect, and mistakes may have serious consequences.
- The inability of AI systems to multitask is a significant challenge. A relatively simple set of tasks is currently impossible for an AI system to accomplish.

The use of AI in warfare should be approached with caution, and the potential disadvantages should be carefully considered and addressed in the development and deployment of military technology.

Challenges of AI Integration

AI technology is a game-changer. The armed forces must look closely at the effect of AI on doctrine, organisation, training, material, leadership and education, personnel, and facilities (DOTMLPF). Integrating AI into the armed forces is a complex and ongoing process. It involves developing and implementing new technologies and training and educating personnel to use them effectively. AI has the potential to meaningfully enhance the effectiveness and efficiency of military operations across all domains.[3]

Doctrine. The armed forces have a rigid formal concept of operations for warfighting. The existing doctrines must be revisited with the introduction of AI technologies in the defence sector.

Organisational Challenges. Challenges here are:-

a. Vast amounts of data are available today. Different services branches must ensure that the data is compatible with other users to share. The armed forces are already drowning in data, but it is in various formats that make it impossible for different users to share. The services must establish common technical standards to ensure their data is compatible.

b. The current process of gathering information through phones, emails, and other means, then sorting and analysing it through chat rooms, sticky notes, and verbal communication is slow and prone to errors. The cycle of OODA loop can take hours or even days, by which point the information may already be out of date.

c. The visible infrared and radio-frequency signatures that facilitate communication are easily identifiable by the enemy through drones and satellites, making the command post a vulnerable target. AI can replace human beings doing cognitive work, watch surveillance videos for enemy forces, track own forces' locations and assignments and supply levels, etc. A single commander could then see the whole battlefield at a glance without the large footprint of a huge headquarters.

Leadership. Any successful AI begins in the minds of the decision-makers. The burden of starting the process is on the decision-makers, not the data scientist. Functional leaders and commanders must ask tough questions: What decisions do I make, what data do I rely on, and how can I have data presented to me in a relevant time and place?[4] The technology should be adapted to the needs of these domain experts rather than expecting them to adapt to the technology.

Personnel. The armed forces need more digital experts or will remain unprepared to buy, build, and use AI and related technologies. They need experts with AI expertise and domain experts in specific fields, such as intelligence analysis, fire support, and logistics, to fully utilise AI capabilities.[5]

Software. In future conflicts, the side that can adapt and update software and AI models faster will have a significant tactical and operational advantage. The quality of the software will determine a military's primacy in collecting and analysing information, developing an operating picture, thwarting enemy attacks, identifying opportunities in time and space to attack and helping with target selection and servicing most effectively.[6] This would include access to cloud computing and storage.[7]

Training. When combined with virtual and augmented reality technologies, AI systems can enhance individualised and customised training by adapting to human behaviour and creating customised training environments or scenarios.

Culture. Adapting from a force focused on hardware and industrial-age methods to one focused on software and digital-age methods can be difficult. However, the biggest challenge to overcome is not technology but the cultural mindset and approach.[8]

Use of AI in Current Conflicts

The First Artificial Intelligence War

Israeli military action, Operation 'Guardian of the Walls' in May 2021 in Gaza, has been described as the first artificial intelligence war. Israel relied heavily on machine learning and data gathering. A senior Israeli officer involved in the digital conflict said, "This is the first time AI was used broadly across an operation."

Israel used AI to coordinate attacks on Gaza. The AI has been fed sufficient raw data related to warfare and intelligence related to the conflict. The IDF used resources, such as signal intelligence (SIGINT), visual intelligence (VISINT), human intelligence (HUMINT), geographical intelligence (GEOINT), data collected through satellites, aerial reconnaissance vehicles, field agents, ground intelligence, and years of information. The Israeli military gathered intelligence reports by adapting readily available AI technologies. Vast amounts of data were analysed for precision attacks. Drawing on satellite imagery, sensors, and other sources, Israel was able to obtain 3D geographical information about Gaza and identify the locations of rocket launchers that Hamas installed.[9]

The IDF set up a multi-disciplinary centre to help identify relevant targets, aiding the military in effective planning and targeting.[10] An advanced AI technological platform was created that centralises all data on the militant groups in the Gaza Strip on one system to help with the analysis and extract intelligence crucial for the operations. According to a report by *Jerusalem Post*, it was IDF's intelligence officers in Unit 8200, an Intelligence Corps unit of the IDF that specialises in code decryption and signal intelligence, who created advanced programmes named "Alchemist", "Gospel", and "Depth of Wisdom", which were developed and used during the conflict.[11] The "Gospel" helped the IDF's military intelligence unit to enhance the intelligence recommendations for the officers and helped them identify 'quality targets', which were then passed to the air force to undertake the strikes. The Israeli Army's J6/C4i Directorate's Lotem Unit specifically creates software for AI and uses machine learning for real-life applications.

Over the years, IDF Unit 9900's satellites have gathered GEOINT. They were able to detect changes in terrain in real time automatically. Unit 8200, the Israeli signals intelligence cell, created multiple algorithms using signal, geographical, and human intelligence to pinpoint strike targets like Hamas missile unit leaders and anti-tank operatives within Gaza, which were then passed to command to order a strike. During the operation, the military could detect launching positions and hit them after firing. The unit used AI algorithms to predict enemy rocket launches, places, and times, helping soldiers on the ground defend against them effectively. The same tool generated 200 military target options for strategic engagement during the military operation, Iron Swords. The system executed this process within seconds, a task that would have previously required the labour of numerous analysts over several weeks.

A part of this technology has been deployed in Israel's Iron Dome System. The Lotem Unit created an app that helped the soldiers predict rocket launch locations, time of launch, and the target for such missiles by studying the data from field sensors, etc. Another app that the Lotem Unit created was used to identify suspicious objects from videos and write down the descriptions, which helped save human resources. Hamas's underground "Metro" tunnel network was heavily damaged in several nights of airstrikes. The Israelis could map the network of hundreds of kilometres under residential areas, where they knew almost everything about them.

Mapping of the underground network was done by a substantial intelligence-gathering process that was helped by technological developments and the use of Big Data to fuse all the intelligence. Once mapped, the IDF could have a full picture of the tunnel with details, such as the tunnels' depth, thickness, and the nature of the routes. With that, the military could construct an attack plan that was used during the operation. Using the data gathered and analysed through AI, the Israel Air Force could use suitable munitions to target an apartment, a tunnel, or a building. The IDF used supercomputing and a swarm of AI-guided drones to comb through data and identify new targets within the Gaza Strip. It is believed that this is the first time a swarm of AI drones has been used in combat.

Use of AI in Recent Wars [12]

AI technology has been utilised in various ways during the ongoing Ukraine conflict, including facial recognition software to identify enemy soldiers and machine learning to enhance the efficiency of military and aid supply chains. Ubiquitous sensors, big data processing, automated orchestration platforms, and drones employed at scale are dramatically compressing detection-to-destruction. Software systems, such as GIS Arta, Delta, and Kropyva, have allowed Ukraine to carefully marshal its resources across large and geographically disconnected fronts. Additionally, AI has been used for propaganda and information warfare, with "deepfake" videos blurring the boundary between real and artificially generated content.

Artificial Intelligence in the Ukraine War. Ukraine has understood the necessity of tapping into today's data-rich battlefields. This has been possible by the following:-

- The sheer amount of available data from the vast number of digital devices, mostly commercial, capturing images, audio, and videos of the war, is utilised.
- There is increased prevalence of open-source intelligence. Each individual, civilian and military, equipped with a smartphone, has become a sensor.
- Opening a Telegram channel that receives tens of thousands of messages per day, where citizens can send videos and photos of Russian troops and material, provides information that complements Ukrainian intelligence-gathering activities.
- Citizens can report Russian troop movements via the national Diia app.

- Other AI applications, such as natural language processing (NLP), have been utilised. For instance, AI company, Primer, utilises AI that uses its algorithms to listen in on intercepted Russian communications and automatically translate and highlight relevant information for Ukrainian forces, like a unit's location, size, equipment, activity, and future intentions, in a searchable text database.
- Now-ubiquitous employment of drones and loitering munitions by both sides offers AI-enhanced autonomous capabilities in flight, targeting, and firing.
- AI is used to analyse satellite images and geolocate and analyse open-source data, such as social media photos, in geopolitically sensitive locations.
- Neural networks are used to combine ground-level photos, drone video footage, and satellite imagery to enhance intelligence to produce strategic and tactical intelligence advantages.
- AI is used for data analytics on the battlefield. It is increasingly and structurally used in the conflict to analyse vast amounts of data to produce battlefield intelligence.
- AI is enhanced by the convergence of other developments, including the growing availability of low-Earth orbit satellites and the unprecedented availability of Big Data from open sources.
- The willingness of foreign geospatial intelligence companies to assist Ukraine by using AI-enhanced systems to convert satellite imagery into intelligence, surveillance and reconnaissance advantages is an important factor.
- U.S. companies like Palantir Technologies have provided AI software to analyse how the war has been unfolding, understand troop movements, and conduct battlefield damage assessments.
- AI is playing an important role in EW and encryption.
- U.S. company Primer has deployed AI tools to analyse unencrypted Russian radio communications.
- AI is employed in cyber warfare. Advances in AI-enhanced threat intelligence and the quick distribution of protective software to cloud services and other computer networks have been utilised.

- Most AI will be deployed in systems far removed from the battlefield, in cloud computing and data analysis systems related to planning, logistics, and preventive maintenance.
- AI-enhanced facial recognition software has been used on a substantial scale. Ukraine has been using Clearview AI to vet individuals at checkpoints and identify deceased soldiers.
- The flip side is the spread of misinformation and the use of deepfakes as part of information warfare. AI systems that can autonomously create and spread messages are becoming more sophisticated.

GIS Arta. Ukrainian forces have used an "Uber-like" application to innovate and speed up their artillery targeting. Named "GIS Arta", the system takes a bottom-up approach to target selection by giving people a well-fused picture of the battlespace, not a recommendation derived opaquely of what to attack.[13]

How GIS Arta works

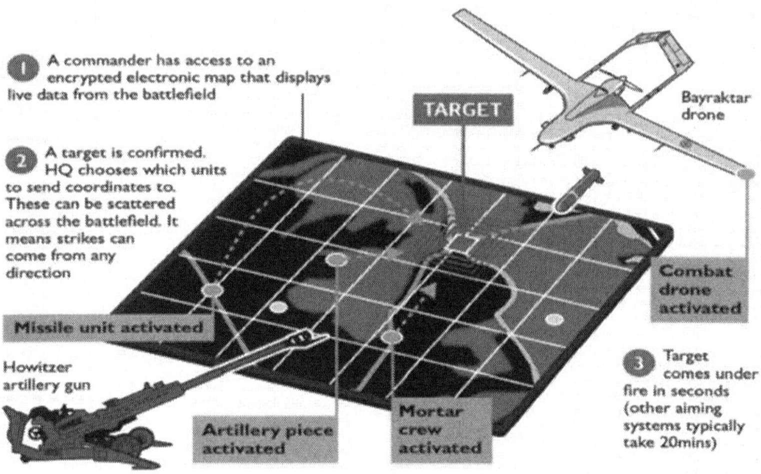

Characteristics of GIS Arta are:[14]

- It uses an algorithm to optimise variables like target type, range, and position to assign "fire missions" to existing artillery units. Users connect to GIS Arta using laptops, phones, and tablets linked to military radios, cellphones, or the Starlink satellite internet system.

- The time from acquisition of target to fire can be reduced to 30 to 45 seconds. Information in GIS Arta is obtained from targets conveyed by forward observers armed with cell phones, counter-battery radars, drones, and satellite-based imagery. GIS Arta even embeds information like munition suitability into its targeting process. For example, a mortar team can be assigned to attack personnel in the open, or an artillery unit can be assigned to attack a vehicle target. Multiple guns in different locations can be brought to bear on the same target simultaneously.
- Ukraine's batteries can "shoot and scoot", setting up, firing, and changing locations within minutes rather than hours. It reduces the opportunities Russia has to engage in devastating counter-battery fire.
- It is a decentralised and distributed command-and-control application.
- It acts as a 'Force Multiplier' improving the effectiveness of each artillery unit by enabling them to engage more targets, more accurately, and with less time and risk.
- It needs human capital and infrastructure to sustain it. Human developers write and maintain the code. They also build and sustain the networked systems on which it lives. With several users spread across a vast physical and cyberspace, GIS Arta has many points of entry that should be secured. Like any computer application or smartphone, it is vulnerable to cyber threats and should be updated continuously to maintain its integrity.

DELTA Battle-Management Software. Ukraine developed a truly connected, high-speed command and control system. The Ukrainian Delta digital C2 system has significantly shortened decision cycles. Delta was developed in collaboration with NATO before 2022. A dramatic improvement in its combat capabilities is its integration of diverse civilian systems into a coherent and highly effective command-and-control system. It has access to near-persistent surveillance of the battlespace. It combines real-time mapping with pictures and locations of enemy units, which can be put as input by anyone with access to a smart device with the Delta app and connection to a network. Artificial intelligence is also part of Delta and is used to speedily send relevant information to the right users. The main features of Delta System are:

- Delta provides a complete understanding of the battlespace in real time and integrates information about the enemy from several sensors and sources, including intelligence on a digital map. It does not require additional settings and can work on any device like a laptop, tablet, or mobile phone. Delta is a modern real-time command map and troop control centre.
- Delta has ties into the NATO system, which draws data from both commercial and classified government systems.
- Delta uses AI developed by Palantir to analyse and send the data to the user speedily. It synthesises knowledge of friendly force weaponry and ranges and then makes suggestions for targeting solutions.
- Ukrainian coders have created a field-expedient, inexpensive version of the Pentagon's ambitious Joint All-Domain Command and Control (JADC2) system for ground commanders.
- Delta pools data on Russian forces from traditional classified intelligence sources, publicly available open-source intelligence, and even crowd-sourced social media.
- Ukraine has leveraged an existing government app, Diia, which was previously employed for civil uses. Diia is installed on 70 per cent of smartphones in Ukraine, allowing most Ukrainian citizens to quickly and easily report enemy movements via encrypted messages and provide real-time intelligence.
- Delta is operated from the innovation centre, whose staff has been drawn mainly from a volunteer organisation of drone operators and programmers called 'Aerorozvidka' (aerial reconnaissance).
- It is a private-public partnership. The people who built it were from the corporate sector who were mobilised to serve in the army, not bureaucrats from the defence ministry. They started to make Delta with their own minds and hands, because they had this agile development culture. The creative process has a short cycle. You develop it, you test it, you launch it.

- Delta is a cloud solution and is already implementing NATO standards and the latest industry trends, such as cloud native environment, zero trust security, and multi-domain operations.
- It is used for planning operations and combat missions, coordination with other units, secure information exchange about enemy forces' location, etc. Delta has integrated chatbots developed by the Ministry of Digital Affairs—"eVorog" and the SSU ("STOP Russian War").
- Allied cyber units are constantly scanning the system for vulnerabilities, intrusion attempts, data leaks, etc.
- The improved web of drones, fighters, and weapons, linked through satellite communications and custom software, gives its soldiers a level of intelligence, coordination, and accuracy that was unheard of earlier.

Other AI Applications. Possible uses of AI applications are as follows:

- The U.S. company Palantir is working with Ukrainian and NATO forces to implement an "electronic kill chain" that uses a data aggregator called Meta Constellation to give Ukrainian soldiers ready access to all available commercial data in a given battlespace. It combines synthetic aperture radar satellites, data from optical pictures, thermal images, and satellite imagery and pieces them together.
- Ukraine's Saker Scout drone can autonomously find, identify, and attack 64 different types of Russian military objects. It has been used in a "human-out-of-the-loop" way to attack Russian targets when radio jamming or interference prevented operator control.
- European military AI-developer Helsing works with Ukrainian armed forces to analyse satellite images, vastly accelerating processing times.
- U.S. firm Scale AI uses machine learning to analyse imagery. This helps Ukrainian armed forces to understand where attacks are coming and assess damage more accurately and quickly than human reporting would do.
- German startup Transversals is analysing publicly available data, from social media, close to the Ukrainian frontline. AI provides

translation and combines data with metadata, geo- and chrono-locate information, and more.

- U.S. firm Clearview has worked with the Ukrainian defence ministry, which uses the company's AI facial recognition to identify deceased Russian personnel through their social media profiles to notify relatives of their deaths, transfer their bodies to their families, and help reunite refugees.
- Private companies like Maxar, BlackSky and Planet (imagery) and HawkEye 360 (signals) are providing AI-enabled space-based services to Ukraine.

Israel's Use of AI in Current Conflicts

Israel has been using AI for a long time. In November 2020, top Iranian nuclear scientist Mohsen Fakhrizadeh was assassinated in a sophisticated attack by a Mossad team. The weapon was a remote-controlled modified Belgian-made FN MAG machine gun attached to an advanced robotic apparatus and powered with AI technology. To account for the delay in the transmission of signals to the weapon, the Mossad used AI software to factor in a time lag, the shaking of the truck caused as each bullet was fired and the speed of Fakhrizadeh's vehicle. The operation required no on-site individual, took less than a minute and did not injure anyone else, including the scientist's wife, who was with him at the time.[15]

Developments in intelligence, surveillance and reconnaissance (ISR) technologies indicate that future ISR capabilities will hinge on AI-powered decision support systems (DSS). The IDF has used this in both the ongoing conflict in Gaza and previous escalations. Some of the systems used are as follows:-

- "The Alchemist" provides unit commanders with real-time alerts of likely threats on the ground, sent directly to their handheld tablets.
- "The Gospel" supports analysis and identification of targets at the brigade and division level. Commanders are given targeting recommendations, which they could verify or discard with the help of human analysts.
- "Depth of Wisdom" was used to map Gaza's tunnel network. This big-data analytical tool provided a complete picture of the network,

both above and below ground, with details, such as the tunnels' depth, thickness, and the nature of the routes.

- "Fire Factory" can meticulously analyse extensive datasets, including historical data about previously authorised strike targets, enabling the calculation of required ammunition quantities, the proposal of optimal timelines and prioritising and allocating targets.
- Israeli company Rafael, recognised for its substantial contributions to the IDF, produced an advanced missile system named "SPIKE LR II" that includes smart target tracking capabilities, AI, and other features to sustain target lock-on in tough conditions, with minimal human intervention required.
- Legion-X platform, an AI-based system like the one developed by Elbit, allows C2 of various unmanned vehicles simultaneously.

The IDF also uses AI for border control through AI-facilitated facial recognition tools. The border system analyses videos, vehicles, and animals, identifying individuals and even armed individuals or specific car models. This system includes not only live video analysis but also combines numerous additional factors, like the historical data of the particular geographical region. However, the October 7 attack by the Hamas raised several red flags concerning this system.

Use of AI-enabled decision-support systems (AI-DSS), in particular Habsora, or "the Gospel", and Lavender,[16] by the IDF in their military operations in Gaza has sparked an enormous outcry. These two systems are used to identify objects and human targets, respectively. They are applied at the very preliminary stages of the chain of creating and authorising a military target. The IDF credited the AI system with the ability to increase the number of targetable sites in Gaza from 50 each year to over 100 each day. The reason for this controversy is the massive civilian casualty inflicted on the population in Gaza.[17]

Concerns and Cautions over Use of AI

AI-enabled emerging technologies have not been a panacea. Though Ukraine has successfully used its technology sector and leveraged the cutting edge of AI-enabled warfare applications, the grim realities of war remain. With all the abilities to increase situational awareness by gaining AI-generated insights into the battlefield, Ukraine's armed forces have had to suffer from communication breakdowns, chaotic withdrawals or fratricide. Some important facts are:

- Networking of the battlefield is much less automated than has been assumed, with data uploaded manually and not instantly actionable.
- Issues with fusing and sharing data streams remain a key problem, resulting in a lack of coordination and mismatches between strategic and tactical-unit situational awareness.

Force modernisation through systems like GIS Arta or DELTA has undoubtedly increased situational awareness and modernised artillery targeting. Nevertheless, it has not lifted the fog of war, decreased the chaos when contact with the enemy is made, or negated the advantage of overwhelming numerical superiority.[18] For its counter-offensives, Ukraine needed more tanks, armoured vehicles, mine-clearing equipment, aircraft, air defence equipment, drones, missiles, personnel, and time to train its personnel, not more AI. Use of advances in AI by bad actors has lowered the barrier to entry for both its constructive and destructive uses. Low-cost, commercial, off-the-shelf AI enables a range of non-state actors to adopt these technologies increasingly. Acquisition of AI-based technologies by non-state actors threatens to destabilise existing state-non-state dynamics on the battlefield.

AI Applications in China

China has taken giant steps to introduce AI in its warfighting concept, introducing intelligentised warfare and cognitive warfare. In large-scale virtual war games, the PLA uses an AI commander who has supreme authority. However, Beijing prohibits AI systems from making choices in live situations. The PLA has introduced the concept of "multi-domain precision warfare (MDMP)" that leverages big data and AI to rapidly identify and destroy key operational systems of adversaries in all domains. Consistent with the CPC's pledge to make China the world leader in AI by 2030, the PLA is matching its ambitions with real commitments. It is spending some 1-2 per cent of its military budget on AI investments, if not more. The PLA is progressing with a clear warfighting concept, institutional reorganisations, and financial commitments that reflect the increasing centrality of AI in the future of warfare.[19]

AI Issues for India

India has some advantages in AI issues. India has a vast pool of human resources with excellent AI knowledge and capabilities. The USA is looking for bright STEM graduates from India. The U.S. has the laboratories, India has the people. India has a vibrant private sector ecosystem of AI, with over 950 startups focused on AI. The number of startups has seen significant growth recently. Data and AI can potentially add $ 450-500 billion to India's economy by 2025. India's government has taken many initiatives to augment AI in the country. Funds have been allocated for research in AI in the Union Budget. India's strength is in:-

- Talent,
- Research,
- Patents,
- AI companies and investments,
- Cloud computing.

Considerations for India

Factors. Before formalising any policy on AI, the Indian Armed Forces need to consider the following factors:-

- What current Armed Forces' policies prohibit or hinder our adaptation of AI systems? How can the Armed Forces allow for the authorised routine access of data to support AI systems while ensuring necessary security and privacy? What network or bandwidth challenges must be overcome to realise the Armed Forces' routine use of AI systems?
- Will preparing Armed Forces personnel to use AI systems increase or decrease training requirements? What must be done in our recruiting and accession programmes to ensure we have the right human capital for the future? What training and education programmes are necessary to ensure that our current human capital is ready for tomorrow's challenges? What incentives are necessary to ensure the Armed Forces retain the right talent?

- What will be the required attributes of soldiers and leaders in a force with widely- fielded AI? How should the Armed Forces talent management programmes evolve so that the Armed Forces are placing the right person in the right job at the right time?
- What can the Armed Forces learn from industry to address this challenge?

Critical Areas. The Indian Armed Forces should give priority to the following critical areas:

- GenAI's potential to enable decision advantage must be prioritised.
- GenAI's potential to enhance current defence operations must be prioritised. Uses of AI for predictive maintenance and back-office support functions to streamline logistics and sustain manpower planning and execution, inform investment and divestment decisions, and facilitate the experimental course of action generation should be exploited.
- Development of technical talent needs to be prioritised. What additional talent needs to be recruited, developed and retained to meet evolving requirements?
- Threats, ranging from misinformation to cyber attacks to chemical and biological weapons, which can be practically expected to arise and grow in complexity, need to be evaluated, and necessary defensive measures to combat and deter them should be identified.
- At the present state, the Indian Armed Forces must develop systems like GIS Arta and DELTA Battle-Management Software in-house. If Ukraine can develop these while fighting a war, there is no reason we cannot develop them with all the expertise that we claim to have.
- Human resources and procurement issues have been under discussion for some time. The problem is known. To fully realise the potential of AI in training, new military training and occupational specialities need to be created. To attract and retain top AI technology professionals, offers of adequate career options should be considered.

Induction of Professionals. The following need to be considered:

- A Defence Experimentation Unit needs to be created to perform much-needed operational experimentation and iteration with AI models. This may be part of the Centre of Excellence on AI.
- An Automated Orchestration Platform, a generative AI-powered interface that can call up relevant tools and datasets, decompose the queries into discrete tasks and semi-autonomously or autonomously complete tasks, needs to be built. AI models should be trained on specific military information, terms, and jargon.
- A digital corps of professionals should be established to organise, train, and equip technologists. The existing Cat. A establishments should start teaching the basics of AI.
- AI experts from across the country could have the option of volunteering, part-time, to serve the armed forces - something like a Territorial Army. Aspiring civilian students can be offered a free college education in exchange for a commitment to serve in the armed forces for at least five years after graduating.

Procurement Proccss

- The current procurement system is not fully geared for buying software-based products and services, including AI. The people handling procurement have been trained to buy complex weapons systems, such as tanks, ships, and aircraft, which requires meticulous attention to whether contractors meet rigid specifications, cost requirements, and scheduled milestones.
- Understandably, most of these professionals are highly risk averse. They are neither trained nor incentivised to buy rapidly developing commercial technologies or to disrupt an existing multi-year acquisition programme to integrate a more effective new technology. The bottom line is that procuring high-tech, software- and AI-related capabilities cannot be delayed due to procedures.
- All modern countries face the same problem. However, they are taking measures to overcome the issue. To devise a process to circumvent this problem on our own, we must learn how other countries manage

the issue. The Ministry of Defence has to take specific cognisance, going beyond the Department of Defence Accounts.

Conclusion

Options like using mass frontal attacks to overwhelm the adversary in a weakly defended area, infiltrating using small assault groups with heavy firepower support, or quickly exploiting some fleeting technological advantage to break through may become practicable as more and more AI-enabled weapon systems enter service.[20] This may prompt a revisionist power like China to seize territory before others can respond, making it difficult to push back.[21]

AI-based systems will, no doubt, revolutionise logistics, dramatically change targeting, and ultimately, power autonomous weapons systems. However, many of the most potent AI-based systems remain unintelligible to their developers and offer unexplained outputs to their users, a phenomenon called the "black-box problem". One of the most famous maxims in AI, the Moravec's Paradox, is that tasks humans take for granted can be confoundingly tricky for a machine. Even humans under stress, in danger, and facing deliberate deception struggle to comprehend what's going on. Ukrainian decoys like fake High Mobility Artillery Rocket System (HIMARS) rocket launchers, anti-aircraft radars, etc., regularly trick Russian drone operators and artillery officers into wasting ordnance on decoys while leaving the well-camouflaged systems alone.

For effective warfighting, networking different systems together and thinking about how they share that information and who's authorised to shoot is very important. Such complex digital decision-making requires sophisticated software to run on high-speed chips, which, in turn, need power, cooling, protection from vibration and electronic interference, and more. None of that is easy for engineers to cram into the kind of small drones being used widely.[22]

Finally, it needs to be appreciated that the ongoing conflicts reveal that cognitive warfare and cyber warfare alone, conducted in non-physical domains, cannot provide extraordinary strategic advantages. The war in Ukraine reveals that such modern era battle support measures have to be assimilated into the classical practices of warfare. Physical battles have to be engaged in to subdue the enemy's will.[23] The theories of Sun Tzu, who idealised subduing the enemy without fighting, and that of the British strategist, B.H. Liddell Hart, who advocated the strategy of indirect approach, have to be translated to specific modern-era propositions.

Notes

1 "Artificial Intelligence and National Security," R45178, Congressional Research Service, November 10, 2020. https://crsreports.congress.gov/product/details?prodcode=R45178. Accessed on January 10, 2023.

2. P.K. Mallick , "Artificial intelligence, national security and the future of warfare," Chapter I. Routledge India, 2024. Available at https://www.taylorfrancis.com/chapters/edit/10.4324/9781003421849-2/artificial-intelligence-national-security-future-warfare-mallick?context=ubx

3. Sydney J. Freedberg Jr., "Building JADC2: Data, AI & Warfighter Insight," *Breaking Defense*, January 13, 2021. Available at https://breakingdefense.com/2021/01/building-jadc2-data-ai-warfighter-insight/. Accessed on January 24, 2023.

4. Michael Groen, "Uncle Sam Needs AI, ASAP: DoD Artificial Intelligence Chief," *Breaking Defense*, January 11, 2021. Available at https://breakingdefense.com/2021/01/uncle-sam-needs-ai-asap-dod-artificial-intelligence-chief/. Accessed on January 14, 2023.

5. Sydney J. Freedberg Jr., "Building JADC2: Data, AI & Warfighter Insight," *Breaking Defense*, January 13, 2021. Available at https://breakingdefense.com/2021/01/building-jadc2-data-ai-warfighter-insight/. Accessed on February 02, 2023.

6. Nand Mulchandani, N.T. John, and Jack Shanahan, "Software-Defined Warfare: Architecting the DOD's Transition to the Digital Age," Center for Strategic and International Studies. Available at https://www.csis.org/analysis/software-defined-warfare-architecting-dods-transition-digital-age. Accessed on January 20, 2023.

7. Final Report, National Security Commission on Artificial Intelligence, March 19, 2021. Available at https://www.nscai.gov/wp-content/uploads/2021/03/Full-Report-Digital-1.pdf. Accessed on January 20, 2023.

8. Michael Groen, "Uncle Sam Needs AI, ASAP: DoD Artificial Intelligence Chief," *Breaking Defense*, January 11, 2021. https://breakingdefense.com/2021/01/uncle-sam-needs-ai-asap-dod-artificial-intelligence-chief/. Accessed on January 27, 2023.

9. Takeshi Kumon, "The first AI conflict? Israel's Gaza operation gives glimpse of future," *Nikkei Asia*, June 28, 2021. https://asia.nikkei.com/Politics/International-relations/The-first-AI-conflict-Israel-s-Gaza-operation-gives-glimpse-of-future. Accessed on February 12, 2023.

10. Anna Ahronheim, "Israel's operation against Hamas was the world's first AI war," *The Jerusalem Post*, May 27, 2021. https://www.jpost.com/arab-israeli-conflict/gaza-news/guardian-of-the-walls-the-first-ai-war-669371. Accessed on February 16, 2023.
11. Younis Dar, "Israel Says It Fought World's First "Artificial Intelligence War" Against Hamas," *The Eurasian Times*, May 29, 2021. https://eurasiantimes.com/israel-sys-it-fought-worlds-first-artificial-intelligence-war-against-hamas/
12. Maj. Gen. P. K. Mallick, VSM (Retd), "Artificial Intelligence in Armed Forces: An Analysis," *CLAWS Journal*, Winter 2018.
13. David Zikusoka, "How Ukraine's "Uber for Artillery" is Leading the Software War Against Russia," May 25, 2023. https://www.newamerica.org/future-frontlines/blogs/how-ukraines-uber-for-artilleryis-leading-the-software-war-against-russia/.
14. Ibid.
15. "Mossad killed Iran's top nuke scientist with remote-operated machine gun—NYT," | *WarSclerotic*, September 18, 2021. https://warsclerotic.com/2021/09/20/mossad-killed-irans-top-nuke-scientist-with-remote-operated-machine-gun-nyt/
16. Simon Frankel Pratt, "When AI Decides Who Lives and Dies," *Foreign Policy*, May 2, 2024. https://foreignpolicy.com/2024/05/02/israel-military-artificial-intelligence-targeting-hamas-gaza-deaths-lavender/
17. Bethan McKernan in Jerusalem and Harry Davies, "'The machine did it coldly': Israel used AI to identify 37,000 Hamas targets," *The Guardian*, April 03, 2024. https://www.theguardian.com/world/2024/apr/03/israel-gaza-ai-database-hamas-airstrikes
18. Maj. Gen. P. K. Mallick, VSM (Retd), "Is Artificial Intelligence (AI) Changing the Nature of War?", VIF, January 18, 2019. https://drive.google.com/file/d/16n9kK2yvPmzKWnfEpAeEWwzZk6F4MqG2/view
19. Maj. Gen. P. K. Mallick, VSM (Retd), "Defining China's Intelligentized Warfare and Role of Artificial Intelligence," VIF, March 2021. https://www.vifindia.org/sites/default/files/defining-china-s-intelligentized-warfare-and-role-of-artificial-intelligence.pdf
20. Ibid.
21. Agence France-Presse, "Japan PM: East Asia Could Be Next Ukraine," *voanews*, January 14, 2023. https://www.voanews.com/a/kishida-says-g7-should-show-strong-will-onrussia-s-ukraine-invasion/6918474.html
22. Frederick W. Kagan and Kimberly Kagan with Mason Clark, Karolina Hird, Nataliya Bugayova, Kateryna Stepanenko, Riley Bailey and George Barros, "Ukraine and the Problem of Restoring Maneuver in Contemporary War," Institute for the Study of War, August 2024. https://www.understandingwar.org/sites/default/files/Ukraine%20and%20the%20Problem%20of%20Restoring%20Maneuver%20in%20Contemporary%20War_final.pdf
23. Ibid.

15. Cyber Warfare

Introduction

Cyber warfare is here to stay. The current conflicts show that cyber warfare is now being carried out in conjunction with conventional warfare. Cyberattacks are being integrated into kinetic strategies and tactics to disrupt opponents' critical infrastructure, weapons systems, and operations by hacking into surveillance and guidance systems, command and control networks, and logistics operations.

The most effective offensive cyber operation during the war will be the most difficult, requiring considerable intelligence, planning, and advanced capabilities guided by experts and commanders with open minds. High levels of uncertainty will limit it. It is difficult to know beforehand which operations might be successful and which will be failures.

Cyber attacks and threats are critical elements of grey-zone warfare, which combines conventional military tactics with irregular methods to intimidate or threaten adversaries, without escalating to open conflict. Cyber threat actors can be categorised into five primary types: state operatives, cyber criminals, hacktivists, terrorist groups, and cyber mercenaries.

Russian cyber operations against Ukraine have been less than fully effective partly because of a successful defence by Ukraine, which was backed by the global technology sector, U.S. Cyber Command, volunteers, and Ukraine's own defensive actions. Ukraine's cyber-defensive effort has shown that a solid and layered cyber defence can be effective against a well-resourced and skilful adversary. We do not know whether the same will happen with Taiwan against the People's Liberation Army (PLA).

The Russian Cyber Attack

Offensive cyber operations were carried out by Russia before and during the invasion of Ukraine in February 2022. A data-wiping malware was found on computers across Ukrainian critical infrastructure sectors, including banking, energy, and communications, on February 22, 2022, the same day Putin announced the military action. This was a wide-ranging attack, using the complete set of Russian cyber capabilities to disrupt Ukraine.

Russia's aim was to weaken Ukraine's political will and ability to fight and collect intelligence to gain tactical, operational, and strategic advantages. Over the next several weeks, Russian actors linked to the GRU, Foreign Intelligence Service (SVR), and Federal Security Service (FSB) conducted numerous cyber attacks. Over the first month and a half of the war, more than 40 per cent of Russia's destructive cyber attacks were targeted at Ukrainian critical infrastructure sectors, while another 32 per cent were aimed at Ukrainian government sites.[1]

Attack on Viasat Inc.'s KA-SAT Satellite. Russia's most significant cyber success was Viasat Inc.'s KA-SAT satellite disruption. On the morning of February 24, 2022, California-based telecommunications company Viasat experienced widespread disruptions in Internet services and hardware located in Ukraine.

The effects were as follows:-

- The system was breached via a virtual private network. The attack rapidly spread internally and affected satellite modems.
- A command was pushed that interrupted connection to the Internet and blocked reconnection.
- The company reported, "Tens of thousands of terminals have been damaged, made inoperable and cannot be repaired."
- The communications of both the government and military were affected.
- The outage spread throughout Europe, knocking the remote monitoring of 5,800 windmills offline in Germany and removing 9,000 French customers and several thousand civilians in five other European countries from the web.

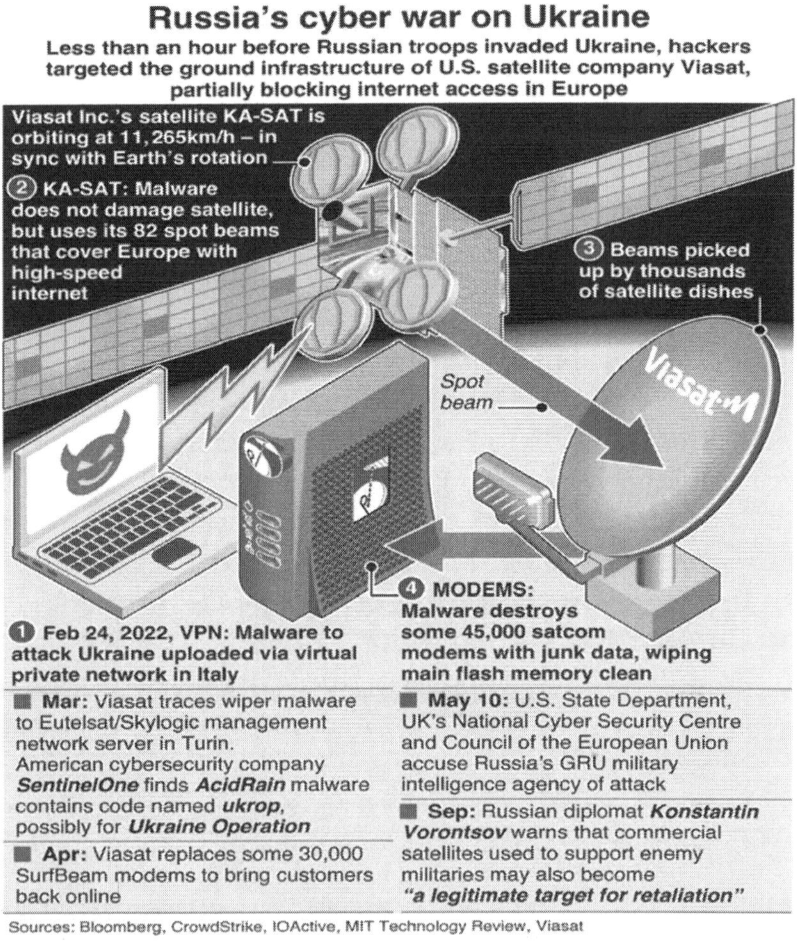

Barely an hour later, a massive column of conventional Russian forces rolled into Ukraine. The attack created a considerable loss in communications at the beginning of the war. Russia had coordinated an attack on the cyber domain to prepare a physical battlefield for a concurrent conventional attack in the first force-on-force war of the 21st century. Other cases of apparently coordinated cyber and kinetic operations include Russia's targeting of the networks of Ukraine's state nuclear power company, Energoatom, before the occupation of the Zaporizhzhia power plant that the company operates and kinetic strikes and cyber attacks against Ukrainian power company DTEK in July 2022.

However, some experts have suggested that the kinetic and cyber components of these attacks were neither coordinated nor served the same objective. Russia did not use cyber attacks for strategic military objectives. The military impact on the Viasat satellite networks is not clear. Military communications did not rely only on the Viasat networks. There were other means of military communication within the country.[2]

Tactics. Initially, Russia concentrated on launching attacks against civilian infrastructure in the region, on the assumption that the war would be short-term. Russian offensive cyber operations have failed to blind the Ukrainian command-and-control set-up or threaten critical infrastructure for a long period and undermine Ukraine's ability or will to fight. Russia has since changed its cyber warfare strategy to shift its priorities, the main features being as follows:[3]

- Russian cyber units now focus on Ukrainian military objectives rather than on strategic civilian targets.
- Russian operatives are targeting military computers and mobiles in particular.
- The devices used by Ukrainian soldiers are being hacked.
- Social engineering attacks are being perpetrated to penetrate Ukrainian command and control systems.
- Compromising placement of webcams in population centres to locate Ukrainian military equipment is being undertaken.

Organisation. Russia does not have a cyber command. The Presidential Administration and the Security Council coordinate cyber operations, but they are not a proper cyber command. Russia expands its cyber capabilities under the GRU, SVR, and FSB. It is likely that Russian organisations, like the GRU, including GRU Unit 26165, or the 85th Main Special Service Center, will recruit additional personnel, build new infrastructure, and increase their offensive cyber activities.

Ukraine's Cyber Defence

Ukraine has learned from the damaging cyber attacks carried out by Russia in 2014 and 2016. The most critical elements of Ukrainian cyber defence are: preparation and hardening of likely targets, partnerships and assistance from foreign cyber actors, and rapid reaction to nullify attacks detected by monitoring critical networks. The main features of Ukraine's cyber defences are:

- Ukrainian agencies played the leading role in defence, but defence did not rely entirely on governmental or Ukrainian assets. It developed relationships and integrated partners during planning and exercises well before any attack.
- Ukraine had a network of partners in governments and companies who could provide training and assistance, including remote monitoring and mitigation, before the invasion and after it began. Tech companies provided invaluable assistance.
- Collective action that combined national and foreign, government and private, gave Ukraine an advantage in monitoring and in rapid reaction to block attacks and repair or eliminate vulnerabilities.

Cyber Defence Measures

Data Security. On February 17, 2022, a week before the Russian invasion, Ukraine's Parliament amended its data protection law to permit government data to be transferred to the cloud, allowing critical government data to be moved into data centres outside the nation. The government, working with Microsoft Cloud, executed a substantial logistical feat of backing up critical data and moving it outside of Ukraine. Amazon supplied Ukraine with "snowball" devices and suitcase-sized computer storage units to help store and transfer data, including the country's land registries. By December 2022, it had helped move some 10 petabytes of data to the cloud. By preserving the integrity of that data, the Ukrainian government preserved its ability to operate and deliver basic services after the Russian invasion. The attacking of Microsoft's data centres located in the USA by Russia is a different ball game altogether.

Partnerships. Ukraine works closely with partners, such as the U.S., the U.K., the EU, and NATO. Throughout 2021, U.S. cyber-security experts and non-profit Civilian Research & Development Foundation Global (CRDF Global) worked with Ukraine's government to draft its national cyber-security strategy. These partners have continued supporting Ukrainian cyber defence during the war by helping to detect attacks and supplying equipment and software. U.S. Cyber Command and the National Security Agency provided help to the Ukrainian government. As General Paul Nakasone, Commander of U.S. Cyber Command and Director of the National Security Agency, remarked, "Coordinating with the Ukrainians in an effort to help them harden their networks, we deployed a hunt team who sat side-by-side with our partners to gain critical insights that have increased homeland defence for both the United States and Ukraine."

Role of Foreign Companies. Ukraine, assisted by Western governments and commercial firms, has demonstrated that collective cyber defence has proven stronger than offensive cyber capabilities. Cyber-security companies, such as Microsoft, Bitdefender, CrowdStrike, and Vectra AI, have enhanced Ukraine's defensive capabilities. They have extended their support to Ukraine to combat Russian ransomware, wipers, spear-phishing, and distributed denial of service (DDoS) attacks. Microsoft provided the following support:[4]

- It established a secure communication link with Ukrainian cyber officials to deliver real-time threat information and offer technical support.
- In January 2022, the Microsoft Threat Intelligence Center recognised wiper malware in over a dozen Ukrainian networks and alerted the Ukrainian government.
- Microsoft worked with Ukrainian government officials to allow controlled folder access, a Microsoft Defender feature, and assisted Ukraine run endpoint detection and response solutions.

Role of Other Technology Giants. Many high-technology concerns have helped Ukrainian cyber defence, providing software to protect against intrusion and sharing information about detected attacks. Google provided access to its free Project Shield software, contributing to an effective cyber canopy that defends Ukraine's websites from attacks. The CRDF Global turned into a platform for the Cyber Defence Assistance Collaborative, an extensive network of U.S. companies and organisations, which helped coordinate many of these efforts alongside the Ukrainian government and critical infrastructure entities.

SpaceX-Starlink. When Viasat was made non-functional by a Russian cyber attack, Ukraine requested Elon Musk for help. Elon Musk's company, SpaceX activated Starlink, a satellite internet group that provides high-speed, low-latency broadband internet using advanced satellites in low- Earth orbit. Elon Musk sent additional network terminals, including over 10,000 dish antennae, to Ukraine. Starlink aided the Ukrainian military to carry out sophisticated intelligence collection and fire support operations against Russian sites. It helped nullify Russia's effort to block the Internet, jam signals, and undermine Ukrainian command and control capabilities. SpaceX's rapid software updates on over 2,000 operational Starlink satellites demonstrated remarkable speed in fending off Russia's cyber attack, a feat that one Pentagon official called "eye-watering".

IT Army of Ukraine. Mykhailo Fedorov, Ukraine's Vice Prime Minister and Minister of Digital Transformation, on February 26, 2022, created the 'IT Army of Ukraine' group. He sent a link to the new group on the chat app, Telegram. Within no time, the Telegram group had grown to almost 300,000 members. The IT Army of Ukraine has mobilised thousands of volunteers to launch high-profile cyber attacks against Russian targets. It has transformed an ad-hoc force of volunteers into a tightly organised operation, with support from Ukrainian government officials, thousands of international participants and industry-leading tools. The hybrid structure of the IT Army is a combination of the operational efficiency of a structured government agency and the versatility of a volunteer force. The IT Army of Ukraine has carried out several high-profile attacks:

- In February 2022, the IT Army shut down the websites for the Moscow Stock Exchange and Sberbank, the largest bank in Russia.
- In October 2022, the IT Army gained access to Loesk, an electrical utility which supplies power to the Leningrad oblast, creating outages throughout the region.
- In November 2022, the IT Army attacked Gazprombank, the bank for Russia's state-owned energy company, with one Gazprom official claiming that the attackers knew the entire pool of the bank's IP addresses.

Ukraine's Cyber Attacks against Russia

While the focus is on Russian cyber operations, it should be noted that cyber attacks are distributed between Russia and Ukraine, with around 331 attacks against Russia and 636 against Ukraine as of December 2023.

In the recent offensive in Russia's Kursk region, Ukraine carried out offensive cyber operations, as detailed under:[5]

- Kursk region was hit by a massive distributed denial-of-service (DDoS) along with Ukraine's surprise cross-border incursion. The unnamed hackers targeted government and business websites and critical infrastructure services, making some of them temporarily unavailable.
- Kursk online services were hit with over 100,000 junk requests per second at the attack's peak.
- The Internet Protocol (IP) addresses involved in the incident were mainly registered in Germany and the U.K. DDoS traffic can originate from multiple sources without signifying the exact origin of the attack.
- It is not clear what hacker group was behind the attack. Well-known Ukrainian hacktivist groups and military intelligence services have not yet claimed responsibility for the incident.

Israel's Cyber Power

Israel is an acknowledged superpower in the cyber domain. Israel has repeatedly shown it can do spectacular harm to the computer networks of its adversaries. Israel's concern is that Iran has provided drones, shells, and other arms to Russia for use in Ukraine. Russia might reciprocate with cyber tools or know-how. Iranian hackers have developed a sophisticated understanding of Israel's social and political fractures, with separate messages aimed at proponents and opponents of the war.[6] 'Predatory Sparrow' is a hacking group suspected to be a front for the Israeli government. In 2021, it disrupted the rail network and petrol stations across Iran and hacked into digital billboards to display messages mocking Mr Khamenei. A follow-up in 2022 damaged three Iranian steel factories, spewing molten steel across the floor of one plant. In December, it struck again, bringing down 70 per cent of the petrol stations in Iran, declaring, "This cyber-attack comes in response to the aggression of the Islamic Republic and its proxies."

Hamas, apart from some early hacking of surveillance cameras in Israel, has been almost irrelevant as a cyber force since December 2023.

Israel has some weaknesses. The IDF finds it difficult to enforce operational security regulations. Despite clear instructions regarding use of smartphones and smartwatches, soldiers and civilians serving at sensitive security sites continue to reveal confidential information about army bases and those serving in them due to the use of smartphones and smartwatches. The information being unwittingly leaked by soldiers and officials enables the enemy to identify which of the soldiers serve at bases, collect and collate other information about them, and then target them by tracking.[7]

Analysis

Even the most advanced military cyber forces struggle to integrate cyber capabilities into conventional military operations effectively. Russia could not do it. It requires planning and waging war in the precise, intelligence-driven manner that is optimal for cyber operations.[8]

Inadequate success of Russian cyber operations could be due to the following:[9]

- *Lack of capacity.* There was unwillingness to use its full capacity in favour of strategic goals.
- *Poor strategy and planning and insufficient intelligence preparation.* Russia was not prepared to repeat sophisticated cyber operations in a long war scenario.
- *Over-burdening secrecy and mistrust that made inter-agency planning difficult.* Russian cyber and conventional forces lacked joint preparation.
- *Possible restraint* because of the potential for a catastrophic attack to escalate the conflict beyond what is intended.
- *Effective cyber defence by Ukraine.*

Cyber operations have been remarkably effective in stealing data, compromising devices and surveillance of targets. Russian cyber elements are moving closer to the front to capitalise on the short-lived tactical intelligence that the mobile devices might provide. Malicious linked devices will continue providing intercepts even when phones are disconnected, destroyed or inactive. Signal messages do not need to route through the target's phone to be delivered to a linked device. Communications will still reach Russian operators even when they may not reach the intended Ukrainian recipient. If 'a soldier from a battalion group gets captured or dies, his phone falls into the hands of the enemy, and the Russians read all the correspondence in this group for another month'. The impact of these operations can be severe. The consequences of these espionage operations can be grave. The lethal strike on Ukraine's 128th Mountain Assault Brigade in November 2023 was traced back to the penetration of a soldier's Signal account.

Mandiant research has highlighted how the GRU's Main Centre for Special Technologies (GTsST), commonly known as APT44 or Sandworm, has provided dedicated infrastructure and technical instructions to Russian ground forces so that they can exfiltrate Telegram and Signal communications from captured devices at the front. The Security Service of Ukraine (SBU) has reported on Sandworm using captured devices as a foothold to deliver malware, known as Infamous Chisel, to penetrate military networks and gather data on connected Starlink terminals and the suite of specialised applications used by the Ukrainian military.

Cyber war in Ukraine brings out the following lessons:

- Cyber war cannot destroy the enemy.
- In the absence of physical combat and violence, cyber warfare cannot provide territorial gains, which is considered one of the main objectives of most modern wars.
- It is hard to bend an adversary by relying on digital means alone.
- Strategic attacks against civilians do not contribute to war-winning objectives.
- Cyber attacks are difficult to orchestrate against thousands of systems that control modern societies' critical functions. Unlike conventional weapons, several cyber operations are target-dependent. They cannot be used indiscriminately against any system.

- With such complex attack chains, there is the risk of failure and unintentional cascade effects that could backfire on the attacker.
- Cyber attacks have not been the game-changer they had long been thought to be.

It is not that militaries shouldn't use destructive or disruptive cyber attacks to their advantage. However, until military leaders understand how to incorporate them with conventional operations effectively, they remain just another tool that some commanders will employ and others will not, depending on their faith in their effectiveness. Cyber weapons are not first-strike weapons but true multipliers on the battlefield.

Cyber operations against Ukraine did not achieve significant strategic effects in reducing Ukraine's capacity to resist. Conventional bombings were able to shut down more than 40 per cent of Ukraine's power grid. Traditional means are often quicker, cheaper, and more precise, and their outcomes are more specific and destructive than those of cyber operations.

Considerations: Cyber Warfare

Cyber attacks are best used with electronic warfare, disinformation campaigns, anti-satellite attacks, and precision-guided munitions. The objective is to degrade informational advantage and intangible assets, such as data, communications, intelligence, and weapons systems, to produce operational advantage. Cyber operations can also be used for political effect by disrupting adversary critical infrastructure to overwhelm defenders' decision-making and create social turmoil.

Planning in the cyber domain requires a whole of government and industry approach. This would require extensive joint exercises. Cyber operations are not a substitution for decisive military action. Since the effects of cyber operations are target-dependent, military planners should have contingency plans in case they fail.[10]

The importance of developing leaders and soldiers who can operate in an analogue world with only a map, compass, and commander's intent in the event of communications or satellite degradation cannot be understated.

Actions required to be taken at various levels are enumerated below:

Strategic Level

- Risk Assessment,
- Cyber-security Strategy Development,
- Cyber Threat Intelligence,
- Partnerships and Alliances.

Operational Level

- Secure Communication Networks,
- Cyber Hygiene Practices,
- Vulnerability Assessments,
- Incident Response Planning,
- Information Sharing on Cyber Threats,
- Red Team Simulations,
- Continuous Monitoring,
- Training and Cyber-security Awareness.

Tactical Level

- Secure Mobile Devices,
- Secure Wireless Communications,
- Endpoint Protection,
- Network Segmentation,
- Regular Software Updates,
- Training and Cyber-security Awareness,
- Tactical Cyber Defence Measures,
- Contingency Planning.

Considerations for India[11]

The whole range of issues, like cyber security, cyber diplomacy, capacity building, espionage, and offensive cyber operations, is too big and important for a national security portfolio not to have a dedicated senior official steering the wider national effort. Priority and allocation of resources for offensive and defensive actions should be clear. Plans should be for long, medium and short term.

A comprehensive cyber strategy should include:

- Measurement of strategic outcomes in terms of advancement of national objectives.
- Adoption of tactics that are actionable, reliable and precise on short notice and the effects are measured by direct and timely impact on digital systems of interest.
- Conduct of cross-government audits across defence, security and intelligence agencies.
- Cooperation with friendly countries. The exchange of technologies with countries like Israel, Taiwan, Japan, Australia, Ukraine, Belarus, South Africa, and Sweden should be explored.
- Continual review of the ongoing operations' effectiveness within a clear legal and ethical framework.
- Clear signals to adversaries, both state and non-state actors and cyber-criminals, about punitive actions by the government should they transgress boundaries.

The role of the armed forces in protecting critical information infrastructure, including the private sector, should be clearly defined to prepare for any call to the aid of civil authorities in case of cyber calamity. The armed forces should:

- Develop theories of cyber operations at strategic, operational and tactical levels.
- Define rules of engagement for armed conflicts.
- Develop and implement professional development courses to build leaders and elite forces in the cyber branches of all services.
- Coordinate within the services and integrate cyber operations and related activities.
- Establish a Centre of Excellence (CoE) for cyber. The Indian Army already has a CoE at the Military College of Telecommunication Engineering (MCTE), Mhow.
- Extensively use cyber training ranges.
- Leverage appropriate expertise outside the military from academia, industry and individuals to augment their cyberspace planning, operation and capability development.

- Encourage open discussion regarding the future evolution of military cyberspace in terms of tasks, authorities, and organisational structures.
- Create a mechanism to ensure that bugs are not present in the procurement of equipment and the supply chain management system.
- Lay down human resource development policies for the armed forces in the cyber domain. Drastic changes will be required to attract and retain talent in such niche technology areas.
- Create a red team to perform operations on MoD critical systems and critical infrastructure.
- Develop cyber capabilities/effects focused on the adversary's military targets, their infrastructure, operational experience and tools.
- Coordinate with MHA, Ministry of Law and intelligence agencies to review existing laws governing action in cyberspace. They should update or draft replacement language to protect own people and promote national interests in cyberspace.

Cyber operations capabilities in the tactical battle area could include the following:

- Developing theories of cyber operations at strategic, operational and tactical levels.
- Collecting intelligence by rapidly exploiting captured digital media and conducting cyberspace intelligence, surveillance and reconnaissance operations.
- Using EW systems as delivery platforms for precision cyber effects and exploiting new emerging devices.
- Countering and exploiting the adversaries' unmanned aerial systems by exploiting data feeds.
- Protecting friendly unmanned aerial systems that function in the area of operations.
- Gaining access to closed networks in or near the area of operations, including extracting and injecting data.
- Engaging in offensive social media operations.
- Developing a deliberate plan and acquisition strategy that leverages existing infrastructure and identifying where new infrastructure and tools are required.

Conclusion

Experts believe that cyber attacks are overrated. While useful for espionage and crime, they are far from being decisive in armed conflict. Cyber attacks may offer greater possibilities for surprise, but their destructive capabilities are suspect. When a missile destroys a power plant, the action and its effects can be observed. It is difficult to find out if a cyber attack has succeeded or how long the effect will remain.

Convergence of cyber capabilities with land, air, sea, and space can produce an effect greater than the sum of its parts. For that, coordinating cyber and kinetic attacks requires a high degree of planning and staff work. For offensive operations, a campaign plan should include a specific and realistic assessment of the benefits and costs of cyber operations, including the cost to intelligence collection and the political effect on both of the combatants and the external parties. This will require both reconnaissance of the target, network and weapons design (writing code for use in the attack) well before any attack, along with testing and refreshing attack tools.[12]

Recent wars have shown that while the cyber domain remains integral to modern warfare, cyber tools have not shown any dramatic kinetic impact; these have not proved to be the 'silver bullet'. Cyber operations can be more active in pre-war phases to gather intelligence and understand the enemy's systems to identify vulnerabilities and exploit them later. Once hostilities start, the phase of shaping or deterring operations is over. Cyber operations complement but are not substitutes for hard military power.[13]

Notes

1. Maj. Gen. P. K. Mallick, VSM (Retd), "War in Ukraine: Are Russia's Cyber Warfare Capabilities Overhyped," Vivekananda International Foundation, May 2, 2022. https://www.vifindia.org/article/2022/may/02/war-in-ukraine
2. Maj. Gen. P. K. Mallick, VSM (Retd), "Decoding Russia's 'Missing' Cyberwar Amid War in Ukraine," Vivekananda International Foundation, VIF Brief, May, 2022.
3. Dan Black, "Russia's Cyber Campaign Shifts to Ukraine's Frontlines," RUSI, July 22, 2024. https://rusi.org/explore-our-research/publications/commentary/russias-cyber-campaign-shifts-ukraines-frontlines
4. Seth G. Jones, "Russia's Ill-Fated Invasion of Ukraine: Lessons in Modern Warfare," CSIS, June 1, 2022. https://www.csis.org/analysis/russias-ill-fated-invasion-ukraine-lessons-modern-warfare

5. Daryna Antoniuk, "Russia's Kursk region suffers 'massive' DdoS attack amid Ukraine offensive," August 8, 2024. https://therecord.media/kursk-military-offensive-ddos-russia-ukraine?utm_medium=email&_hsenc=p2ANqtz-_9eydCGdrIIIIN_5-w2XgqTtmCgmva
6. "Iran's electronic confrontation with Israel," *The Economist*, August 15, 2024. https://www.economist.com/middle-east-and-africa/2024/08/15/irans-electronic-confrontation-with-israel
7. Omer Benjakob, "How Israeli Soldiers on Sensitive Bases Reveal Their Identity and Location," *The HAARETZ*, August 8, 2024. https://www.haaretz.com/israel-news/security-aviation/2024-08-08/ty-article/.premium/israeli-soldiers-at-sensitive-security-sites-reveal-their-identity
8. Matthias Schulze and Mika Kerttunen, "Cyber Operations in Russia's War against Ukraine," *Stiftung Wissenschaft und Politik*, *SWP*, April 17, 2023. https://www.swp-berlin.org/publikation/cyber-operations-in-russias-war-against-ukraine
9. Maj. Gen. P. K. Mallick, VSM (Retd), "War in Ukraine: Are Russia's Cyber Warfare Capabilities Overhyped," Vivekananda International Foundation, May 2, 2022. https://www.vifindia.org/article/2022/may/02/war-in-ukraine
10. Matthias Schulze and Mika Kerttunen, "Cyber Operations in Russia's War against Ukraine", *Stiftung Wissenschaft und Politik, SWP,* April 17, 2023. https://www.swp-berlin.org/10.18449/2023C23/
11. Maj. Gen. P. K. Mallick, VSM (Retd), "Cyber and Space Strategy for India," Chapter in CLAWS Book, *Military Strategy for India in the 21st Century*. Cyber and Space Strategy for India. https://drive.google.com/file/d/1tzcDdEENIiC9AX2nep7i1NOxaSOzKtCQ/view
12. James A. Lewis, "Cyber War and Ukraine," June 2022. https://csis-website-prod.s3.amazonaws.com/s3fs-public/publication/220616_Lewis_Cyber_War.pdf?S.iEKeom79Inugn YWlc ZL4r3Ljuq.ash
13. Eric Schmidt, "Ukraine Is Losing the Drone War," January 22, 2024. https://www.foreignaffairs.com/ukraine/ukraine-losing-drone-war-eric-schmidt 5/9

16. Information Warfare (IW)

Introduction

Since the beginning of human history, warfare has always had a psychological dimension. Today, people, specifically the technology-savvy younger generation, can easily be deceived and manipulated. The tactics employed by state and non-state actors have progressed to exploit the speed, reach and addictive qualities of digital platforms. They use AI-powered algorithms, micro-target populations, and the amplification of information campaigns to a great extent.

Information Warfare (IW) aims to create a narrative or propaganda among the enemy's population using various psychological operations, widely called PSYOPS. In the 21st century, access to information has become very easy because of the extensive use and availability of the Internet, which makes IW easier. Social media has become an essential facet of war and a key battleground on which the information war is fought at a never-before-seen scale, affecting how war is chronicled, experienced, and understood. Commercial satellite images have circulated information about troop movements, while smartphones have led to a proliferation of direct live-feed videos from the battlefield.

The increasing sophistication of AI-powered social-media algorithms that enable and dictate the diffusion of information online has been instrumentalised both by Ukraine and Russia. Social media platforms like X (formerly Twitter) and TikTok have emerged as primary news sources for many worldwide. In the first week of the Ukraine war, videos on TikTok with the hashtags #Ukraine and #Russia garnered over 40 billion views. This wealth of information and a significant amount of misinformation complicates an individual's ability to discern the truth.

The ability to influence information and its human dimensions are no longer limited to powerful nations and traditional news organisations. State and non-state actors are developing methods to utilise emerging technologies like deepfakes or synthetic media content—photos, videos, or audio clips—that have been digitally manipulated or fabricated to mislead and to challenge their adversaries.

In future wars, we must consider public access to satellite imagery, the ubiquity of mobile phone cameras, and communications intercepts using online services like WebSDR. These public, non-governmental sources of information weaken any effort to control the narrative while providing real intelligence advantage.[1] Secret intelligence is now publicly available.

Nations would need to plan for this battle with a wide variety of means from traditional to modern social media, and to wage it among diverse global audiences, after considering the local differences, especially between societies with 'open' and 'closed' media environments.

Conflict Narratives

Misinformation refers to false information shared without harmful intent. Disinformation involves deliberately spreading false information to deceive and cause harm or mislead. Information can be manipulated in diverse ways, contributing to the complexity and instability of the digital landscape. At the local level, state-sponsored disinformation campaigns can cynically manipulate genuine grassroots movements to sow discord. They can also be used to shape larger geopolitical narratives. Though new technologies have not fundamentally changed IW, the availability of satellite data and commercial satellite imagery has made it more difficult for disinformation campaigns to be successful. For example, the *Maxar News Bureau* released satellite imagery to global media, countering the Russian narrative that they were pulling their troops back from the border before the start of the invasion.

Use of Artificial Intelligence (AI) in IW Campaigns

AI and its sub-components, algorithms and machine learning, are powerful tools for generating and amplifying disinformation, particularly on social media channels. In addition to bots, deepfake videos that use

AI to create false images and audio of real people have circulated online throughout the Ukraine conflict. Experts have expressed concern that beyond deepfakes, AI could be leveraged for sophisticated disinformation techniques. Using techniques like Natural Language Processing (NLP), AI can produce fake social media posts, articles, and documents that are nearly indistinguishable from those made by humans.[2]

AI tools also show promise for combating disinformation. They are significantly more effective than human content moderators. The sheer volume of information uploaded to social media daily makes developing AI tools essential to accurately identify and remove disinformation. According to Facebook, 99.5 per cent of terrorist-related content removals and 98.5 per cent of fake accounts are recognised and removed mainly using AI trained with data from their content-moderation teams. Presently, AI aimed at combating disinformation on social media relies on both human and computer elements.

The current technical limitations on proactively identifying and removing false information, combined with the scale of information uploaded online, produce a challenge for restricting disinformation on social media in the Russia-Ukraine war.

IW in Ukraine[3]

Ukrainian President Volodymyr Zelenskyy gave a master class on controlling the conflict narrative. From his statement, "Ukraine will fight for its freedom against a brutal Russian regime", to squad-level TikTok videos, the messages have been well articulated and consistent. Getting the right external message out immediately has been key in sustaining Western support for sanctions. Devastated Russian helicopters and armour columns were highlighted by effective Ukrainian social media feeds. Photos, videos and memes of Russian losses and Ukrainian successes regularly appear online within hours.[4] Part of Ukraine's success in slowing Russia's early advance was its ability to muster international, mainly Western, public opinion. President Zelensky capitalised on the narrative that depicts this conflict as the fight between democracy and autocracy and made it politically costly for Western leaders to adopt any other political line than full support for Ukraine's war effort.

Russia uses disinformation and propaganda as a tool of war both domestically and within its sphere of influence and against its adversaries. Russia has spread disinformation through troll farms and bot accounts to spread its narrative of the war. During the conflict with Ukraine, Russia has undertaken massive influence campaigns targeting both Ukraine and its Western allies. As connectivity and technology continue to improve, Russia will probably refine its techniques for using operations to influence information systems and networks and for crafting narratives to impact target audiences' perceptions. At home, Russia wields strict control over the Russian information ecosystem, harshly stifling dissent and passing new legislation criminalising critique of the war.

However, the claim of Ukraine's unilateral victory in the information war early in the conflict is too narrow and Western-centric. While it is true that Ukraine managed to gain Western public opinion, Russian war narratives hit their target in places like China, India, Pakistan, Iran or South Africa, where genuine antipathy towards the West creates sympathy for Russia's cause. Outcomes of the votes on the UN resolutions condemning Russia's invasion of Ukraine and expelling it from the Human Rights Council show that about half of the world's governments aligned with Russia or at least, did not condemn Russia's actions. This was further aggravated by the escalation of the Israeli-Palestinian conflict, through which Russia was able to instrumentalise the inconsistencies felt by much of the world regarding the West's reaction to the conflict.

Use of Hardcore Intelligence for IW in the Ukraine War

The U.S. released highly classified intelligence on Russian troop movements and positions to the public about their planned aggression and telegraphed the Russian military's future moves before they occurred. This was very effective in shaping and influencing public perception. This release of intelligence was strategically more important than keeping it confined behind classification barriers. Normally, intelligence leaders would oppose vehemently the release of such sensitive intelligence as this would dry out their source of information. In very few cases, like the Cuban Crisis, 1973 Arab- Israel War and the Kargil conflict, this type of action was taken.

Individualisation of War in the Ukraine War

Advanced AI and Big Data analytics can exploit personal preferences and vulnerabilities on a grand scale, enabling actors to manipulate public opinion, sow discord and influence behaviours with unprecedented efficiency and scope. Proliferation of sensors, which collect the data that individuals leave on the Internet through everyday search, reading, watching, shopping, etc., and the speed with which AI-enabled systems can analyse vast amounts of harvested data can position militaries to micro-target individuals. In the Ukraine War, the Ukrainians have repeatedly and effectively tracked and targeted Russian military leaders.[5]

This individualisation of war will change the psychology of war. The reach of new tech-enabled systems can easily target individual combatants, leaders and even their family members. The Russians, in the initial stage of the war, targeted the family members of Ukrainian soldiers through social media and email. They sent messages to the parents that their children would face sure destruction, and they should desist from sending their children to battle. Soldiers, commanders and their families may come under constant individualised threats.

While individual targeting is not new, the scale, precision, and speed at which individuals can be targeted is new. Before the recent advances in AI, it would have been tough to use data to identify and micro-target many individuals simultaneously at such a scale.

Israel's IW in the Gaza Conflict

Since October 7, 2023, Israel has faced extensive information and propaganda attacks accompanied by organised global campaigns from government and non-governmental organisations. These efforts seek to challenge Israel's right to defend itself against terrorist attacks, portraying Hamas and Palestinians as the actual victims and Israel as the aggressor, often accusing Israel of committing war crimes against Palestine. One outcome of this situation is the emergence of the "tent intifada" phenomenon on various university campuses across the Western world, especially in the U.S. These highly violent occurrences involve students seizing university grounds and erecting protest tents, denouncing "Israel's crimes against the residents of Gaza". These protests are fuelled by fake news, disinformation, misinformation, and propaganda disseminated by Hamas, Russia, China, and Iran.

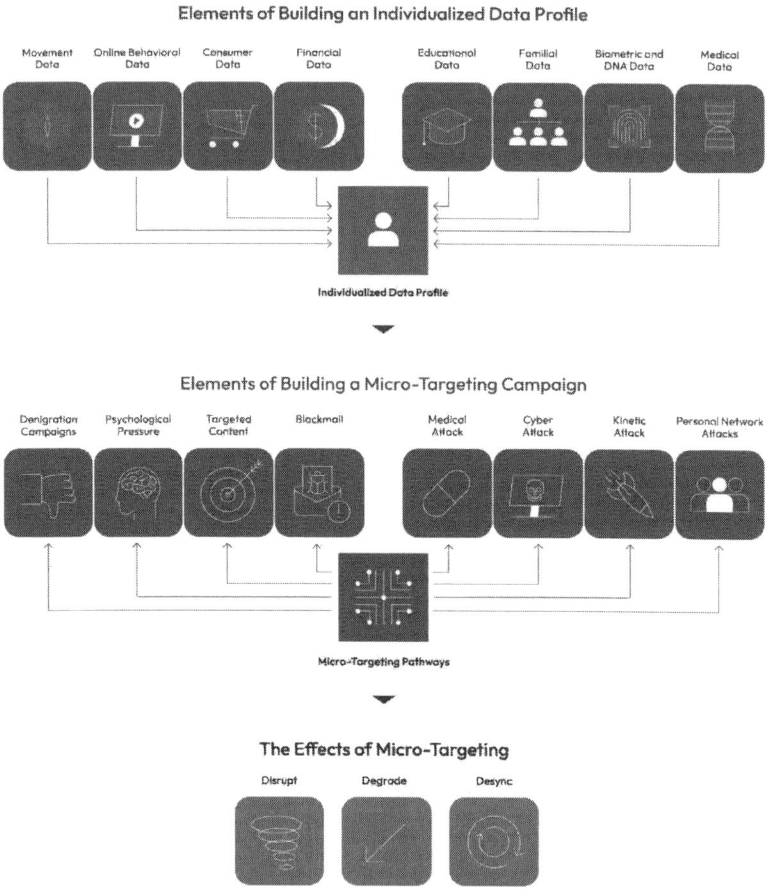

Source: https://www.scsp.ai/wp-content/uploads/2022/10/Defense-Panel-IPR-Final.pdf

Since the October 7 attack, Hamas's cognitive war against Israel has been a significant weapon. It leaves a lasting impact on the international public and has led to a surge in anti-semitism globally. Under Iran's supervision, Hamas and other terrorist groups use social and mainstream media to portray themselves as legitimate political entities and freedom fighters. This strategy shapes perceptions among various audiences, including Israelis, Palestinians, and Western political circles.

Israel's Counter-Information Operations (IO)

Since October 7, 2023, Israel has been put under widespread campaigns of disinformation, misinformation, fake news, and IO orchestrated by its adversaries in the digital media landscape. To counter this threat, Israel has activated several government ministries and agencies, including the Ministry of Foreign Affairs, the Public Diplomacy Directorate within the Prime Minister's Office, the Prime Minister's Office itself, the Israeli Defence Forces (IDF) spokesperson, the Ministry of Justice, the Ministry of Diaspora, and the Office of the President of the State.

These governmental entities employ various strategies and platforms to counter IW against Israel. Their approach includes:-

- Leveraging digital media;
- Maintaining ongoing communication with international media outlets;
- Establishing connections and briefings with influencers and public figures globally;
- Providing briefings to government officials and representatives in various countries and international organisations;
- Issuing prompt and well-substantiated responses to false reports;
- Submitting requests to social media platforms for the removal of inflammatory and false content;
- Disseminating proactive materials to counteract the tarnishing of Israel's image worldwide.

China's IW: Influence Operations[6]

The Chinese Communist Party (CCP) initially viewed social media as a threat to its regime but has since recognised its potential to shape public opinion, both domestically and internationally, in its favour. Although China restricts foreign platforms like Facebook and Twitter (now X) from operating within the country, it actively utilises these and other platforms for overt propaganda and covert cyber influence operations abroad. While these efforts have seen limited success so far, the emergence of generative artificial intelligence (AI) could significantly boost China's capabilities in the future, posing a heightened risk to global democracies.

The People's Liberation Army (PLA) has likely to have:

- Begin advancing its social media manipulation strategies;
- Show interest in using AI for social media manipulation, with some Chinese military researchers already engaged in advanced work in this field;
- With both the PLA and the broader Party-state being well-positioned, leverage generative AI and employ social bots for large-scale social media influence operations.

The PLA justifies these efforts based on its perception that the United States seeks to destabilise the CCP regime. The April 2024 restructuring of the PLA Strategic Support Force (PLASSF) could also influence China's use of AI in influence operations. Since the newly established PLA Cyber Support Force (PLACSF) will report directly to the Central Military Commission (CMC), this closer connection may result in enhanced support—such as increased resources and authority—facilitating quicker adoption of technologies like AI. Alternatively, increased scrutiny from the CMC may lead to more cautious use of such capabilities.

In 2023 and early 2024, Microsoft identified various types of generative AI content used by Chinese influence operations actors, including AI-generated anchors, specifically 'Spamouflage' (which China has employed since late 2022), as well as AI-enhanced videos and 'deepfakes', which have become more prevalent over time.[7]

Information Operations (IO)/Public Information (PI) in India

Organisation

The Ministry of External Affairs has the Public Diplomacy Division, which was established in May 2006 to "educate and influence global and domestic opinion on key policy issues and project a better image of the country commensurate with its rising international standing." The Public Diplomacy Division also partners with major domestic and international universities, think tanks and research organisations to organise seminars and conferences. The Ministry of Information and Broadcasting lends support to the public diplomacy initiative with the ministry's strategic use of the media. However, currently, this MEA organisation lies dormant and low key.

Defining the Right Terms

Currently, the Indian Armed Forces and the strategic community follow U.S. jargon rather blindly. If we want to influence people's minds across the border and the leaders of the adversary, what terminology should we use? Would it be information/influence/psychological/strategic/communications/perception management/public information operations/public field diplomacy or some other terms? These terms are being used interchangeably, but these are not synonyms. The Indian Armed Forces must coin standard terms and take appropriate actions to customise concepts, tactics, techniques, and procedures accordingly. The term 'Psychological Operations' could be used for operations across the border while 'Perception Management' might be appropriate for CI/CT Ops within the country.

Responsibilities for Conduct of IO

The most critical issue is as to who is in charge of Information/Psychological/Influence operations? In the U.K., it is the foreign ministry. In the U.S., the DoD takes the lead for the simple reason that they have got the funds. Recently, the state department is being given importance, and funds are being transferred from the Department of Defence to the state department to carry out psychological operations. However, the cyber part for content delivery is still with the DoD.

In the case of India, it is not clear who is overall responsible. The army does a good job at operational and tactical levels. However, there is no formalised mechanism. It is the personality of the commander on the ground which drives the operation. In the counter-insurgency/counter-terrorism (CI/CT) environment, the army, intelligence agencies of both central and state governments, central and local police and the paramilitary organisations, and the ministries concerned, all come together and carry out influence operations, including winning hearts and minds (WHAM) of the population. Invariably, they do a good job taking an ad-hoc approach.

For information operations, the various stakeholders are the Ministry of Home Affairs and the intelligence agencies, the Ministry of Defence, the Ministry of External Affairs, the Ministry of Information and Broadcasting, the Ministry of Electronics and Information Technology, the Ministry of Communications, the Ministry of Education, and the Ministry of Law and Justice, among others. Close coordination between these ministries will be needed to conduct information operations against an adversary. However, currently, there is no central agency to coordinate and direct such a task.

To carry out psychological operations at the strategic level, the central government has to take a whole-of-government and whole-of-society approach. The strategy has to be chalked out at the highest level. The lead agency, in Indian circumstances, should be the MHA or a specific organisation under the NSA, working within the NSCS. The National Security Council Secretariat is the appropriate agency to be made responsible for information operations, given India's notoriously stove-piped bureaucracy. The organisation should have experts in psychology, sociology, media, armed forces, political science, foreign affairs, communication, social media, language, and law besides area specialists and country experts.

Suggested Organisation and Tasks at the Apex Level

At the apex level, the establishment of a Centre for Cognitive Security may be considered, which will bring together experts working in fields, such as computer science, cognitive science, social science, engineering, political campaigning, security, marketing, public policy, and psychology, to advance a theoretical and an applied engineering methodology to manage the full spectrum of information environment and security issues. It should have close ties with government, industry, academia, think tanks, and public interest groups. It should have the following functions:

- Develop Cognitive Security strategies, policies and implementation methods;

- Assign technology objectives in support of the policies and strategies developed;
- Identify and evaluate pertinent research results and commercial technologies and develop and execute strategies for transitioning them into practice;
- Maintain a response team to coordinate with all communities to identify influence campaigns and distribute alerts and warnings.

Use of social media by our adversaries, both external and internal, has to be checked. The most obvious tool is the law. The present recent action by the government against Twitter is a case in point. IW against the armed forces threatens the morale of service personnel, command and control of forces, and relations with local people in the area of operations.

The Indian Armed Forces

India's Armed Forces and other agencies have some sort of organisation for cyber warfare. However, no such organisation exists specifically for psychological operations. The Ministry of Defence has an old organisation named the 'Directorate of Public Relations'. This is meant for the dissemination of Public Information (PI). The respective service headquarters have their organisations for PI Operations. In the army, the Additional Directorate General of Public Information (ADGPI), now renamed the ADG Strategic Communications (StratCom), comes under the Directorate General of Military Intelligence. It deals with Public Relations activities, Media Relations and Monitoring of Information Domain, Information Release, Publicity, Image Projection and Perception Management. It aims to establish conditions that lead to confidence in our army and its readiness to conduct operations in peacetime and war.

Recently, there has been some reorganisation in this field. A new post of Director General of IW has been created under the Deputy Chief of Army Staff (Strategy).[8] He will be the 'single point of advice' to the Vice Chief of Army Staff (VCOAS). He will have the Director Generals of Military Operations, Intelligence, Perspective Planning and Strategic Communication reporting to him. From the outside, an additional layer has been included in the processing chain. However, it is too early to judge the efficacy of the organisation.

Strategy and Doctrine. An integrated strategy for psychological operations, encompassing all its facets related to international, national, concerned ministries and armed forces, may be enunciated. The armed forces should then chalk out their tactics, techniques, and procedures for this operation in their respective service domain. The Indian Army should take the lead role in CI/CT Ops-infested areas.

Talent Management. There is a general shortage of talent in this critical field. It is the same for all armies of the world. We must study how others try to solve this problem and improve our system. The present system is incapable of maturing talents in critical capabilities and maintaining the talent to be competitive and win. Industry experts possess a perspective vastly different from that of government or army professionals. Sending junior officers to the industry would expose individuals to leading technology and bring their experiences and relationships back to the army. In some cases, hiring from traditional government contractors is a solution.

Intelligence Organisation. We have intelligence organisations and staff at every level. They already have well-developed doctrine and analytic processes honed over a period of time. They must be part of the IW battlefield, not fringe players. Intelligence people should also get acquainted with the requirements for an operational information environment (OIE) and provide adequate support for these operations through focused data collection, analysis, and intelligence products. Training in OIE should be formalised and expanded. Cross-functional analytic teams should be created to integrate intelligence functions better and increase IE attention.

Conclusion

The information domain and the rise of social media are here to stay. Public Affairs (PA) is now a key feature of multi-domain operations. The armed forces cannot and should not cede ground in that domain. Collection and dissemination of information and countering misinformation are deliberate professional activities. These are but military operations in the information domain and should be regarded with a big-picture, operational approach.

Notes

1. James Andrew Lewis, "Cyber War and Ukraine," CSIS, June 16, 2022. https://www.csis.org/analysis/cyber-war-and-ukraine
2. Christian Perez and Anjana Nair, "Information Warfare in Russia's War in Ukraine," *Foreign Policy.* https://foreignpolicy.com/2022/08/22/information-warfare-in-russias-war-in-ukraine/?tpcc=recirc_trending062921
3. Maj. Gen. P. K. Mallick, VSM (Retd), "Ukraine is Winning the Information War Against Russia on Social Media: But Experts Say It Is Far From Over!!", *CLAWS*, March 2022.
4. Lt. Col. John Q. Bolton, U.S. Army, "The More Things Change ... Russia's War in Ukraine Mirrors the Past as Much as It Shows the Future," *Military Review Online Exclusive*, July 2023. https://www.armyupress.army.mil/Portals/7/military-review/Archives/English/Online-Exclusive/2023/The-More-Things-Change/Bolton-AWC-Ukraine-Observations-UA.pdf
5. Mykhaylo Zabrodskyi, Jack Watling, Oleksandr V. Danylyuk, and Nick Reynolds, "Preliminary Lessons in Conventional Warfighting from Russia's Invasion of Ukraine: February–July 2022," RUSI, November 30, 2022. https://static.rusi.org/359-SR-Ukraine-Preliminary-Lessons-Feb-July-2022-web-final.pdf
6. Maj. Gen. P. K. Mallick, VSM (Retd), "China's Cyber-Influence Operations," Vivekananda International Foundation, VIF Paper, May 2021.
7. Microsoft Threat Intelligence, 2024.
8. Manvendra Singh, "Army has a new head of information warfare. But first, stop hiding facts from Indians," *The Print*, December 07, 2020. https://theprint.in/opinion/army-has-new-head-of-information-warfare-but-stop-hiding-facts-from-indians/561524/

17. Electronic Warfare (EW)

Introduction

Electronic warfare (EW) has been a component of military operations since the introduction of the radio at the beginning of the 20th century. EW is the use of electromagnetic (EM) energy to control the electromagnetic spectrum (EMS)—range of frequencies of electromagnetic energy—in own favour. EW supports command and control (C2) by allowing military commanders' access to the spectrum to communicate with forces, while preventing potential adversaries from accessing the spectrum to develop an operational picture and communicate with their forces.[1]

EMS is at the heart of modern military operations and the essential link between the land, air, naval, space, and cyber domains. Since the advent of two-way radios, militaries have become dependent on the spectrum. Modern militaries require access to the electromagnetic (EM) spectrum for all operations. This reliance has extended over the past century to include nearly every weapon system. Applications of EMS include:

- Radio frequencies to communicate with friendly forces
- Microwaves for tactical data links, radars, and satellite communications;
- Infrared for intelligence and to target enemies;
- Lasers across the entire spectrum to transmit data, communicate and potentially destroy a target.

Management of the Electromagnetic Spectrum (EMS)

EMS comprises all man-made and naturally occurring electromagnetic energy, arranged according to wavelength and frequency from zero to infinity. Common bands include radio waves, infrared (IR) radiation, visible light, ultraviolet radiation, x-rays, and gamma rays. It consists of all EM radiation from below the Earth's surface (e.g., extremely low-frequency radio to communicate with submarines) and continuing deep into space (e.g., X-band communications with deep space probes).

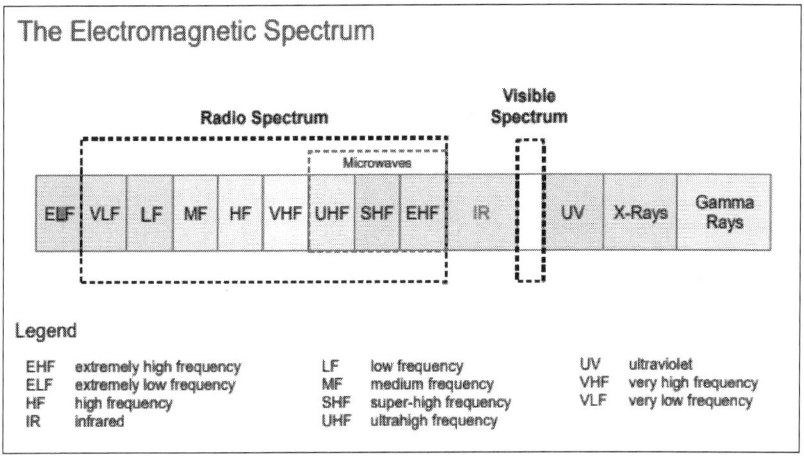

EMS is physical, pervasive, congested, constrained, contested, and dynamic. One of the main causes of congestion in EMS is its extensive use for commercial and non-commercial civilian applications. This general interest in exploiting EMS has led to increased densification of transmitting systems, mainly in the frequency bands between 500MHz and 10GHz. Some bands, for example, the 2 to 4GHz band, are particularly congested with developing technologies, such as Bluetooth, Wifi, WiMax, 4G networks, and 5G. This situation leads to many complications that affect military systems, as given below:

- Competition between private companies and state agencies;
- Inter-system interference;
- Increasingly complex management of this resource.

Confronted with the economic and social stakes of these civilian needs, the political leadership is increasingly asking military authorities to accept compromises like reducing or abandoning frequency bands or finding technical solutions to enable these developments for the public. Developments in high-speed communications, Internet of

visible light, ultraviolet radiation, x-rays, and gamma rays. It consists of all EM radiation from below the Earth's surface (e.g., extremely low-frequency radio to communicate with submarines) and continuing deep into space (e.g., X-band communications with deep space probes).

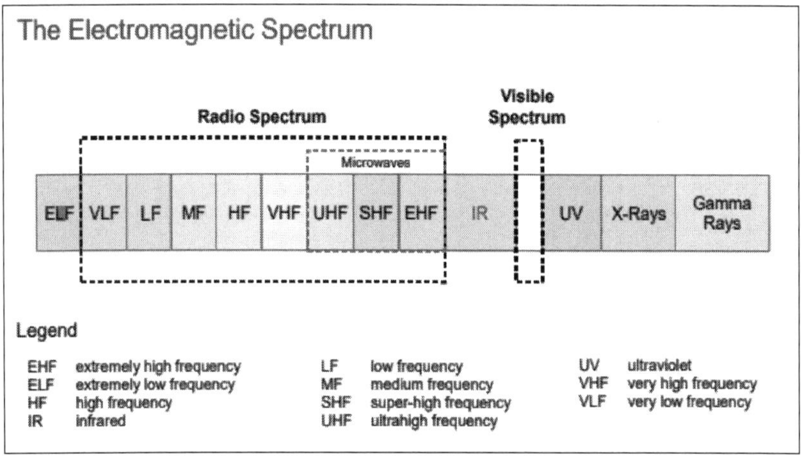

EMS is physical, pervasive, congested, constrained, contested, and dynamic. One of the main causes of congestion in EMS is its extensive use for commercial and non-commercial civilian applications. This general interest in exploiting EMS has led to increased densification of transmitting systems, mainly in the frequency bands between 500MHz and 10GHz. Some bands, for example, the 2 to 4GHz band, are particularly congested with developing technologies, such as Bluetooth, Wifi, WiMax, 4G networks, and 5G. This situation leads to many complications that affect military systems, as given below:

- Competition between private companies and state agencies;
- Inter-system interference;
- Increasingly complex management of this resource.

Confronted with the economic and social stakes of these civilian needs, the political leadership is increasingly asking military authorities to accept compromises like reducing or abandoning frequency bands or finding technical solutions to enable these developments for the public. Developments in high-speed communications, Internet of

Some more actions can be taken to mitigate this growing risk:

- Adapting the existing EMS military systems by employing waveforms that allow coexistence with public systems using the same frequency bands;
- Improving collaboration with political and civil actors to defend military interests directly within the decision-making body for frequency band allocation and management;
- Encouraging the development of future capabilities that are increasingly flexible in terms of waveform and frequency band;
- Reviewing the Electromagnetic Battle Management (EMBM) tools to ensure compatibility with this modern environment. This will require better interoperability between systems.

Russia's Application of EW

Russia's EW capabilities are among the most advanced internationally. Developed over decades, Russia has consistently prioritised the improvement of EW technologies and their integration into the broader military strategies. Its new, more agile EW doctrine was not devised in isolation. It was designed to deliver its full potential in hybrid warfare. The Ukrainian Donbass conflict of 2014-2015 proved its effectiveness.

Russia has invested heavily in EW systems capable of shutting down communications and signals across a broad spectrum. This ability is grouped under the concept of the Radio Electronic Battery.[2] Within the Russian Army, maximum investments were made in jammers and SIGINT capabilities. Deployed in Syria and Ukraine, these systems have proved their worth in gaining complete control of GSM networks, giving an offensive jamming and self-protection capability at the lowest tactical level and countering the ground-to-air threat by distorting encrypted data of aircraft location.

The Russian Concept of Electronic Warfare

Over the preceding few years, Russia had developed EW systems capable of shutting down the adversary's modern systems of communications and signals. The ongoing conflict in Ukraine serves as a clear example of the formidable nature of Russia's EW, demonstrating its ability to neutralise even the advanced NATO-supplied systems. Russia had invested heavily in new EW vehicles a decade ago and battle-tested many in Ukraine in 2014 and Syria in 2015. Russian forces have instituted an integrated system that employs a mix of electronic warfare, missile systems, and connected sensors to degrade Ukrainian use of drones and loitering munitions.

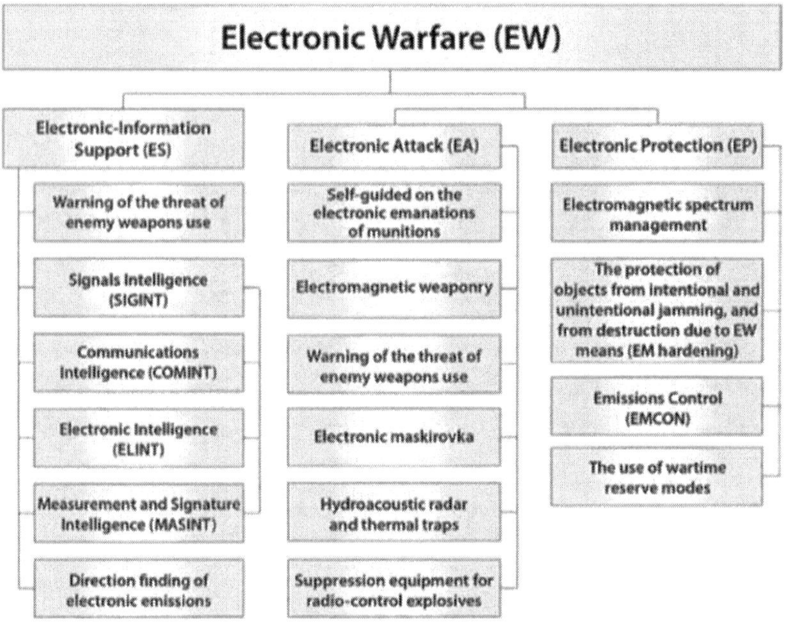

Source: Dr. Lester W. Grau and Charles K. Bartles, *The Russian Way of War; Force Structure, Tactics and Modernisation of the Russian Ground Force*, FMSO: Kansas, Fort Leavenworth, 2016, p. 290.

Russia's EW in Ukraine

Russia has saturated the battlefield of Ukraine with EW. Truck-mounted EW systems, mainly focused on jamming drones, are located every six to nine miles on Ukraine's frontline.

During the opening phase of the war, Russian forces failed to conduct effective EW. Unencrypted Russian communications provided Ukraine with a wealth of intelligence. Initially, the Russian jets found that their communications, navigation, and radar were all disrupted and, in some cases, knocked out. Only after deploying three of its five EW brigades into the theatre did Russian forces effectively use EW. In the early morning of February 24, 2022, Russia jammed Ukrainian air defence radar across all frequency bands. Russian E95M UAVs, which simulated Russian aircraft, exposed the Ukrainian air defences. As the lines stabilised in the east, Russian EW was credited with most of the kills.

The reasons for Russia not being able to effectively conduct EW to its full capacity are as follows:

- There was confusion caused by a lack of planning time when many Russian EW systems were kept off, leading to fratricide and poor command coordination. Russian forces faced numerous command and control problems, including a lack of secure communications, undermining their ability to synchronise and coordinate attacks.
- Russia was unwilling to push sensitive EW systems into Ukraine, in case these were captured.
- Russian soldiers frequently used unencrypted communications, including civilian cell phones, which allowed Ukrainian intelligence and military units to target them.

Subsequently, the Russian forces have been able to pinpoint Ukrainian headquarters, cut the link between drones and their operators, find drone operator stations, and jam or degrade the effectiveness of Ukraine's drones and precision weapons. The Russian side has learned from these successes and scaled-up its EW capabilities by focusing on increased industrial production of EW equipment. Russia has leveraged a traditional strength in EW systems and improved these through collaboration with its strategic defence industry. Russia's signals intelligence (SIGINT) systems have also become proficient in intercepting and decrypting signals, even from Motorola radios using 256-bit encryption. These can also jam Motorola radios to a depth of six miles from the frontline. Russia's military employs eight specialised Mi-17 helicopters to conduct longer-range jamming.

Russia increasingly uses a technique to generate many fake drone signatures for the enemy sensors to detect. This technique may be used to shield the real drones from fire or cause Ukrainian troops to waste valuable missiles shooting at the ghosts.

Russian forces have also integrated at least one counter-drone system, typically a drone jammer gun, into every Russian platoon. Such weapons may become a standard attachment to even small combat units.

Russia's EW Capabilities

Russia's strength is in its ground-based EW systems, which have proven highly effective in Ukraine in countering close-air support operations and disrupting large-scale UAV attacks. Some of these are:

The Krasukha-4. With an effective range of up to 300 km, it has demonstrated its ability to jam radar signals from NATO-supplied systems like the AN/TPQ-36 Firefinder and AN/TPQ-37 counter-battery radars, rendering them obsolete.

Shipovnik-Aero. A truck-mounted jamming system optimised for targeting UAVs and capable of suppressing a range of communications networks, Shipovnik-Aero provided a more active layer in the Russian EW defence architecture. The system has a range of 15 km. It takes approximately 25 seconds to analyse the control frequencies of newly encountered UAVs and around two seconds to reconfirm the control frequencies of previously encountered UAVs. It then jams the command frequency.

TORN-MDM Signals Intelligence Vehicle. It is capable of direction-finding and triangulating tactical communications within a radius of between 30 and 70 km, depending on frequency. This system can also record and analyse communications. Motorola radios used extensively by Ukrainian forces are susceptible to jamming.

Leer-3 EW Payloads. This payload is mounted on Orlan-10 UAVs to target cell phone networks. While widely employed, the effect of these systems has been limited by their protracted employment over the past eight years in Donbas so that Ukrainian forces are familiar with the system's risks and have effective countermeasures.

1RL257. It has proven more effective in the preparatory jamming of radar and other defensive systems in preparation for large-scale artillery or air strikes.

Weaknesses Observed in Russia's EW

Satellite Communication. Ukrainian forces have maintained reliable satellite connections across tactical formations, courtesy Starlink satellites. Russia has not been able to close that option.

Lack of Training and Expertise. The sinking of the Russian warship *Moskva*, the Russian Air Force's inability to achieve air superiority against an adversary with far fewer combat aircraft and continued logistics failures show a glaring lack of training and expertise.

Command and Control Issues. Significant weaknesses in command and control multiplied Russia's inability to gain control of the air. Lack of planning and preparedness and issues with encryption key distribution has forced many units to use civilian handheld radios and mobile phones instead of secure, jam-resistant tactical radios. Ukrainian EW forces exploited these weaknesses by eavesdropping on Russia's unencrypted transmissions, jamming their communications, and targeting by using direction-finding techniques. These issues adversely affected Russia's ability to conduct joint air and land operations and to make real-time tactical decisions on the battlefield. The failure to de-conflict EW activities with the rest of their operations has also led to fratricides. The resultant confusion and disruption caused by this electronic fratricide led Russia to scale back its electronic attack efforts, thus enabling Ukrainian Ground Based Air Defence (GBAD) to become more effective.

Ukraine's EW

If Ukraine has to defeat Russian fires through a combination of range and precision, its armed forces would need a kill chain that can identify and communicate the position of Russian targets. Reconnaissance teams, UAVs, or electronic direction finding can deliver this. All these methods, however, are affected by Russia's EW complexes, which are integral to Russian concepts of operation. It is essential to assess how these means are being used by Ukraine, their limitations, and where they present tactical challenges that must be overcome.[3]

Ukrainian Forces are using Portable Counter-drone Jammers like this one supplied by the U.S.

Source: US DOD.

Ukraine finds that Russian direction finding is extremely capable, and where it is not possible for Russia to suppress Ukrainian UAVs, it often targets the ground control stations. Due to the measures adopted by Russian EW forces, the lifespan of Ukrainian UAVs is approximately seven days. Yet, Russia's EW has not been able to stop Ukrainian communications and deny them access to the electromagnetic spectrum. However, it is disrupting, diverting, slowing down the kill chains, and imposing significant limitations on Ukraine's reconnaissance in depth. As long-range strikes depend on precision systems, Russian EW is a critical obstacle to Ukrainian forces' performance.

In Ukraine, the war of drones versus jammers has been a constant arms race of upgrades as each move to evade jammed frequencies is countered by new jammers. The Ukraine Army has been able to bring down Russia's screen of aircraft-type reconnaissance drones, effectively blinding the latter's commanders to what was happening. This may have been done by the new interceptor FPVs linked to air-defence radar. Then, under the cover of a temporary observation blackout, Ukraine's short-range jammers were brought forward to the frontline. These were programmed with data previously obtained from EW reconnaissance. According to a Russian blogger, "They discovered the main frequencies of our border radio communication networks and drone control frequencies, and deployed powerful jammers to crush our communications." This could also have been possible because the Russians might have considered some areas as low priority and not supplied these with the latest equipment.

Ukraine has distributed its EW capabilities across the forces to provide dedicated support on critical axes. But there had been insufficient training to employ these troops suitably. The Ukraine Armed Forces (UAF) has, therefore, formed a Cyber and Electromagnetic Activities Command to manage capability development, electronic payload preparation and delivery, force protection, and direction finding.

Developments in Kursk

The Ukraine Army launched a stunning offensive into Kursk, Russia, starting on August 6, 2024. This rapid Ukrainian advance, pushing deep into the enemy territory and threatening the city of Kursk, had taken Russia as well as the Western analysts by surprise. While it is difficult to tell what exactly is happening, success seems to have been achieved by Ukraine's mastery of a new style of warfare.

In Kursk, the Ukrainians took advantage of their technical knowledge to gain a lead in battlefield tactics. Using various electronic sensing systems, they figured out the critical Russian radio frequencies along the invasion route. They jammed these frequencies, creating a series of 'electronic bubbles' that kept enemy drones away from their forces, thus allowing their reconnaissance units, tanks, and mechanised infantry to breach the Russian border, mostly undetected. This is a glimpse of the chaotic ways of modern combat—a choreography of lightweight, unmanned systems driven by a spider web of electronic signals.

Observations

Doctrine. Technology development and equipment acquisition are equally important. Cyber and electromagnetic activities cannot be an afterthought; they must be tightly woven into joint force plans.

Training

- For a contested electromagnetic environment, training is critical for leaders. Developing and maintaining resilient systems with operators capable of rapidly reacting to evolving enemy threats would allow forces to maintain technological superiority.
- If the soldiers accustomed to using a particular EW system find that the enemy degrades the system, they must be prepared to function in the blind.
- In the event of degraded or compromised communications or satellites, the soldiers must be capable of operating across a dispersed and tactical footprint in an analogue world with only a map, compass, and the commander's intent.

Frequency Management. This crucial issue does not get the necessary importance it deserves. The following factors need to be taken into account:

- The number of systems communicating is increasing. EMS is becoming crowded.
- Forces cannot accept loss of communications. In defence, ground-laid cable and other primitive methods can be used to limit signal traffic, signature, and vulnerability. In an offensive, these are not viable options.
- Without careful frequency management, forces are liable to engage in widespread fratricide in the EMS, including degrading the efficiency and survivability of their own UAVs. This may cause commanders to limit electronic protection to their forces, thus giving freedom to enemy ISR and fires.
- Russian forces would reset their frequencies every 24 hours, deconflicting UAV orbits and would synchronise EW with the manoeuvre.

Updating of Systems. Having a technological advantage requires the ability to rapidly update systems on the battlefield.

Electronic Protection. Because of precision fires, all units require electronic protection. Offensive formations should be able to create electronic barriers. Since sub-units are unlikely to have dedicated air defence, systems must be multifunctional and able to engage small aerial targets. Electronic protection is at risk if kept on a small number of dedicated platforms. Instead, electronic protection modules must be programmable, relatively autonomous, and widely distributed.

Use of Smartphones. Smartphones are now ubiquitous in operations. Soldiers do not want to part with them, even when engaged in battle. Through their electromagnetic signature, smartphone transmitters can betray a unit's nature, volume, and position. In 2014, during the Donbas conflict, a Ukrainian artillery battalion was destroyed within fifteen minutes by Russian counter-battery fire. The unit's location was given out by an application installed on the smartphones of the unit's soldiers. Protection against electromagnetic attacks is not a matter for specialists. It is the responsibility of each soldier and requires individual discipline and awareness to reduce collective vulnerabilities.

Resilience. In March 2022, when Russia jammed a Starlink network, SpaceX immediately responded with additional code that broke the jamming within 24 hours. This resilience, rapid reaction, and civil-military partnership across the cyber domain and the electromagnetic spectrum will be critical for military satellites during war.

Cost. Ukraine and Russia have learned that uncrewed systems can cost their forces considerably. Armed forces require a new generation of cheaper counter-autonomy systems that can be deployed widely. The aim should be for the next generation of counter-autonomy approaches to be generally equal to or cheaper than the uncrewed systems they face. Militaries that master this combination will be successful in future conflicts; those that don't will suffer extreme attrition.

Considerations for India

A SWOT analysis of India's EW systems shows significant capability requirements in the fields of EM spectrum denial, quantum technology, and AI/ML.

EW Capabilities. India's defence R&D expenditure is about three per cent of the defence budget, and its Research & Development (R&D) capabilities in the EW domain are limited. At present, India is importing substantial parts of EW hardware. With the combination of Defence Public Sector Undertakings (DPSU), Micro, Small & Medium

Enterprises (MSME), and start-ups active in this domain, India can innovate the development of EW systems. However, the following capabilities are required:

- Self-reliance in the production of electronics and hardware. Enhancing operational efficiencies by building the next-generation AI/ML-enabled EW products;
- Increased focus on R&D for non-kinetic technologies;
- Attraction, retention, and focus on talent development and upskilling;
- Establishment of shared infrastructure;
- Forming alliances with other countries and between industry and academia in India and abroad to develop capabilities to limit the adversaries from using the EM spectrum;
- Enabling widespread development and adoption of quantum computing that will create a new generation of satellites, radars, and communication systems, which can render even the most modern EW systems redundant.

These capabilities will address the demands of defence systems by providing advanced functionalities, such as spoofing, jamming, and deception and help advance nano-electronics.

Doctrines and Concepts. India may formalise her EW doctrines, consolidate the capabilities, and re-align the organisational culture. The critical steps for implementing doctrine-level reforms are as follows:-

- Adaptation of military doctrines and concepts for non-kinetic operations, increasing the lethality of weapon systems, and tightening the OODA loop;
- Strengthen the organisational structure and realign its culture to address norms, behaviour, leadership, and innovation to leverage non-kinetic means in future warfare across all levels and formations;
- Consolidation of cyber and IT capabilities through capability and competency-based training and education. Beyond the doctrinal and technological development, the ability to win in a contested Electromagnetic Environment (EME) will rest on how well troops have prepared for it through training and drilling.[4]

R&D.[5] India needs to build an R&D strategy and revise R&D institutional structures to make them more dynamic and efficient, supported by mixed funding models for increasing investments in start-ups, academia, and CoEs. Developed countries spend around 10–13 per cent of their defence budget on R&D.

Notes

1. "Defense Primer: Electronic Warfare," Congressional Research Service (CRS), November 14, 2022. https://crsreports.congress.gov/product/pdf/IF/IF11118
2. Seth G. Jones, "Russia's Ill-Fated Invasion of Ukraine: Lessons in Modern Warfare," *CSIS Briefs*, June 1, 2022. https://www.csis.org/analysis/russias-ill-fated-invasion-ukraine-lessons-modern-warfare
3. Greg Waldron, "Russia poses tough EW problem for Ukrainian UAVs: RUSI," FlightGlobal, July 7, 2022. https://www.flightglobal.com/military-uavs/russia-poses-tough-ew-problem-for-ukrainian-uavs-rusi/149311.article
4. "Modern Electromagnetic Spectrum Battlefield," National Defense University Press News Article View. https://ndupress.ndu.edu/Media/News/News-Article-View/Article/2846737/modern-electromagnetic-spectrum-battlefield/
5. "A roadmap for making India a leader in non-kinetic warfare solutions," PWC Report, December 2023.

18. Command, Control, Communications, Computers, Intelligence, Surveillance and Reconnaissance (C4ISR)

Introduction

The modern battlefield is growing progressively more transparent because of the proliferation of advanced technologies like smart devices, sensors, emitters, etc. and the emergence of hyper-connected global communications and social media. The following technologies are improving the surveillance mechanisms of the battlefield:-

- Long-range sensors from surveillance planes and medium and high-altitude drones are now equipped with much higher levels of resolution and image fidelity, allowing them to zoom in closely and gather precise data from extraordinary distances.
- Drone swarms are multiplying exponentially with the specific aim of blanketing areas with surveillance, overwhelming enemy air defences, and launching suicide strikes.
- Low and Medium-Earth Orbit satellites are emerging by the hundreds to bring about additional surveillance, imagery, throughput, and networking.

Battlefield Transparency

The modern battlefield is becoming increasingly transparent due to advanced technologies of modern sensors, a plethora of modern smart devices, wide ambit of social media and accessibility to global communications. Historically, high-quality targeting and surveillance were reserved for well-resourced states, but now even lesser actors can use commercial technologies to locate and strike high-value targets. For example, Ukraine successfully targeted Russian forces by exploiting unauthorised cell phone signals, including a rocket attack that killed 63 personnel.

Technological growth in areas like the Internet of Things, commercial space platforms, and autonomous systems will further increase battlefield transparency. Nations with advanced command, control, and surveillance capabilities will leverage commercial off-the-shelf technologies, open-source data, and artificial intelligence to make the battlefield more transparent.

Personal devices and social media can reveal troop locations and operations, enabling adversaries to quickly refine targeting using data from unmanned aerial systems (UAS) and other sources. Warfare is becoming a contest between "hiders" and "finders", with fleeting opportunities to strike. The ability to protect forces and hide in plain sight is crucial for survival, especially as modern weapons grow more precise and powerful.

Thousands of unmanned ground, air, and surface platforms, robots, sensors, and vehicles will likely span across a multi-domain war zone, leaving nowhere for the forces to hide from view. Advanced high-tech heat sensors will detect thermal signatures through heavy vegetation and weather hiding. The secure networking of surveillance data and image collection will allow high-speed data transfer from inside buildings, behind ridges, across mountains, or in many otherwise undetectable locations.[1] The ability to hide takes on even greater importance with the mass and precision of modern weapons systems.

A large concern is that advanced, AI-enabled computer algorithms have become capable of processing and analysing massive pools of incoming sensor data to identify moments and objects of great relevance.[2] The process of gathering, analysing, processing, exploiting, and disseminating information, called PED, is becoming faster, more efficient, multi-domain, and ubiquitous.

Battlefield Surveillance

Ukrainian forces have gained access to pervasive surveillance primarily due to their employment of commercial satellites and drones. *Maxar* has been providing imagery to the U.S. government for over two decades and others for the past few years.[3] The main features of this pervasive surveillance are as follows:-

- By December, Ukraine could tap into the roughly 40 commercial satellites a day that pass over the area in 24 hours.
- Ukraine and other countries can tap into more than a dozen companies competing to provide ever faster, more precise multispectral products to commercial customers and real-time transparency to a global audience.
- Several companies now offer interpreted Synthetic Aperture Radar (SAR) imagery of any point on Earth on demand at least every six hours to see through the darkness, cloud cover, and light foliage.
- Soon, a satellite formation will be able to locate a specific radio frequency signature with an accuracy of three km every twenty minutes.
- Earth observation from space-based visual, infrared, radar, and electromagnetic sensors is available virtually continuously. Companies have also developed the 'change detection' software.

Ukraine exemplifies this shift by forming the world's first UAV strike companies. These units, using both commercial and military drones, enhance surveillance and targeting capabilities, helping Ukraine to effectively counter the Russian forces. Ukraine's Ministry of Digital Transformation started training civilian drone operators in flying and hiding skills. Using both off-the-shelf drones and U.S.-supplied military unmanned aerial vehicles, this Army of Drones would deploy on the battlefield to boost surveillance and targeting of Russian assets. As stated, modern armies can now fly drones instead of having to send out personnel every time to do the reconnaissance, and gain near-perfect situational awareness. Then depending on the target profile, they can fix the targets to neutralise with long-range missiles, modern High Mobility Artillery Rocket Systems, armed drones, and fighter aircraft.

Command & Control

The Russia-Ukraine War revealed that the electromagnetic signature emitted from the command posts cannot survive against the pace and precision of an adversary that possesses unmanned aerial systems, sensor-based technologies, and Electronic Warfare (EW) and has access to satellite imagery. Resultantly, modern militaries have to focus on the following:

- Development of command-and-control systems and mobile command posts is required that enable continuous movement, allow distributed collaboration, and synchronise across all warfighting functions to minimise electronic signature.
- Ability to construct, dismantle, and move command posts in quick time would be mandatory in modern warfare.
- A cultural shift is required to embrace distributed C2 systems, more commonly known as 'mission command'.
- Development of effective counter-reconnaissance capability is required to reduce sustained enemy observation of the intended axes of advance. The inability to screen axes of advance from enemy ISR risks sustained exposure to precision fires, producing an unacceptable rate of equipment loss.

Ukraine's Example. Ukraine has developed a truly connected, high-speed command and control (C2) system:

- A dramatic improvement in its combat capabilities is its integration of diverse civilian systems into a coherent and highly effective command-and-control system. It has access to near-persistent surveillance of the battlespace.
- Skilled use of precision artillery, drones, and loitering munitions demonstrated how its smaller, lighter forces could defeat Russia's offensive.
- In the first weeks of the war, the Ministry of Digital Transformation of Ukraine team created the chatbot 'eVerog'. Everyone with a smartphone can share photos of enemy equipment and report collaborators or mines. Almost half a million Ukrainians have used the chatbot.

- Ukraine has refined its system with the creation of 'Delta'. Delta provides a comprehensive understanding of the battlespace in real time, integrates information about the enemy from various sensors and sources on a digital map, does not require additional settings, and can work on any device—laptop, tablet, or even on a mobile phone. 'Delta' is a modern real-time command map and troop control centre.
- Delta is tied to the NATO system, which draws data from commercial and classified government systems. Delta uses AI developed by Palantir to analyse and send data to the user speedily.
- Ukrainian coders have created a field-expedient, inexpensive version of the Pentagon's ambitious Joint All-Domain Command and Control (JADC2) system for ground commanders.

Communications

Since the introduction of the first two-way radios in the Second World War, the armed forces have been increasingly relying on the electromagnetic spectrum (EMS) rather than physical cables for their communications. The ongoing war in Ukraine offers a modern-day case study of battlefield communication.

Today, military operations depend on access to the EMS for communications, navigation, and overall C2. Adversaries try to deny each other the use of the EMS. Using legacy communications is less costly than developing a secure, robust, resilient wireless architecture in a highly contested environment. By reducing reliance on the EMS for its wireless communications, the armed forces can try spectrum denial at the battlefield, jamming across radio frequencies without fear of disrupting communication.

In the initial stages of the 2022 Russian invasion of Ukraine, Russian forces used EW at all levels to target Ukrainian radio communications. However, these tactics were anticipated mainly because of Russia's aggression in 2014. Ukraine was less reliant on the EMS for tactical communications and readily shifted to historical methods, including runners and despatch riders.

Russia's special operations forces have access to sophisticated tactical communications equipment using strong encryption. However, these were in short supply and unavailable to all the forces. Some Russian units even relied on Ukraine's commercial telecommunication infrastructure. The destruction of Ukrainian telecommunications infrastructure hindered their own communications. The reason for the high casualty rate among Russian Generals could be that their locations could be pinpointed due to vulnerable communication networks.

Russia suffered severely from its own jamming, which affected its ability to command the battlefield. EMS denial greatly impacted the attacking force, which had a higher dependence on technology. Russia realised this and, after the first week of conflict, relaxed the suppression of Ukrainian radar and communications. While EW superiority was preferable, Ukraine demonstrated how a reduced reliance on the EMS diminished Russia's substantial EW advantage in the opening stage of the war.

Tactical Communications. A tactical hardwired network of a legacy technique could be leveraged in a contested electromagnetic environment. Wired networks require physical tapping to intercept signals and cannot be jammed by adversary interference. Spiral-bound cables can be reeled out rapidly and have been utilised in previous conflicts to communicate over long distances. Modern, purpose-built vehicles, such as cable-laying trucks, could increase the speed of creating vast wire networks. This is mainly useful for static defensive positions that can be identified prior to or at the beginning of conflict. But wires can be physically cut while parallel paths can create redundancy. In the worst case, runners and drivers can be leveraged for the last tactical mile of communications.

High Frequency (HF) Communications. Radio communications across the Russian forces were poor, leading to use of unencrypted high-frequency (HF) radio for distant communications and mobile phones for local communications. Unlike Very High Frequency (VHF) or Ultra High Frequency (UHF), HF can perform beyond line-of-sight communications. It uses the ionosphere to bounce radio transmissions over the horizon. The Russian Air Force (RuAF) places a high premium on HF. The RuAF has access to domestic military-grade SATCOM. However, the preference for HF is because it is difficult to jam high-frequency radio, although not impossible.[4] Russian military HF radio transmissions are comparatively easy to find, as they are made in the clear without encryption. They seem oblivious to the risk that these transmissions may be intercepted and exploited for intelligence. This raises some possibilities:-

- Russian military HF users may not care if eavesdropping takes place.
- HF may be used for deliberately transmitting false information. However, intercepted traffic has correlated with Russian tactical actions.
- The RuAF has difficulty encrypting its HF traffic. Encryption equipment may not have been supplied to the forces *en masse* or are of poor quality.
- The Ukrainian EW cadres could exploit Russian use of HF communication by the following ways:
    - ♦ Detecting the source of communication and the position of Russian units, they could locate the position of RuAF command posts and attack them electronically.
    - ♦ While HF jamming is difficult, it is not impossible. They could jam them to hamper C2.
    - ♦ They could also use communications for false, misleading and demoralising traffic.

Radio Relay. Russian radio-relay vehicles are impressive systems. The R-142, the Russians' main relay vehicle during the later decades of the Cold War, packed as many as five separate long-range radios in a single 3.5-ton GAZ-66 truck with space for up to five crew. The Russians used this R-416GM extensively over the 700-kilometre frontage. With some discipline, a radio relay crew could deceive its location by limiting the duration of its broadcasts and frequently changing position to thwart Ukrainian efforts to trace the vehicle's coordinates. Rosoboronexport, the Russian export agency, has developed the newer R-419L1 a few years ago, describing it as "equal in quality to digital cable and fibre-optic communication lines." The Russian Army deployed relay vehicles, including dozens of R-416GMs that were factory-fresh, in and around Ukraine as part of the initial concentration of forces in early 2022.

Tropo-scatter Radio. The Russian network of tropospheric radios depends on special relay vehicles that, positioned scores or hundreds of miles apart between the frontline and various military headquarters, receive and re-transmit the weak signals radiating from the troposphere.

Jamming Equipment.[5] The RuAF can jam civilian V/UHF communications, including two-way radios and mobile phone networks. The RB-314V Leer-3 EW system deployed at the operational/tactical level can target mobile phone transmissions. RP-377U/UA EW systems that the RuAF deploys at the tactical level can target V/UHF transmissions.

Lessons

It seems strange that units moving into Ukraine during the first phase of the operation would not be outfitted with the best radios that Russia's defence industry had to offer. Russia's MoD has made diverse claims about the capabilities of its C2 network. It indicated that target data can be quickly shared between systems, and communication between units has been improved. But the current operations in Ukraine show that Russia does not have as many modern radios in service as it has claimed.

Russia has learned the following lessons from the initial stage of war:-

- Balancing modern technology, legacy techniques, and pre-existing infrastructure may offer a more gainful approach to resilient communications for the armed forces operating within a heavily contested EMS.[6]
- Command posts at the brigade and higher level are positioned further back, typically about 12 miles.
- Use of more secure lines of communication based on hijacked Ukrainian telecom infrastructure and extensive use of field cable and micro-link relays may be more gainful.

However, Russian forces suffer from the following shortcomings:-

- Smaller units and sub-units still rely on unencrypted radios and cellphones. They often do not use code words while communicating.
- They cannot horizontally integrate their C2 organisation, nor can they communicate the commanders' decisions and share information across different units in real time.
- Russian units deployed in proximity cannot effectively communicate with one another if they belong to different formations. Often, they

cannot support one another because they have separate chains of command.

- The Russian Army does not have enough access to satellites for long-range communication.
- The success of Ukraine's communication is mainly due to its tech-savvy human capital. Ukraine also had a good defence industrial base, which had existed since the days of Soviet Russia.

Use of Satellite Communication by Ukraine[7]

'SpaceX', founded by Elon Musk, makes very cheap, reusable rockets. 'Starshield' is SpaceX's military business unit, which provides access to the company's Starlink constellation, a fleet of more than 6,000 satellites in Low Earth Orbit (LEO), about 1,200 miles above Earth's surface. The growing network of spacecraft provides internet service for private consumers as well as militaries around the world. Ukraine's military has relied heavily on 'Starlink' in its war with Russia. Soldiers use it to communicate, identify targets, and upload video footage.

Starlink represents a quantum change in two ways:

- It offers a sheer amount of capacity. Senior officers, headquarters, and drone pilots largely used earlier satellite links. Frontline troops can now use Starlink in real time, even as they advance beyond the reach of mobile networks. This provides tactical agility, which is vital to modern warfare.
- Starlink has resistance to attack—it has survived attempts to jam or hack it. Traditional satellite networks comprising small numbers of big, complicated satellites are vulnerable to anti-satellite missiles whereas Starlink is not so. The number of satellites and the speed with which SpaceX can replace them makes it futile to try to shoot these down.

  Nevertheless, there are problems in relying on a whimsical tycoon like Elon Musk for vital infrastructure.

The Ukraine Army, particularly its network team, has worked meticulously over the last few years to mask electronic signals from command posts as part of its modernisation strategy. It has modernised its network with a range of networking tools, including radios and waveforms, to reduce an adversary's ability to locate troops using the electromagnetic spectrum.

Data Superiority

The ongoing Russia-Ukraine War demonstrates the significance of 'data superiority' in modern warfare. Both the forces have utilised advanced technologies to gather intelligence and conduct operations. Key lessons about data superiority are as follows:-

- Integration of diverse data sources is essential for comprehensive situational awareness. Armed forces need to invest in technologies that facilitate the collection and analysis of data from multiple platforms.
- Speed of data processing and dissemination is crucial. The ability to convert raw data into actionable intelligence can determine the outcome of engagements.
- Training personnel to interpret and utilise data effectively is paramount. As warfare becomes increasingly data-driven, armed forces have to prioritise the development of skills that are necessary to harness data superiority for strategic advantage.

Network Warfare

Battle network, or 'kill chain', is a model for understanding the Command and Control warfighting function. There are five essential steps between identifying a threat and effecting a solution:-

- Sensors that collect information on a threat or situation;
- Communicators that relay information between network nodes;
- Processors that analyse the information;
- A decider node that elects a course of action;
- Effector nodes that execute the decision.

Each of these is a necessary component for the network to function. Therefore, each institutes an exploitable vulnerability. Communicating among various platforms and network nodes presents several significant inefficiencies, causing a dangerous lag in the engagement process. For the army's platforms to effectively share information or network with those of the air force or the navy to achieve a greater unified effect, multiple intermediary nodes and communications networks are required to connect the platforms.

At the tactical level, Russia has fought a form of networked warfare. It uses computerised command and control to knit together drones and artillery batteries. It has good human intelligence and satellites of its own. But Russia's air force failed to take out Ukraine's air defences in the initial days of fighting. It was not due to poor training and preparation but because it took two days and more for the Russian military intelligence to send target information to a command centre in Moscow and onwards to the fighter aircraft. The targets were typically long gone by then.[8]

Survivability

Force survivability is becoming increasingly difficult amid satellite (both military and civilian) observation and widespread communications networks. Thin frontlines are easier to break through. New sensors, more accurate munitions, and better digital networks make finding and striking targets easier. The trick is that attackers have to concentrate their forces to pierce well-defended frontlines. Such concentrations can be detected and struck, not always, but more often than in the past. The advantage is shifting from offence to defence:

- The proliferation of cheap firepower and redundant communication tools potentially dulls the operational offensive.
- Abundant battlefield sensors and commercial satellite imagery mean mass and surprise may not be possible without communication blackouts or science fiction-like stealth technology.

Speed and precision have consequences for tactics. The forces have to fight under constant observation and contact. There is no break. There is no sanctuary. Responses can be in the form of the following:

- Resorting to age-old methods is one tactic. Trenches and fortifications have been built for hundreds of kilometres across eastern Ukraine.
- Camouflage and concealment is another tactic, though it is getting more difficult as sensors are combined. A thermal blanket might

confuse an infrared camera, but radar satellites will pick up subtle tyre tracks leading to a concealed position.

- The best way of surviving is to disperse and move more quickly before the enemy can spot and target. Russian drones have found the Ukrainian Special Forces operating in small teams when they stay in one place for too long.

Consideration for India

Connectivity. Optimising the data flow between sensors, aviation, fires, and manoeuvre presents several challenges, but these are addressable with strategic approaches. Instead of fixating on specific hardware, the focus should be on data accessibility and integration, ensuring that any soldier at any echelon can access the necessary information to complete their mission. That means valuing software advancements and understanding that even partial solutions can offer significant improvements over existing capabilities. This approach requires a shift in acquisition processes and contracting, allowing for more flexible and rapid development cycles. To explore alternative connectivity options, we have to consider possession of:

- Hardware for high-speed internet via satellite constellation;
- Hard-to-detect atmospheric laser communication terminals;
- A software platform for arranging networks across land, sea, air, and space;
- A decentralised wireless telecom network with fifth generation (5G) capabilities that allows users to share bandwidth from their personal Wi-Fi networks;
- Mobile mesh networks to extend connectivity or enable communications when Wi-Fi and satellite are unavailable;
- Traditional tools, such as virtual private networks (VPNs), personal VPN servers, and mesh networking applications.

Hardwired Networks. A tactical hardwired legacy network could be leveraged in a contested electromagnetic environment. For battlefield communications resilience, Ukraine has shown that legacy systems and techniques can provide cheaper and simpler alternatives to keep critical lines of communication open.[9] We could focus on building a baseline understanding of data and technology, gradually increasing comfort and proficiency to create an environment where new systems and software can be tested and iterated rapidly. Soldiers can then quickly learn and adapt to these tools, demonstrating the importance of user-friendly technology.

Cautionary Approach. However, far from making victory easy, these technologies impede military operations. The sheer volume of information transiting the modern battlefield and entering military command posts is often too much to address. It can result in paralysis of analysis.

Notes

1. U.S. Naval Institute Staff, Report to Congress on China Naval Modernization, USNI News, August 20, 2024. https://news.usni.org/2024/08/20/report-to-congress-on-china-naval-modernization-2
2. Colton Jones, "US Army secures $322M for M10 Booker production," Defence Blog, Aug. 25, 2024. https://defence-blog.com/us-army-secures-322m-for-m10-booker-production/
3. "Maxar Awarded G-EGD Contract Renewal to Provide Mission-Ready Satellite Imagery for U.S. government," *Investing News Network*, September 20, 2022. https://investingnews.com/maxar-awarded-g-egd-contract-renewal-to-provide-mission-ready-satellite-imagery-for-u-s-government/.
4. Withington, "Thinking about the Unthinkable," in *Military Technology*, Issue 1, 2022. https://monch.com/ebooks/military-technology/2023/MilTech_2023-02/
5. Grau and Bartles, *The Russian Way of War: Force Structure, Tactics and Modernisation of the Russian Ground Forces*, 2016, pp. 289-300. https://www.armyupress.army.mil/portals/7/hot%20spots/documents/russia/2017-07-the-russian-way-of-war-grau-bartles.pdf
6. Nicholas Johnson, *Back to the Future of Comms*, Rand Corporation, July 30, 2024. https://www.rand.org/pubs/commentary/2024/07/back-to-the-future-of-comms.html
7. "Starlink's performance in Ukraine has ignited a new space race," *The Economist*, January 5, 2023. https://www.economist.com/leaders/2023/01/05/starlinks-performance-in-ukraine-has-ignited-a-new-space-race
8. WW3 - some handy phrases. (Page 8) | Politics Forum on Dover.UK.com. https://www.dover.uk.com/ forums/politics-forum/ww3-some-handy-phrases?p=8
9. Nicholas Johnson, *Back to the Future of Comms*, Rand Corporation, July 30, 2024. https://www.rand.org/pubs/commentary/2024/07/back-to-the-future-of-comms.html

19. Mechanised Forces in Recent Wars

Introduction

The tank was introduced in 1916. The Cold War lasted for 30 years, but today's tanks still look and feel familiar to those of the Cold War era. America's M1 Abrams, Russia's T-72 and T-90, Germany's Leopard 2, Britain's Challenger, and Israel's Merkava have not changed much, though these machines have been upgraded over the years.

There is an argument that the tank has become obsolete due to technological improvements in anti-tank weapons. Is the tank the horse cavalry of the 21st century? Or is it a useful supporting system? Or is it still, with adaptation, the weapon of choice for ground combat?[1]

This argument has been commonplace for over 50 years. Yet, in 2025, both sides in Ukraine continue to rely on tanks and are doing everything they can to get their hands on more of them.

Before any mis-conceived epitaph of the tank is written, the following questions must be addressed:[2]

- Is there a role for mobile, protected lethality on future battlefields?
- If the answer is yes, then the next act of how to protect the tank is to enable it to do what only the tank can do.

Modern Tanks

The new tanks won't be unfamiliar. They will probably resemble today's tanks, with rotating turrets and caterpillar tracks. Instead of incurring the huge expense of developing and manufacturing a brand new design, nations like the U.S. and Germany are building from existing models.

Tanks in the mid-21st century will have plenty of new features. They will:

1. Be smaller and lighter, more mobile and easier to transport by air or sea;
2. Have hybrid or electric engines;
3. Launch their own drones;
4. Have defensive systems to stop enemy drones;
5. Be highly digital and automated, including extensive reliance on artificial intelligence.

Anti-Tank Weaponry

The ongoing conflicts have also highlighted the value of having large numbers of widely deployed precision weapons. From man-portable anti-tank weapons to artillery to strike drones, widely deployed precision weapons have allowed small units to inflict heavy damage to the Mechanised Forces.

Early in the conflict, the Ukrainians had amazing success using a variety of man-portable anti-tank weapons to blunt Russian attacks. While the Javelin received most of the publicity, it was augmented by Stugna-P anti-tank guided missiles, Next-generation Light Anti-tank Weapons (NLAWs), Carl Gustav recoilless rifles, and rocket-propelled grenades (RPGs). Effective combined-arms tactics could have neutralised these weapons, especially using infantry to support the armour. While this may have been true in the past, the extended range of new systems makes infantry screens impractical.

Since World War II, the 1967 Arab-Israeli War was the first war that saw the large-scale employment of tank formations on a mobile battlefield. The outright Israeli victory in this conflict confirmed that the tank was the dominant force on the battlefield. Although outnumbered, the Israel Defense Forces demonstrated that well-trained, led, and equipped militaries could defeat numerically larger forces.

Two technologies changed the ball game between 1967 and the 1973 Yom Kippur War. The development of the Sagger and other anti-tank guided missiles (ATGM) allowed the infantry to engage tanks at long ranges for the first time. After the 1973 Yom Kippur War, the first 'obituaries of the tank' were published.

Armour Protection Measures

The Israel Defense Forces (IDF) and the U.S. Army realised that neutralising the Sagger and other ATGMs was the first priority. The tactical solution was to resort to combined arms operations, with particular emphasis on suppressing the ATGMs. The IDF installed mortars on their tanks. Smoke canister dischargers were mounted on the combat vehicles to screen them from fire. When a tank crew detected a Sagger in combat, it began suppressing it immediately with mortar fire. That fire would quickly be joined by larger mortars and field artillery. Artillery units would lay guns on potential Sagger locations to rapidly engage them with immediate suppression missions. Moreover, the Sagger required the dismounted gunner to track the missile to the target. High explosive rounds near his position would make him cringe, break the lock-on the target and cause the ATGM to miss.

An important technical improvement was the use of improved armour to replace the World War II-era rolled homogeneous steel. Chobham armour and explosive Reactive armour were developed. Also, to solve the Surface-to-Air Missiles (SAM) challenge to air, the IDF learned that suppression by artillery fire was the tactical solution to neutralising enemy missiles. The tank and the aeroplane regained their ascendancy on the battlefield.

Second Lebanon War of 2006. During the Second Lebanon War of 2006, the tank faced a significant new challenge. The challenge came from the 9M133 Kornet MISSILE, which had a much longer range than the Sagger. This tandem warhead can defeat all known armour, and most significantly, it has a laser-beam guidance system that is simple to operate. Thus, the 'end of the tank' was again announced. But the IDF also realised that only the tank had the potential to survive on the battlefield against hybrid adversaries like Hezbollah. If tanks were vulnerable, then dismounted infantry had no chance. That led the IDF to take the following measures:

- Tank crews needed to be trained in high-intensity combat and air-ground integration battle drills.
- Artillery suppression of ground fire came to the fore as a key capability requirement.
- The adversary's weapons had to be further suppressed to enable armoured formations to get the infantry into the close battle, the last 100-metre fight. Given the range and guidance system of new ATGMs, a technical solution and a doctrinal/tactical approach were needed as even one ATGM surviving to engage meant losing an expensive system and casualties. The technical solution was the 'Trophy' active protection system. The Trophy uses a sophisticated radar-directed weapon mounted on the tank to shoot down any incoming ATGM. It provides other networked systems and the crew with the site of the ATGM launcher. It quickly proved its worth in Israel's operations against Hamas in Gaza to neutralise threats from the ATGM and rocket-propelled grenades. The U.S., the U.K., and Germany have all fielded the Trophy. Other states have developed soft and hard-kill active protection systems, e.g., the Russian 'Arena' and the German 'MUSS'.[3]

Ukraine War. The overall ATGM threat in Ukraine is somewhat different. It uses top attack to penetrate the thin top armour of the targeted tanks. This is a technical problem whose solution will enable the tank to provide decisive shock action by skilful application of mobility and protected lethality as parts of combined arms teams. Drones, however, are a different matter. The growing ubiquity of unmanned aerial systems on the battlefield, like the Predators, Reapers, Switchblades, Turkish TB2s, loitering munitions, or weaponised toys, has been stunning.

Armour in Combined Arms Operations

The role of tanks, infantry, and artillery in modern combined arms warfare continues to be crucial. During the Russia-Ukraine War, it has been observed with keen interest that the destruction of Russian mechanised formations was achieved by the power of defence predominant operations and the lethality of infantry armed with modern anti-tank weapons. In this case, the reasons for the poor performance of the Russian Forces were:

- Lack of warning and preparation for battle;
- Poor strategy that worsened the logistics issues;
- Incompetence in combined arms fire and manoeuvre;
- Lack of close infantry support to the tank formations to bust the ambushes laid by the Ukrainian forces;
- Unavailability of suppressive artillery, mortar and close air support fires.

Tanks in Nagorno-Karabakh War

Tanks were critical to Azerbaijan's success in breaking through Armenian defence and exploiting that success. Azerbaijan was able to protect its tanks and employ them effectively, while Armenia was unable to do so. This was one of the main reasons for Azerbaijan's success in the war. The war demonstrated that Armenia's air defences were inadequate to defend its tanks and artillery from Azerbaijan's air power. Heavy Armenian tank losses during the Second Nagorno-Karabakh War in 2021 have ignited debate about their continued relevance. Armenia and its allies lost a substantial share of their tanks in that war. However, attributing this to the tank's obsolescence is a misreading of the data.

Tanks in Ukraine War

Available data from Ukraine and the recent war in Nagorno Karabakh show that tanks are still critical in modern warfare. Their vulnerabilities have been exaggerated. The following reasons can explain Russia's heavy tank losses:

- *Logistics Issues*. Tanks require routine maintenance, spare parts, and substantial fuel to keep them operational. Logistics planning is more important for tank units than nearly any other type of military unit. Russia's disorganised invasion aggravated these logistical challenges.
- *Secrecy*. Extreme efforts at compartmentalisation and secrecy marked Russia's operation. Commanders and soldiers found out they were going to war only a few hours before the invasion.

Advancing at a rapid pace. Russian Ground Forces units were ordered to advance at an extremely rapid pace. Russian forces regularly moved beyond artillery, EW, and air defence coverage, further exacerbating logistics issues. Russia had longer and more exposed supply lines; its logistics convoys were unable to handle ambushes from territorial defence forces.

Notably, the Ukrainian forces equipped with the best Western tanks saw many of them incapacitated within hours. Others are now used only sparingly. The Abrams has a 500-gallon fuel tank and needs several gallons just to start up, making it a behemoth in the U.S. arsenal. At $10 million each, tanks like the Abrams aren't easy to replace. Abrams tanks are yet to be used in the Kursk region.

Tank Protection Measures

A tank commander's skill is determined by their ability to fire and quickly retreat covertly. The rise of drones has increased the focus of training on the need for constant movement.

The Ukraine Armed Forces (UAF) have modified the traditional approaches and developed techniques for indirect fire. The use of modern technologies, in the form of graphic and calculation complexes, developed in Ukraine with the function of automated transmission of information to other tanks participating in the combat mission. This made it possible to achieve high accuracy at distances of up to 10 km and reduced the time to calculate fire corrections to a few seconds. This technique blurs the line between artillery and tanks. It allowed tanks to concentrate fire over a wide area while they could manoeuvre without the protection and screening needed by artillery guns. Ukraine planned to use armour as mobile reserves, capable of offering blunting fire against enemy movements and supporting counterattacks, if conditions permitted, to support its formations.

Some Ukrainian tank crews have installed metal cages around their tank's turret to guard against drones. Tanks are more vulnerable to drones than other armoured vehicles because of their sheer size and their large turrets, the top of which is thinly armoured. A tank's cannon also isn't suited to shooting down drones, and the vehicles typically carry only 30 to 40 shells.

Close protection by infantry is an important issue. The extended range of new anti-tank systems makes infantry screens infeasible. To cover the advance against an NLAW's 800-metre range, the infantry would have to form a perimeter of 5,000 metres around the armour. Against a Javelin's 4,000-metre range, the infantry would have to create a perimeter of 25,000 metres. From where will the infantry come to provide support to the tank?

Features Needed in Modern Tanks

Notwithstanding the re-emergence of the repeatedly belied tank vs. anti-tank debates of the past, tanks have been instrumental to the Ukrainian forces in sweeping into Russian mainland—the Kursk region. Ukrainian forces were met by lightly armed conscripts with little drone cover till Russian forces geared up for counter-offensive operations. Following Ukraine's military exhaustion, the retaliatory Russian counter-offensive, too, is an armour- predominant operation.

Use of tanks continues to have a predominant role in fast-paced manoeuvres. Against lightly armed adversaries like Hamas in Gaza, tanks have a major role in seizure of key objectives. To that end, there are certain key features to be added in the modern tanks.

In the Short Term:

- Tanks that are lighter to ease the logistics with V-shaped floors, crewless turrets, minor heat signature, Advanced Protection Systems (APS) against drones, and equal armour thickness all around since now top-hitting kamikaze drones and missiles are the main enemy, would be developed.
- Tanks would be armed with high-trajectory indirect-fire weapons like missiles, rockets or mortars. Many tank models would have added secondary weapons like anti-infantry explosive strips on the sides, rotary multi-barrelled autocannons, machine guns, side-firing ports for internally carried soldiers or crew, etc. They would also

have various advanced computer brains, communications, systems, and sensors.

Long Term Measures

- Tanks will be AI or remotely controlled crewless vehicles with light armour and a focus on mass manufacture and low maintenance.
- The Russian T-14 Armata is the first MBT designed with eventual automation in mind. The Russians are developing the Tachanka-B, a robotic addition to the Armata platform. They are retrofitting existing manned units for automation. The crew compartment will be replaced with additional fuel and ammunition.
- However, modern defence production is not simply applying resources. It involves engagement of a vast and complex and diffused global supply chain. Modern electronics rely on rare earth materials, which are in high demand and under strict import/export restrictions even during peacetime.[4]

Considerations for India

India's mechanised forces have to consider the recent developments in the ongoing conflicts and modify their doctrine, concepts of operation, tactics, training and procedures, and measured equipment profiling.

Some of the crucial factors to be considered are:

In Ground Warfare

- Due to battlefield transparency, big armoured formations are difficult to hide—if observed, these would be hit. Formations have to be dispersed in a wider area and yet be effective at the point of decision quickly and then disperse again.
- Logistic load has to be reduced. Mobility of the logistics chain has to be compatible.
- India's adversaries have integrated tiered air defence systems. Favourable Air Situation for a selected time can no longer be taken for granted. It would need to be carefully crafted.

- Effectiveness of traditional weapons and equipment should not be overlooked. A big chunk of Ukrainian tank losses has been from the land mines.
- India's armoured forces have primarily Russian-made T-series tanks. Development of top attack capabilities has exposed serious shortcomings in T-72 series tanks. Russian T-72 series tanks are no match for the NLAWs, Javelins, and Turkish Bayraktar TB2 Drones. These tanks need to be able to thwart the threats from such anti-tank weapons.
- As per the latest Military Balance Reports, India has 3740 MBTs, including 122 Arjun, 2418 T-72 M1, and 1200 T-90. India has placed orders to OFB for 118 Arjun Mk-1A tanks worth Rs. 7,523 crore in September 2021, 156 BMP 2 worth Rs. 1094 crore in June 2020, and 464 T-90S worth Rs 20,000 crore in November 2019. Russian OEM were to be paid $1.2 billion for technology transfer. These tanks will come into service over five to ten years and would be in service for at least the next 30 to 50 years. Investments of such huge amounts for a tank that has shown its vulnerability and shortcomings in the ongoing Ukraine war need to be reconciled.
- Mechanised forces are vulnerable in close space against small infantry teams with MANPADS. Especially against our western neighbours, the terrain will be predominantly urban. How to get adequate infantry when operating against an adversary who can fire anti-tank missiles from a range of six km?
- Indian forces need to be capable of fighting in a communication void even without the GPS.

In the Naval Domain

- Attack submarines, frigates, support ships and corvettes are here to stay. The tactical packaging of crewed or uncrewed systems remains to be seen.
- Ukraine, a country essentially without a navy, could still chase down Russia from the Black Sea and its traditional home base in Crimea. The Russian Fleet had to go out of range of Ukraine's cruise missiles and airborne and sea-based drones.

- Low-cost drones and cruise missiles have destroyed about a third of Russia's surface fleet or 20 warships, besides a submarine, and even destroyed the Russian Black Sea Flagship, the cruiser *Moskva*. It has severely impaired the Russian Black Sea Fleet's amphibious capability and considerably reduced Russia's ability to carry out precision sea-based strikes from the southern waters, which was so far viewed as a 'Russian Lake'.

In Air Warfare

- The value of space-borne assets as well as air superiority and multi-role fighters, ground attack aircraft, bombers and drones has increased manifold. Ground-based missiles and drones are vital instruments of air power. Whether all these systems remain crewed, uncrewed, or a mix is an open question.
- Ukraine has begged the Western countries for supply of their fourth-generation fighter planes like the F-16 with its combat training and maintenance support.
- Passive defence measures like painted decoys on runways, camouflage on aircraft, screens and barrage-type balloons to intercept drones are most helpful and cheap.
- Some analysts believe that modern air defence systems can create an area of air denial where crewed aircraft cannot operate. Russian and Ukrainian crewed aircraft rarely attempt to penetrate the multilayered air defence of the other side.[5]

Combat Engineering. Recent wars have shown that defensive works, anti-tank ditches, camouflage, mines, booby-traps, dragon's teeth, barbed wire and other obstacles in depth can absorb the heaviest of offensives and render the battlefield as killing grounds. Defeating these measures takes feats of combat engineering and will require innovative technologies and explosives.

Command and Control. An extremely capable central hub of command is required to control many systems operating on the battlefield. The Command Posts (CPs) are highly vulnerable to electronic warfare, satellite imagery, electromagnetic signal detection, and surveillance UASs.

Conventionally, CPs have been largely stationary, bigger, and indifferent to their electromagnetic footprints and have relied on emitting technology to supervise operations. Such weaknesses would be exploited in any future conflict.

Conclusion

Autonomous weapons systems and powerful algorithms would dominate future warfare. The armed forces will have to reform their structures, tactics, leadership development, training and procurement processes.

In the ongoing conflicts, major changes—the integration of cutting-edge technologies with traditional ways of fighting, proliferation of sensors, smart and loitering munitions, AI-enabled analytical tools, and widely-available space-based imaging and communications—are taking place. Battlefields have become increasingly transparent. It is extremely difficult to mass or move large formations and yet remain undetected on land, air, underwater or in space. The Ukrainian battlefield is full of deep trenches and bunkers as troops from both sides have been forced to go underground or huddle in cellars to survive.[6]

In transparent battlefields, those forces with the shortest response time from detection to destruction will win. The armed forces are creating operational opportunities by using long-range precision fires to destroy higher echelon headquarters and disrupt enemy logistics and operations rather than relying primarily on concentration of forces and tempo.

Drones are changing fire and manoeuvre. They are used as expendable intelligence, surveillance, and reconnaissance (ISR) systems, munitions, or to correct long-range artillery fires with pinpoint accuracy. Cheap, expendable drones play an important role in degrading costly, advanced air defence systems by forcing these to expend expensive and limited missile stocks while exposing themselves to follow-on attacks by more sophisticated drones, aircraft, and higher-end missiles. Drones are also vulnerable to air defences and electronic warfare.

From sensing targets to decision-making and battle damage assessment, software is now integral to every part of combat. The quality of the software will determine who will have an edge on the battlefield. The wars in Gaza and Ukraine have shown that in the next major conflict,

AI will integrate every aspect of military planning and execution. In conjunction with satellite imagery, Ukraine has used artificial intelligence to create software that helps artillery locate, aim, and destroy targets in the most efficient and lethal manner possible.[7]

Intelligence can be searched for and gathered quickly. OSINT is very useful to provide immediate information. Beyond the need for updated intelligence, intelligence management systems integrating AI will be critical for disseminating information across domains in a future conflict.

However, the paradox of the war is that mass and technology are intimately bound together. As stated earlier, Jack Watling of the Royal United Services Institute has reiterated that "What blunted the Russians north of Kyiv, was two brigades of artillery firing all their barrels every day."[8] In similar vein, Excalibur shells with a small, rugged chip inside could receive GPS signals from America's navigation satellites that could be precise and disproportionately effective. These have reduced the number of shells required, thus lowering the logistical burden. However, the chips inside the Excalibur shells have been tampered with; many are missing the designated targets.

Non-State Forces. Violent non-state actors and terrorists can pose significant threats by exploiting low-cost, commercially available technologies and automated systems like AI, drones and digital platforms. Groups like the Islamic State, Hezbollah and Houthis exploit these technologies to conduct attacks at low costs and yet avoid detection. These forces increasingly leverage crypto-currencies and new fin-tech tools, exploiting the relative obscurity and lack of regulation to finance their nefarious activities. Insurgent groups and terrorist organisations can use encrypted messaging apps and social media to ask for crypto-currency donations to sustain operations, to purchase weapons, and to recruit new fanatics and their training. As state, non-state and hybrid forces continue to exploit disruptive technologies, the international community must remain vigilant, adaptable, and united in promoting peace and security in the digital age.

The Private Sector. Today, private firms drive most of the investments in AI, drone development, satellite surveillance, and advanced manufacturing. The Indian defence establishment needs to engage the private sector as a critical source of technology and innovation. Most of the technologies in use on the battlefield, like AI and modern drones, were derived from commercial developments. Therefore, these will advance more rapidly than most government projects. India needs appropriate organisational structure to experiment with these developments and integrate these at a rate faster than adversaries.

Defence innovation is an inherently risky process. The innovation process goes wrong when the armed forces disassemble an old capability to create a new one, ignore its associated risks, or rush the vetting process to speed up deployment. Private developers are unlikely to have the necessary capability to evaluate all the risks due to lack of access to classified data and specific analytic expertise held by armed forces or intelligence agencies.[9]

The current conflicts have many dimensions. There is violent fighting on land, sea, and air, while the electromagnetic domain, cyberspace, IW, and space also play a vital role. However, the conflicts are mainly about defending, conquering, and retaking territory where the armies lead. The main task of all the other means of power of the state is to support such decisive battles.

Modern era warfare is not just about emerging or disruptive new technologies. Some of Ukraine's most urgent demands have been for tanks, artillery, munitions, and fighter aircraft. War is a human endeavour, and the war in Ukraine has highlighted the importance of the humans behind the technology. Modern warfare demands an army that can use the technology available under optimal conditions while functioning independently when this capability has been compromised or destroyed.

Finally, notwithstanding the ability of technology to create more robust systems that improve upon the existing ranges of weaponry and equipment, quantity still matters. To repeat the former Estonian president Kersti Kaljulaid, "There is no point in having one fancy weapon if the enemy has 10,000 non-fancy ones."[10]

Notes

1. "The Tank Is Dead: Long Live the Javelin, the Switchblade, the … ?", *War on the Rocks*. https://warontherocks.com/2022/04/the-tank-is-dead-long-live-the-javelin-the-switchblade-the/

2. David Johnson, "The tank is dead: long live the javelin, the switchblade, the …?", *War on the Rocks*, April 18, 2022. https://warontherocks.com/2022/04/the-tank-is-dead-long-live-the-javelin-the-switchblade-the/
3. Rob Lee, "The Tank Is Not Obsolete, and Other Observations About the Future of Combat," *War on the Rocks*, September 6, 2022. https://warontherocks.com/2022/09/the-tank-is-not-obsolete-and-other-observations-about-the-future-of-combat/
4 Lt. Col. John Q. Bolton, U.S. Army, "The More Things Change … Russia's War in Ukraine Mirrors the Past as Much as It Shows the Future," *Military Review* Online Exclusive, July 2023. https://www.armyupress.army.mil/Portals/7/military-review/Archives/English/Online-Exclusive/2023/The-More-Things-Change/Bolton-AWC-Ukraine-Observations-UA.pdf
5. T.X. Hammes, "The Tactical Defense Becomes Dominant Again," *Joint Force Quarterly*, no. 103 (October 14, 2021). https://www.960cyber.afrc.af.mil/News/Article-Display/Article/2810962/the-tactical-defense-becomes-dominant-again/
6. "Human-machine teams driven by AI are about to reshape warfare," *The Frontier Post.* https://thefrontierpost.com/human-machine-teams-driven-by-ai-are-about-to-reshape-warfare/
7. "How Ukraine Is Remaking War: Technological Advancements Are Helping Kyiv Succeed." https://www.foreignaffairs.com/ukraine/how-ukraine-remaking-war?mod=djemCapitalJournalDaybreak
8. "What Western armour gives Ukraine in the next round of the war," | Royal United Services Institute. https://www.rusi.org/news-and-comment/in-the-news/what-western-armour-gives-ukraine-next-round-war/
9. "Ukrainian Innovation in a War of Attrition." https://www.csis.org/analysis/ukrainian-innovation-war-attrition?ref=readthemaple.com
10. "Star tech enterprise: Emerging technologies in Russia's war on Ukraine," | ECFR. https://ecfr.eu/publication/star-tech-enterprise-emerging-technologies-in-russias-war-on-ukraine/

Index